METHODS OF HUMAN RIGHTS RESEARCH

METHODS OF
HUMAN RIGHTS RESEARCH

Edited by
Fons COOMANS
Fred GRÜNFELD
Menno T. KAMMINGA

intersentia

Antwerp – Oxford – Portland

Distribution for the UK:
Hart Publishing
16C Worcester Place
Oxford OX1 2JW
UK
Tel.: +44 1865 51 75 30
Fax: +44 1865 51 07 10

Distribution for the USA and Canada:
International Specialized Book Services
920 NE 58th Ave Suite 300
Portland, OR 97213
USA
Tel.: +1 800 944 6190 (toll free)
Tel.: +1 503 287 3093
Fax: +1 503 280 8832
Email: info@isbs.com

Distribution for Switzerland and Germany:
Schulthess Verlag
Zwingliplatz 2
CH-8022 Zürich
Switzerland
Tel: + 41 1 251 93 36
Fax: + 41 1 261 63 94

Distribution for other countries:
Intersentia Publishers
Groenstraat 31
BE-2640 Mortsel
Belgium
Tel: + 32 3 680 15 50
Fax: + 32 3 658 71 21

Methods of Human Rights Research
Fons Coomans, Fred Grünfeld and Menno T. Kamminga (eds.)

Cover illustration: © Danny Juchtmans

© 2009 Intersentia
Antwerp – Oxford – Portland
www.intersentia.com

ISBN 978-90-5095-879-0
D/2009/7849/65
NUR 828

TABLE OF CONTENTS

A PRIMER
FONS COOMANS, FRED GRÜNFELD and MENNO T. KAMMINGA 11

1. Problems with Methods of Human Rights Research...12
2. Some Suggestions..14

SOCIAL SCIENCE METHODS AND HUMAN RIGHTS
TODD LANDMAN 19

1. Introduction..19
2. Human Rights as an 'Object of Inquiry' 21
2.1. Absence of Agreed Philosophical Foundations..21
2.2. Contestation over the Meaning of Human Rights...22
2.3. Applicability of the Social Sciences...24
3. Methods in Social Science...25
3.1. Dimensions of Social Science Research 26
3.1.1. Epistemological Continuum..26
3.1.2. Cross-National Generalisations and Comparative Methods...........................31
3.1.2.1. Global Comparative Analysis 31
3.1.2.2. Few-Country Comparisons 33
3.1.2.3. Single-Country Studies..36
3.2. Quantitative and Qualitative Evidence 39
4. Conclusion: Methods Matter 41

REDEFINING NORMATIVE LEGAL SCIENCE: TOWARDS AN
ARGUMENTATIVE DISCIPLINE
JAN M. SMITS..45

1. Introduction..45
2. From Internal to External Approaches of Legal Science 46
3. Towards a Redefinition of Normative Legal Scholarship:
the *Homo Juridicus* 48
4. The Methodology of Normative Legal Scholarship 50
4.1. Law as the Science of Competing Arguments..50

4.2. How Can the Better Arguments Be Found?..51
4.3. Three Consequences..54
5. Two Examples: Fundamental Rights in Relationships between Private Parties 55
6. Conclusions: Legal Science as a Scholarly Discipline 57

HUMAN RIGHTS STUDIES: ON THE DANGERS OF
LEGALISTIC ASSUMPTIONS
DAVID P. FORSYTHE...59

1. Introduction..59
2. Legalistic Studies 62
2.1. General Overview 63
2.2. A Focus on Impact...70
2.3. A Focus on Legal Obligation...71
3. Conclusion 74

METHODS IN LEGAL HUMAN RIGHTS RESEARCH
EVA BREMS...77

1. Introduction..77
2. Research Question(s) and Method...77
2.1. Research Questions 77
2.2. Method...78
2.2.1. Examining the Attitudes and Practice of Researchers.....................78
2.2.2. Examining the Research Output..82
3. Results of the Empirical Research 83
3.1. Questionnaire 83
3.1.1. Who?..83
3.1.2. The Importance of Methodology..83
3.1.3. Training and Guidance..84
3.1.4. Methods Used 85
3.1.5. Empirical vs. Normative Research..86
3.1.6. Some Conclusions from the Questionnaire......................................87
3.2. Examination of the Corpus 87
4. Normative Conclusions..89

THE NEED FOR EVIDENCE-BASED HUMAN RIGHTS RESEARCH
HANS-OTTO SANO and HATLA THELLE..91

1. Introduction..91
2. The Sources of Human Rights Research...95

3. Empowerment and Making Claims — Two Different Contexts..........................101
4. Evidence-Based Research: an Example of the Complexities Involved 104
5. Conclusion 108

**MEASURE FOR MEASURE: UTILIZING LEGAL NORMS AND
HEALTH DATA IN MEASURING THE RIGHT TO HEALTH**
DABNEY EVANS and MEGAN PRICE 111

1. Introduction..111
2. Global Health Inequalities Between States 112
3. Establishment of Right to Health under International Human Rights Law.........114
4. A New Theoretical Model: The Synergistic Approach.....................................117
4.1. The International Convention on the Elimination of all Forms of
Racial Discrimination...119
4.2. Special Rapporteur on the Right to the Highest Attainable Standard
of Physical and Mental Health 120
4.3. General Comment 14 121
5. Applying the Synergistic Approach..123
6. Barriers and Challenges to the Approach...130
7. Conclusion and Implications 131

**METHODS IN HEALTH AND HUMAN RIGHTS RESEARCH:
TOWARDS A SPIRAL OF CO-LEARNING**
MARIA STUTTAFORD 135

1. Introduction..135
2. Health and Human Rights 136
3. Review of Methods Used in Health and Human Rights Research......................137
3.1. Methods Used in Research into Developing Policy and Programmes..............138
3.2. Methods Used in Research into Analysing and Critique Government
Performance 139
3.3. Methods Used in Research Providing Evidence in Redress for those
who Suffer Violations of their Rights..140
3.4. Methods Used in Research into Supporting Advocacy and Civil
Society Mobilization..141
4 Reflections on Research Design and Methods Used to Explore Health
and Human Rights...142
4.1. Exploring Collective Rights to Public Health for Homeless People 144
4.2. Towards Establishing a Learning Network to Advance Health Equity
Through Human Rights Strategies 145

4.3. Learning by Doing and Doing by Learning: A Civil Society Network
to Realise the Right to Health..146
4.4. Strengths and Weaknesses of Methods used in the Completed
Research Projects...146
5. A Learning Network to Facilitate a Spiral of Co-Learning....................148
6. Mixed Methods of Research in the Learning by Doing Network..........153
7. Conclusions..156

TELLING TRUTH? THE METHODOLOGICAL CHALLENGES OF TRUTH COMMISSIONS
PAUL GREADY 159

1. Introduction...159
2. Concepts and Methods..160
3. Qualitative and Quantitative Methods..163
4. Truth as Genre...167
5. Legitimacy and Impacts Beyond Report 'Fetishization' 170
6. Speaking Truth with and to Power 175
7. History as Saviour?..179
8. Conclusion 184

METHODOLOGICAL CHALLENGES IN COUNTRY OF ORIGIN RESEARCH
MARCO FORMISANO...187

1. Introduction...187
2. A Definition of Country of Origin Information 189
3. The Quasi-Judicial Character of Country of Origin Information and
Its Role in Asylum Law..191
4. The Three Elements of COI Research: the Observer, the Facts and
the Research Instruments 196
4.1. The Observer 196
4.2. The Facts..197
4.3. The Research Strategy..198
4.4. Procedural Principles 200
4.4.1. Impartiality and Objectivity 200
4.4.2. Public vs. Anonymous Sources 201
4.4.3. Assessing Sources..202
4.5. Substantive Principles 203
4.5.1. Relevance...203
4.5.2. Accuracy 204
4.5.3. Reliability...206

4.5.4. Currency 207
4.6. Presenting Research Results 208
5. Conclusions..210

TREATY INTERPRETATION AND THE SOCIAL SCIENCES
    KOEN DE FEYTER...213

1. Introduction...213
2. Multidisciplinarity in Treaty Interpretation 213
3. The *Awas Tingni* Judgment 219
4. Subsequent Case Law 226
5. Lessons for Human Rights Research...230

METHODS OF PHILOSOPHICAL RESEARCH ON HUMAN RIGHTS
    ANDREAS FOLLESDAL 233

1. Introduction...233
2. Amartya Sen 235
3. Charles Beitz 237
4. The Method of Reflective Equilibrium 237
4.1. Three Main Features 238
4.1.1. The Aim of Arriving at Reflective Equilibrium is Practical: To Attain
Agreement on Specific Moral Issues...238
4.1.2. The Starting Points of the Procedure are Non-Foundational Empirical
and Normative 'Considered Judgments' 238
4.1.3. The Theory Claims That There Is a rational Procedure by Which This Aim
Sometimes Can Be Reached. 239
4.2. Elaboration...240
4.2.1. Partial, Wide, Ideal Reflective Equilibrium 240
4.2.2. The Method of Reflective Equilibrium 240
4.2.3. Justification by Reflective Equilibrium 241
4.2.4. Four Norms that Guide the Method of Reflective Equilibrium 241
5. The Method of Reflective Equilibrium applied: Sen and Beitz............................242
5.1. On Sen: Why are Philosophical Human Rights Overriding?.........................243
5.2. On Beitz: The Complexity of Object-dependent Theories and of
Multiple Roles for Human Rights...243
6. Conclusions...245

About the Authors...247

Subject Index 253

Intersentia

A PRIMER

FONS COOMANS, FRED GRÜNFELD and MENNO T. KAMMINGA

This book was prompted by our impression that scholarship in the field of human rights is often lacking in attention to methodology. We were certainly not the first to have this impression. According to one commentator, for example, '[w]ishful thinking and sloppy legal analysis tend to be too common in international human rights law'.[1] Rather than simply dismissing such criticisms as biased and ill-informed we felt they should be taken seriously and examined more closely.

Human rights research encompasses a very broad range of topics and approaches. It may be about the content of human rights standards, the effectiveness of international and domestic enforcement mechanisms, compliance with human rights standards by states and non-state actors, the role of human rights in foreign policy, the history of human rights and philosophical questions, to mention just some examples. Although human rights scholarship is often regarded as the exclusive province of lawyers it therefore covers a much wider range of disciplines than merely the law.

There appear to be very few books specifically on the methodology of human rights research that could be recommended to, say, a Ph.D. candidate embarking on a dissertation.[2] We therefore set out to fill this gap and decided to convene an international conference to examine methodological questions in the field of human rights research. Because we felt that different disciplines could learn methodological lessons from each other we published a call for papers inviting scholars from disciplines varying from law to health sciences, philosophy, political science, international relations and sociology to identify what are in their view the criteria for sound human rights research. We asked them: How are you able to distinguish a sound piece of human rights research from a bad one? We also invited the participants to identify the methodological standards that are typical for human rights research. Are they different from research standards in other fields?

---

[1]   J. CROOK, 'The International Court of Justice and Human Rights', 1 *Northwestern Journal of International Human Rights Law* (2004) 1, 8.

[2]   Exceptions include T. LANDMAN, Studying Human Rights (London, 2006) and T. LANDMAN & E. CARVALHO, *Measuring Human Rights* (London, 2009).

The call for papers produced an overwhelming response. This strengthened us in our conviction that there is indeed a need for more reflection on the methods of human rights research. We made a selection from the offers that seemed to best encapsulate our intentions and these papers were presented at a conference that was held at Maastricht University under the auspices of the Maastricht Centre for Human Rights in November 2007. The present book contains revised and edited versions of the best papers that were presented at the conference. In this introduction we attempt to briefly summarize what are the key findings that may be derived from these papers and from the discussions that were held at the conference.

1. PROBLEMS WITH METHODS OF HUMAN RIGHTS RESEARCH

One initial finding is that if there is indeed a methodological deficit in human rights scholarship it is more urgent in respect of legal research than in respect of research by social scientists. This distinction may be caused by the difference in approach of these two disciplines. Lawyers are system builders; they rely on logic to determine whether arguments are compatible with an existing normative setting. Human rights may be but are not necessarily part of this normative setting.[3] Legal scholarship therefore has little to say on the impact of legal systems on the ground. It makes implicit assumptions in this regard and runs the risk of remaining aloof from reality. Social scientists, on the other hand, attempt to understand and explain social phenomena. Their findings can be empirically challenged and verified. However, they run the risk of ignoring or misinterpreting applicable legal standards.

A survey carried out among 28 human rights scholars who are lawyers by training found that only half of them had received any formal training in methodology.[4] The others had simply learned by doing. Even more alarmingly, only 13 of the respondents said they always reflected on the most appropriate research method when starting work on a new research topic. And only three responded that as a rule they included in their published work information on the research method used. An additional survey of scholarly articles contained in the 2006 volume of seven leading human rights law journals found that 22 out of 90 articles contained no explicit information on the method used.[5]

We are not aware of a similar survey of human rights scholarship by social scientists. Our impression, however, is that while social scientists conducting

---

[3]   See the contribution by J. SMITS, Redefining Normative Legal Science: Towards an Argumentative Discipline, in the present volume.

[4]   See the contribution by E. BREMS, Methods in Legal Human Rights Research, in the present volume.

[5]   *Ibid.* A recent study of methodological choices made in legal Ph.D. dissertations in the Netherlands found a similar trend. H. TIJSSEN, *De verantwoording van methodologische keuzes in juridische dissertaties* (Den Haag, 2009).

research in the field of human rights tend to do better than their legal colleagues their work also frequently leaves something to be desired from a methodological point of view. They similarly demonstrate a tendency, for example, not to spell out their research methods in any detail in their publications. A survey of articles published in the interdisciplinary human rights journals the Human Rights Quarterly and the Netherlands Quarterly of Human Rights found a further worrying phenomenon: a tendency by authors from all disciplines to rely on secondary rather than primary sources.[6]

Why would human rights scholarship have such an above average tendency towards methodological sloppiness? Our hypothesis — subscribed to by several of the authors contributing to this book — is that human rights scholars tend to passionately believe that human rights are a good thing. Many of them are activists or former activists in the field of human rights. Without saying so explicitly the aim of their research is to contribute to improved respect for human rights. They therefore risk ignoring the fact that human rights are not a goal in themselves but merely one instrument to help improve respect for human dignity.[7] They may forget that human rights standards are the result of compromises concluded by states and may therefore be less than perfect. They may also overlook the fact that the mere adoption of resolutions by international bodies and the mere establishment of new international institutions will not necessarily result in improvement of the enjoyment of human rights on the ground.

The mission statement of the Netherlands Research School on Human Rights (the collaborative framework of human rights scholars in the Netherlands) is a case in point. It provides that the School's purpose is 'to contribute to the development and the strengthening of international, regional and domestic systems for the protection of human rights.' In accordance with these terms there is therefore little room for research challenging the conventional wisdom that such systems are to be applauded.

An unfortunate inclination among some human rights lawyers is to show excessive deference towards the case law emanating from international human rights bodies. This may be done so as not to weaken these bodies by criticisms, especially when the bodies in question are newly established or dependent on the annual renewal of their mandates. Such a sympathetic attitude may also be based on the implicit assumption that international supervision mechanisms in the field of human rights should be supported whatever they are saying and especially if they are adopting 'progressive' opinions. In our view this approach confuses scholarship

---

[6]   See the contribution by H-O. SANO & H. THELLE, The Need of Evidence Based Human Rights Research, in the present volume.

[7]   See the contribution by D. P. FORSYTHE, Human Rights Studies: On the Dangers of Legalistic Assumptions, in the present volume.

with activism. If the output from some international bodies is not up to standard human rights scholars have a duty to say so.

Because human rights scholars often already know which conclusions they want to arrive at the temptation may be great to engage in wishful thinking. This may involve limiting sources to those that support the desired conclusion and ignoring literature or findings that point in the opposite direction. In most disciplines it is encouraged to be contrarian and to attempt to demonstrate that conventional wisdom is wrong. In human rights scholarship, on the other the hand, it often appears to be considered an achievement to come up with findings that support conventional wisdom. In other words, there appears to be a marked absence of internal critical reflection among human rights scholars.[8]

There are of course positive exceptions to this tendency. Just one example is a study by Oona Hathaway — a legal scholar by the way — that demonstrated that non-democratic states that practice torture are more likely to become parties to the UN Convention against Torture than those that do not systematically do so.[9] Moreover, after having become parties torture in these states does not decrease. These findings of course challenge the conventional wisdom that states parties to the Convention will be less inclined to tolerate torture because they are subjected to the Convention's supervisory mechanisms. This assumption is the underlying reason for campaigns encouraging states to become parties to human rights treaties. In fact, as the author points out, states may become parties to the Convention against Torture not with the intention to combat torture but in order to improve their international reputation and thereby to increase their chances of obtaining development assistance.

The lack of methodological rigor in human rights scholarship has some undesirable consequences. Most importantly of course, it undermines the credibility and the validity of its findings. But it also has a negative impact on the chances of success in funding competitions. Because it is difficult to compare the quality of research proposals from different disciplines proposals in such competitions are often compared on the basis of their methodologies. Proposals that seem thin methodologically are unlikely to receive grants.

2. SOME SUGGESTIONS

Methodology stands for 'approach'. It addresses the question how to find relevant information; how to organize it; and how to interpret the results. Methodology therefore is crucial for any branch of scholarship because an unreliable method

---

[8]   See the contribution by A. FOLLESDAL, Methods of Philosophical Research on Human Rights, in the present volume.

[9]   O. A. HATHAWAY, 'The Promise and Limits of the International Law of Torture', in S. LEVINSON (ED.), *Torture: A Collection* (Oxford, 2004) 199-212.

produces unreliable results. It follows that reflection on methodology is not a luxury, not something that detracts from time devoted to one's substantive research efforts. There is no contradiction between method and substance. Method is the substance.[10] Method is the very essence of scholarship. Arguably, the section describing the methodology used is the most interesting and revealing part of any academic paper (or research proposal).

A description of the method that has been adopted for a research project should not be confused with a description of the sources of information that have been used. Such a list is useful in itself, especially if it is accompanied by an explanation why these sources have been chosen and how they have been used. But the essence of a description of the methodology is that it also sets out how the information emanating from these sources has been organized and interpreted.

Another mistake that is frequently made is to confuse what has been investigated with how it has been done. In the introduction of their book or paper authors may provide an elaborate summary in the contributions that follow. Useful as that may be, such a 'road map' is to be distinguished from the paper's methodology. The methodology cannot be derived from the table of contents. It requires a detailed description of the steps that have been taken to arrive from the problem statement to the conclusion.

The method chosen for a research project should follow logically from the project's research question. It may also depend on such practical considerations as the information, the financial resources and the time that is available, as well as the qualifications of the researcher. Again, this should be explained.

There is therefore not a single, preferred research method. There also is no typical, preferred method for carrying out research in the field of human rights. The method chosen to answer a given research question may, for example, be quantitative or qualitative, inductive or deductive, a case study or an attempt to draw general conclusions, covering just one country or comparing more countries, be based merely on written sources ('desk top research') or on field study and interviews. A combination of methods, if expertly employed, may of course produce more reliable results.

The method used for a research project should not be hidden between the lines but be spelled out explicitly and in plenty of detail. Each step in the research process should be identified and justified. If the method employed is not carefully explained the validity of the outcome of a research project cannot be judged. It is not good enough, for example, to mention in passing that 'the usual methods of legal research' have been relied upon.

---

[10] See the contribution by T. LANDMAN, Social Science Methods and Human Rights, in the present volume.

The description of the method adopted should also discuss which alternative methods have been considered and why these have been rejected. The purpose here is to demonstrate that the researcher has reflected on the proper method of research for the project and has made a choice that is justifiable.

Normative research projects in the field of human rights should make sure to clearly distinguish the law as it (lex lata) or the law which is likely to stand up in a court of law from the law as it should be in the opinion of the author (lex ferenda). A device that is all too often used to blur the lines between lex lata and lex ferenda is that of 'emerging' human rights or 'emerging' interpretations of such rights. The term 'emerging' in this context may provide a smokescreen for wishful thinking and should be employed only sparingly.

When evaluating the impact of policies conclusions should be drawn very cautiously. This applies generally but in the field of human rights this is particularly tricky.[11] This is because it is difficult to demonstrate causality. Even if suitable indicators can be found to measure change it is hard to determine the effect of, for example, NGO campaigns or UN sanctions because numerous other factors besides these policies may also have had an impact.

Quantitative methods should also be employed with great care. They may appear attractive because they may seem to provide certainty when qualitative methods are unable to do so. This is especially relevant in the field of social, economic and cultural rights. States are required to take measures to respect, protect and fulfill these rights. To determine whether a state has complied with its duty to respect a right is comparatively straightforward. There must have been an absence of state interference with the enjoyment of the right. But to determine whether a state has taken sufficient positive measures to protect and to fulfill a right is less easy. It may then make sense to turn to statistical indicators without keeping in mind that these may produce misleading results. For example, an increase in the number of children attending primary schools does not tell us whether or not girls or pupils from poor parents are being discriminated against.

Applied research poses its own methodological risks because researchers may be under considerable pressure to support a desired outcome. One example is the collection and assessment of country of origin information to determine the status of asylum-seekers and refugees.[12] This process often functions in a politicized context but should nevertheless be guided by principles of impartiality, objectivity and reliability of information. Another example is research undertaken in support of

---

[11]   PH. ALSTON, 'Appraising the United Nations Human Rights Regime', in PH. ALSTON (ed.), *The United Nations and Human Rights: A Critical Appraisal* (Oxford, 1992) 19.

[12]   See the contribution by M. FORMISANO, Methodological Challenges in Country of Origin Research, in the present volume.

truth and reconciliation commissions.[13] Such commissions are essentially hybrid institutions with one foot in academia and another in practice. Research of this type similarly runs the risk of attempting to justify politically informed mandates or goals. A third example discussed in the present book is research specifically aimed at overcoming existing inequalities and supporting social change and empowerment of certain groups.[14] This may be acceptable as long as it is clearly stated and explained.

Interdisciplinarity is an indispensable element of human rights research if only because lawyers are needed to clarify the legal framework and social scientists are needed to assess the situation in the field. But genuine, high quality interdisciplinary research is rare because few researchers are fully qualified in more than one discipline. In our view, it is generally best for researchers to work within their own disciplines and not to moonlight in other domains. Researchers should however attempt to make the results of their research accessible to readers outside their field of specialization and avoid unnecessary jargon. In order to be able to appreciate the results from research carried out in other disciplines than their own, it is important for researchers to make an effort to comprehend the methods of research of those other disciplines.

We are indebted to Maastricht University's Faculty of Law and the Royal Netherlands Academy of Arts and Sciences for their financial support for the conference that led to the present book. We are also very grateful to Martine Boersma and Jennifer Sellin for having prepared the conference report, to Aafke Kok and Laura Visser for their editorial assistance and to Chantal Kuypers for her skill in transforming the manuscript into a book.

---

[13] See the contribution by P. GREADY, Telling Truth? The Methodological Challenges of Truth Commissions, in the present volume.

[14] See the contribution by M. STUTTAFORD, Methods in Health and Human Rights Research: Towards a Spiral of Co-Learning, in the present volume.

SOCIAL SCIENCE METHODS AND HUMAN RIGHTS

TODD LANDMAN

1. INTRODUCTION

The social sciences have a long tradition in analysing the conditions under which human beings live, interact with one another, and form social relations; develop ideas, norms, and beliefs; struggle for social transformations, peace, and prosperity; and create systems of governance and institutional arrangements designed to realise more fully the idea of the 'good life'. While not addressing human rights explicitly (and for that matter consistently) until more recently, the social sciences have generated considerable knowledge about the human condition relevant to rights-based research, while at the same time making tremendous progress in developing methods that are applicable to a range of topics in the field of human rights. Moreover, the social sciences have problematized human rights in ways that have challenged the predominance of law and opened up new avenues of inquiry that provide greater insight into the fundamental challenges that need to be overcome for a truly global implementation of human rights norms.

The main aim of the social sciences is to provide explanation and understanding of social phenomena, which for human rights research comprises a broad and complex array of topics relating to the promotion, protection, and enhancement of human dignity. Social science theories and the analytical categories and variables derived from them map well onto the different *categories* and *dimensions* of human rights, and much progress has been made in operationalising them for systematic analysis.[1] Increasingly, social science research is moving beyond the academy to inform larger policy debates within the international community and among practitioners in the non-governmental sector. For example, the World Organisation Against Torture (OMCT) carried out an international research project on the causes of violence; the Centre for Economic and Social Rights (CESCR) is conducting

---

[1]   T. LANDMAN, 'Measuring Human Rights: Principle, Practice, and Policy', 26 *Human Rights Quarterly* (2004) 906-931; T. LANDMAN, *Studying Human Rights* (London, 2006); UNDP, *Indicators for Human Rights Based Approaches to Development in UNDP Programming: A User's Guide* (New York and Oslo, 2006).

research on better ways to measure, monitor, and advocate for economic and social rights;[2] the International Council on Human Rights Policy recently engaged social scientists in a series of research papers on the relationship between corruption and human rights;[3] and Oxfam along with Saferworld and the International Action Network on Small Arms conducted an impact assessment of Africa's multiple armed conflicts, which estimates the financial and human costs of war between 1990 and 2005.[4]

Central to any social scientific analysis of significant research areas in human rights (as in any topic) is the need for good method. Method establishes a direct connection between the main research question, the empirical theories used to provide possible answers to the question, the propositions they make about the social phenomena under investigation (or the observable implications of a particular theory), and the collection of evidence that may or may not support these propositions.[5] In this way, methods establish the ground rules of any inquiry, specify the types of knowledge that are possible given the theoretical expectations and assumptions of the researcher, and set the parameters for how evidence is collected and analysed. There is thus no one preferred method. Rather, method is a function of the research question that is posed, the theories used to help answer the question, and the epistemological orientation of the researcher.

This paper examines the contribution that social science methods can make to sound human rights research in an effort to provide explanation of different human rights experiences in the world; deeper understanding of the conditions under which the promotion, protection, and perception of human rights vary; and a better evidence base for continued human rights scholarship, advocacy, and policy prescription. The first section of the paper discusses why human rights continue to be a difficult 'object of inquiry' for the social sciences given the absence of agreed philosophical foundations, contested nature of their full content, and the possible tension between the use of social science methods to research questions that are fundamentally moral in nature. The second section provides a brief outline of the

---

[2] See, <http://cesr.org/about/methodology>.

[3] T. LANDMAN and C.W. SCHUDEL, 'Corruption and Human Rights: Empirical Relationships and Policy Advice', Working Paper Prepared for the International Council for Human Rights Policy (Geneva, 2007). The full catalogue of working papers is available here: <http://www.ichrp.org/public/workingpapers.php?id_ projet=1125&lang=AN>.

[4] C. MCGREAL, 'The devastating cost of Africa's wars: £150 billion and millions of lives', *The Guardian*, 11 October 2007, 17.

[5] G. KING, R.O. KEOHANE and S. VERBA, *Designing Social Inquiry: Scientific Inference in Qualitative Research*, (Princeton, 1994); T. LANDMAN, 'Comparative Politics and Human Rights', 24 *Human Rights Quarterly* (2002) 890-923; T. LANDMAN, *Issues and Methods in Comparative Politics: An Introduction (2nd ed.)* (London, 2003); LANDMAN, *supra* n. 1; T. LANDMAN, *Issues and Methods in Comparative Politics: An Introduction (3th ed.)* (London, 2008).

dimensions of social science with respect to the epistemological range of approaches, the different kinds of cross-national comparisons in the search for empirical generalizations, and the use of qualitative and quantitative data. The final section concludes the paper with an argument on why method matters for the social science of human rights.

2. HUMAN RIGHTS AS AN 'OBJECT OF INQUIRY'

A social science that seeks to make human rights its main object of inquiry must confront three significant and complementary challenges: (1) the absence of agreed philosophical foundations for the existence of human rights and their uncertain character, (2) contestation over the meaning and core content of human rights, and (3) the applicability of the social sciences to the study of human rights. The first challenge involves the fact that normative political theory and philosophy have failed to establish an agreed consensus on the grounds for the existence of human rights.[6] Appeals to God, nature and reason have all in their own ways failed to provide the definitive source for human rights, while significant normative and empirical critiques have variously characterised human rights as 'nonsense',[7] 'fantasy',[8] 'bourgeois',[9] and 'relative'.[10] Moreover, the empirical record on human rights protection around the world and the significant 'gap between the theory and reality of human rights' means for some that they are indeed a 'fiction'.[11]

2.1. ABSENCE OF AGREED PHILOSOPHICAL FOUNDATIONS

In the absence of agreed philosophical foundations and against the more vociferous criticisms of human rights, two broad responses have been offered to this first challenge. Legal responses cite the growth and proliferation in human rights norms, instruments, and declarations as evidence that there is an emerging global consensus on the need to promote and protect human rights,[12] as well as a 'language of

---

[6]   S. MENDUS, 'Human Rights in Political Theory', 43 *Political Studies* 10-24.

[7]   J. WALDRON (ed.), *'Nonsense Upon Stilts': Bentham, Burke, and Marx on the Rights of Man* (London, 1987).

[8]   A. MACINTYRE, *After Virtue (2nd ed.)* (South Bend, 1984).

[9]   K. MARX, 'The Eighteenth Brumaire of Louis Bonaparte', in R.C. TUCKER (ed.), *The Marx-Engels Reader (2nd ed.)* (New York, 1978) 594-617.

[10] R. RORTY, 'Human Rights, Rationality, and Sentimentality', in S. SHUTE and S. HURLEY (eds.), *On Human Rights: The Oxford Amnesty Lectures* (New York, 1993) 112-134.

[11] J.S. WATSON, *Theory and Reality in the International Protection of Human Rights*, (Ardsley, 1999) 1-16.

[12] M. FREEMAN, 'Is a Political Science of Human Rights Possible?', 19 *The Netherlands Quarterly of Human Rights* (2001) 121-137.

commitment' from state and non-state actors in the international community.[13] Social and political responses argue that rights 'made' initially through domestically based struggles in the 18th, 19th, and early 20th Centuries have been joined by international advocacy efforts at standard setting and implementation which created the international human rights system as we now know it.[14] This 'making' of rights has led to more general and pragmatic claims that human rights represent 'bulwarks against the permanent threat of human evil',[15] 'necessary legal guarantees for the exercise of human agency',[16] or as an 'important political lever for the realization of global justice'.[17] And is it these pragmatic functions and dimensions of human rights, the ways in which they are contested, and the ways in which the variation in their promotion and protection can be explained that have become the main quest for the social science of human rights.

2.2. CONTESTATION OVER THE MEANING OF HUMAN RIGHTS

The second challenge concerns the contestation over the full meaning and content of human rights. It is probably unfair to say that human rights are 'essentially contested',[18] since the international law of human rights and its associated jurisprudence has made great strides in clarifying the content of human rights in ways that have not been done for other contested concepts. But that for purposes of social scientific research, there remain definitional problems that have presented significant obstacles for their operationalisation. The international instruments have in many ways established both *categories* and *dimensions* of human rights that ought to be protected. The categories are well known and range across civil, political, economic, social, and cultural rights. The notion of human rights *dimensions* has evolved from understanding human rights in 'positive' and 'negative' terms to 'generations' of rights, to a more useful formulation that comprises the

---

13   K. BOYLE, 'Stock-taking on Human Rights: The World Conference on Human Rights, Vienna 1993', 43 *Political Studies* (1995) 79-95 at 81.

14   T.H. MARSHALL, 'Citizenship and Social Class', in T.H. MARSHALL, *Sociology at the Crossroads and Other Essays* (London, 1963); C. TILLY, L. TILLY and R. TILLY, *The Rebellious Century 1830-1930*, (Cambridge, 1975); R.P. CLAUDE, 'The Classical Model of Human Rights Development', in R.P. CLAUDE (ed.), *Comparative Human Rights* (Baltimore and London, 1976); J.M. BARBALET, *Citizenship: Rights, Struggle and Class Inequality* (Milton Keynes, 1988); J. FOWERAKER and T. LANDMAN, *Citizenship Rights and Social Movements: A Comparative and Statistical Analysis* (Oxford, 1997); M. ISHAY, *The History of Human Rights: From Ancient Times to the Globalization Era* (Berkeley, 2004).

15   MENDUS, *supra* n. 6, 23-24.

16   M. IGNATIEFF, *Human Rights as Politics and Idolatry* (Princeton, 2001).

17   R. FALK, *Human Rights Horizons* (London, 2000).

18   W.B. GALLIE, 'Essentially Contested Concepts', 51 *Proceedings of the Aristotelian Society* (1956) 167-198.

separate dimensions of *respect, protect* and *fulfil,* which arise from the legal obligations of states party to international human rights instruments.[19]

The obligation to *respect* human rights requires the state and all its organs and agents to abstain from carrying out, sponsoring or tolerating any practice, policy or legal measure violating the integrity of individuals or impinging on their freedom to access resources to satisfy their needs. It also requires that legislative and administrative codes take account of guaranteed rights. The obligation to *protect* requires the state and its agents to prevent the violation of rights by other individuals or non-state actors. Where violations do occur, the state must guarantee access to legal remedies. The obligation to *fulfil* involves issues of advocacy, public expenditure, governmental regulation of the economy, the provision of basic services and related infrastructure, and redistributive measures. The duty of fulfilment comprises those active measures necessary for guaranteeing opportunities to access entitlements.[20]

Combining these categories and dimensions produces a simple matrix of the scope of human rights, and provides a good starting point from which to operationalise human rights for social science analysis (see Figure 1). To date in the social sciences, more attention has been given to civil and political rights across the two dimensions of respect and protect. Such attempts can be seen as a function of larger ideological and methodological reasons that go beyond the scope of this paper.[21]

Figure 1. The Scope of Human Rights

Dimensions of human rights

		Respect No interference in the exercise of the right	**Protect** Prevent violations from third parties	**Fulfil** Provision of resources and the outcomes of policies
Categories of human rights	Civil and political	Torture, extra-judicial killings, disappearances, arbitrary detention, unfair trials, electoral intimidation, disenfranchisement	Measure to prevent non-state actors from committing violations, such as militias, uncivil movements, or private sector firms and organisations.	Investment in judiciaries, prisons, police forces, electoral authorities, and resource allocations to ability.
	Economic, social and cultural	Ethnic, racial, gender, or linguistic discrimination in health, education, and welfare, and resource allocations below ability.	Measures to prevent non-state actors from engaging in discriminatory behaviour that limits access to services and conditions.	Progressive realisation Investment in health, education and welfare, and resource allocations to ability.

Source: adapted from UNDP22

---

[19]   UNITED NATIONS, *Economic and Social Council, 'The right to adequate food: General Comment 12',* UN Doc. E/C.12/1999/5, New York, 1999.

[20]   UNDP, *supra* n. 1, 4.

[21]   T. LANDMAN, 'Review Article: the Political Science of Human Rights', (July) *British Journal of Political Science* (2005a).

2.3. APPLICABILITY OF THE SOCIAL SCIENCES

The third challenge for a social science of human rights involves the fundamental *moral* nature of human rights, which has led some to question whether the theories and methods of contemporary social science can be applied to their study, especially those approaches that are more positivistic in their stance.[22] Over the last three decades, scholars have queried the degree to which the social sciences can engage in the cross-national comparison of government practices, which would include human rights,[23] as well as the applicability of the social sciences,[24] or in particular, *political* science to the study of human rights.[25] Their doubts arise from the difficulty associated with the types of universal assumptions required for cross-national comparison, the capacity for social scientific tools for analysing human rights problems, and the tension between the natural law foundations of human rights and the positivist origins of modern social science.

While strict positivists may eschew making ethical judgements and may well want to pursue 'value-free' scientific research, social scientists of human rights, consistent with Max Weber, carry out research on topics that have been *influenced* by values but the research process itself has not been so influenced. Moreover, to ignore the actual practice of human rights violations carried out by state and non-state actors for some notion of objective scientific purism would have precluded a large body of research in social and political science carried out since the 1960s, such as the comparative work on political violence, social protest, state repression, and the dynamics of economic development. The cross-national comparison of countries is predicated on analysing similarities and differences across countries and the necessary trade-offs in making large empirical generalisations based on the analysis of a large number of countries, a smaller sample of countries, and single-country analysis. And as will be shown below, extant studies differ across the types of knowledge claims that they are making, the type of analytical reasoning that is adopted, the range of countries that feature in the analysis, and the ways in which evidence is used to make inferences. Nonetheless, these different methods for comparing human rights practices assume that there is some consensus on what constitutes the scope of rights in the ways that have been outlined above.

---

[22] FREEMAN, *supra* n. 12; M. FREEMAN, 'Anthropology and the Democratisation of Human Rights', 6 *The International Journal of Human Rights* (2002a) 37-54; M. FREEMAN, *Human Rights: An Interdisciplinary Approach* (Cambridge, 2002b).

[23] A. MACINTYRE, 'Is a Science of Comparative Politics Possible?', in A. MACINTYRE, *Against the Self-Images of the Age* (London, 1971) 260-279.

[24] J.F. McCAMANT, 'Social Science and Human Rights', 35 *International Organization* (1981) 531-552.

[25] FREEMAN, *supra* n. 12.

3. METHODS IN SOCIAL SCIENCE

The primary aim of the social sciences is to provide *explanation* and *understanding*[26] of observed (and in many cases unobserved) social phenomena. Such phenomena variously include events, actions, outcomes, conditions, processes, and perceptions. Social scientific *explanation* seeks to provide general accounts of why things happen and why certain conditions or state of affairs persist, or change. Such explanations rely on the systematic analysis of evidence to make inferences. Social science contributions to *understanding*, on the other hand, seek to provide deeper meanings of what has happened, persisted, or changed, where systematic analysis of evidence provides the foundation for arriving at overarching interpretations. Central to both of these social scientific goals is the need to pay significant attention to method, in terms of the need to provide clear rules of inquiry, strategies for collecting and analysing data, a well formulated research design, and the ability to draw inferences from the evidence that has been gathered. This general claim, however, leaves room for a variety of different methods that nonetheless establish a direct connection between the research question, the theoretical considerations, propositions that may have been derived and formulated, and the evidence used to make inferences and build strong argument.

While this is a position of methodological pluralism, I do not subscribe to methodological or epistemic relativism,[27] which is to say my position is one that is committed to the evidence-inference methodological core of the social sciences.[28] There are rules of inquiry that seek to achieve fairness and rigour in the collection and analysis of evidence and that are reflective of the limitations in the inferences that can be made given the methods that have been adopted. As the ensuing discussion will show, there are a number of trade-offs associated with the scope of countries under comparison, the level of conceptual abstraction, and the use of qualitative and quantitative techniques, all of which are directly linked to the types of knowledge claims about the world that can be made in any one research project.

---

[26] G.H. VON WRIGHT, *Explanation and Understanding* (London, 1971).

[27] See, *e.g.* P. FEYERABEND, *Against Method* (London, 1993); B. FLYVBJERG, *Making Social Science Matter*, (Cambridge, 2001); S. S. SCHRAM and B. CATERINO (eds.), *Making Political Science Matter: Debating Knowledge, Research, and Method* (New York, 2006); P. BOGHOSSIAN, *Fear of Knowledge: Against Relativism and Constructivism* (Oxford, 2006); J.W. MOSES and T.L. KNUTSEN, *Ways of Knowing: Competing Methodologies in Social and Political Research* (London, 2007).

[28] T. LANDMAN, *Issues and Methods in Comparative Politics: An Introduction* (London, 2000); LANDMAN, *supra* n. 5, 2003; LANDMAN, *supra* n. 5, 2008.

3.1. DIMENSIONS OF SOCIAL SCIENCE RESEARCH

There are three main dimensions of social science research. The first dimension is the 'epistemological continuum' ranging across methodological approaches that vary according to the types of knowledge claims they make (universal vs. particular), the type of reasoning that connects their theory and evidence (inductive vs. deductive), the balance between evidence and inference, and the scope of coverage for their evidence (from sub-national units and single countries to global comparisons). The second dimension deepens the discussion concerning the degree to which cross-national comparisons and empirical generalizations frame the analysis of human rights problems; examining the general methodological trade-off between the 'ladder of abstraction'[29] in the concepts that are used and the scope of units that form the basis of the analysis (Landman 2002; 2003).[30] The third dimension concerns the relative balance or mix between quantitative and qualitative evidence used in making inferences about human rights problems.

3.1.1. Epistemological Continuum

Table 1 lays out an epistemological continuum by specifying seven main categories of social science methods ranging from 'soft' hermeneutic approaches to 'hard' nomothetic approaches, which are further broken down by (1) their type of reasoning, (2) the balance between the use of evidence and the making of inferences, (3) the nature of the knowledge claims that each purports to make, and (4) the scope of their empirical coverage. The table also includes examples from extant human rights research that fall within each of these different categories of analysis.

---

[29] G. SARTORI, 'Concept Misinformation in Comparative Politics', 64 *American Political Science Review* (1970) 1033–1053; P. MAIR, 'Comparative Politics: An Overview', in R.E. GOODIN and H. KLINGEMANN (eds.), *The New Handbook of Political Science* (Oxford, 1996) 309–335.
[30] LANDMAN, *supra* n. 5, 2002; LANDMAN, *supra* n. 5, 2003.

Table 1. The Epistomenological/Methodological Continuum of the Social Sciences

Range	I	II	III	IV	V	VI	VII
Type of approach	Hermeneutic/thick description	Discourse analysis	Theory-driven empirical	Theory-driven empirical	Theory-driven empirical	Theory-driven empirical	Nomothetic
Reasoning	Inductive	Inductive and analytical	Inductive and analytical	Inductive and analytical	Inductive and analytical	Deductive and analytical	Deductive
Evidence vs. inference	'Evidence without inference'	Meaning and understanding from language and action	Qualitative evidence and inference	Quantitative/ qualitative evidence and inference	Quantitative evidence and inference	Inference with confirmatory evidence	Inference without evidence'
Nature of knowledge claim	Particular Context specific	Particular Context specific	Universal with room for exceptions	Universal with room for exceptions	Universal with room for exceptions	Universal	Universal
Scope of coverage	Single countries Subnational analysis	Single countries Limited comparison	Comparative and single case analysis	Comparative	Global comparative	Small-N comparative	Theoretical constructs only
Examples in human rights research	Goldstein (2004) *The Spectacular City* Huggins et al (2002) *Violence Workers*	Norval (1996) *Deconstructing Apartheid Discourse* Roniger and Sznajder (1999) *The Legacy of Human Rights Violations in the Southern Cone*	Risse, Ropp, and Sikkink (1999) *The Power of Human Rights* Hawkins (2002) *International Human Rights and Authoritarian Rule in Chile*	Foweraker and Landman (1997) *Citizenship Rights and Social Movements* Gómez (2003) *Human Rights in Cuba, Nicaragua, and El Salvador*	Poe and Carey (2004) *Understanding Human Rights Violations* Landman (2005) *Protecting Human Rights*	Mitchell (2004) *Agents of Atrocity*	Wantchekon and Healy (1999) 'The "Game" of Torture'

Source: Landman.[31]

The hermeneutic and 'thick-description'[32] end of the continuum (Column I) comprises those approaches that rely on descriptive and interpretative analysis of the social world, using a variety of qualitative methods such as participant observation, in-depth interviews and ethnographic methods, oral histories and narratives, archival documentation, and formal and informal discourses of individuals, as well as images, symbols, constructs, and architectures.[33] The goal of research that adopts these methods is to *understand* the nature and meaning of the social world that is constructed by the subject population under investigation. Less emphasis is placed on *explanation* of that social world, and there is rarely an attempt to make generalizations that extend too far beyond the evidence that has been examined. There is thus greater attention to primary evidence and less attempt to use that evidence to make inferences that extend far beyond the context in which a particular research project or study has taken place.

In this way, these approaches make knowledge claims that are limited to the particular social phenomena under investigation rather than make knowledge claims

---

[31] LANDMAN, *supra* n. 1, 2006, 60.

[32] C. GEERTZ, 'Thick Description: Toward an Interpretative Theory of Culture', in C. GEERTZ, *The Interpretation of Cultures* (New York, 1973) 3-30.

[33] F. DEVINE, 'Qualitative Analysis', in D. MARSH and G. STOKER (eds.), *Theories and Methods in Political Science* (London, 1995) 137-153; M. TRAVERS, *Qualitative Research Through Case Studies* (London, 2001); D. HOWARTH, 'Applying Discourse Theory: The Method of Articulation', in D. HOWART and J. TORFING (eds.), *Discourse Theory in European Politics: Identity, Policy, and Governance* (London, 2005) 316-349, at 335-343.

that have universal applicability. In both the Goldstein[34] and Huggins[35] examples, the primary aim of the research is to understand particular sets of practices using primary data that is highly intensive and collected from relatively small number of individuals combined with general observations of the researcher. Goldstein[36] investigates public vigilante violence in a small peripheral section of Cochabamba Bolivia, while Huggins[37] examines the different roles played by state agents that carried out torture and other human rights abuses in Brazil under the auspices of the military government. The units of analysis in such approaches tend to be individuals and groups that share common features and identities, sub-national units and geographical spaces, and single countries. Methodological criticisms of these approaches argue that pure descriptive studies have little social scientific value, since they are 'atheoretical' and 'interpretative',[38] 'configurative-ideographic',[39] and may simply provide 'evidence without inference'.[40] But scholars who adopt these approaches (and many who do not) argue that such in-depth studies, while not seeking universal applicability, have tremendous inherent value, are full of inferences that add to our pool of knowledge about the social world, and have significant practical and policy implications.[41]

The next category in the continuum (Column II) includes those approaches that adopt discourse analytic techniques to problem areas in the social sciences. Such analysis is much akin to hermeneutic analysis in that it seeks to elucidate 'problematized objects of study by seeking their description, understanding, and interpretation'.[42] The goal of such analysis is to produce new interpretations about specific objects of investigation through either uncovering phenomena previously obscured and undetected by dominant social scientific theories and approaches or by 'problematizing existing accounts and articulating alternative interpretations'.[43] Such analysis relies on inductive and analytical reasoning that examines the social and

---

[34]   D. GOLDSTEIN, *The Spectacular City: Violence and Performance in Urban Bolivia* (Durham, 2004).

[35]   M. HUGGINS, *Violence Workers: Police Torturers and Murderers Reconstruct Brazilian Atrocities* (Berkeley, 2002).

[36]   GOLDSTEIN, *supra* n. 35.

[37]   HUGGINS, *supra* n. 36.

[38]   A. LIJPHART, 'Comparative Politics and Comparative Method', 65 *The American Political Science Review* (1971) 682-693 at 691.

[39]   H. ECKSTEIN, 'Case-study and Theory in Political Science', in F.I. GREENSTEIN and N.S. POLSBY (eds.), *Handbook of Political Science, Vol. 7: Strategies of Inquiry* (Reading, 1975) 79-137.

[40]   G. ALMOND, 'Political Science: The History of the Discipline', in R.E. GOODIN and H. KLINGEMANN (eds.), *The New Handbook of Political Science* (Oxford, 1996) 50-96, at 52. (Hirschman 1970; Geertz 1973, Almond 1996; Landman 2000, 2003; Flyvberg 2001)

[41]   A. HIRSCHMAN, 'The Search for Paradigms as a Hindrance to Understanding,' 22 *World Politics* (1970) 329-343; GEERTZ, *supra* n. 33; ALMOND, *supra* n. 41; LANDMAN, *supra* n. 29; LANDMAN, *supra* n. 5, 2003; FLYVBJERG, *supra* n. 28.

[42]   HOWARTH, *supra* n. 34, 319.

[43]   HOWARTH, *supra* n. 34, 320.

political 'logics' at work in the construction of meanings, understandings, and articulatory practices. The analysis thus moves to a second-order assessment in applying post-modern analytical categories drawn from linguistic, psychological, and post-structuralist theory.

Such meanings and understandings are obtained through an analysis of language and action, which are seen as mutually constitutive phenomena. Like its hermeneutic counterpart, discourse analysis eschews making universal generalizations and tends to analyse small sub-national units and single-countries, although it has begun to explore ways in which to carry out comparative analysis that is at once 'problem-driven', but does not sacrifice attention to historical context and concrete specificities of the cases under comparison.[44] Such approaches thus seek to strike a balance or indeed reside in the tension between universality and particularity in ways that elucidate the broader sets of meanings associated with human rights problems. Both the Norval[45] and Roniger and Sznajder[46] studies examine how political actors construct, deconstruct, and reconstruct meanings in ways that hegemonise human rights and other discourses under the larger sets of national concerns and political evolution.

The next three categories in the continuum (Columns III, IV, and V) share a general orientation to providing theory-driven empirical analysis that is inductive, comparative, and seeks to make broad generalizations that still leave room for some exceptions. While they differ in the degree to which they use qualitative and quantitative analysis and in the number of countries that feature in their comparisons, they are all self-conscious about research methods and the strength of the inferences that are drawn from their analyses. The Column III studies use qualitative evidence collected systematically and compared across a small collection of countries[47] or a single country.[48] The goal of these comparisons is to draw larger inferences about processes of norms socialisation through and examination of transnational mobilization for rights, pressure on national states, and regime reform that ultimately leads to the internalisation of human rights norms. Column IV mix qualitative and quantitative analysis in a small number of countries, while those in Column V use purely quantitative analysis across a large number of countries to establish a set of universal empirical generalizations about the relationships between and among different variables.

---

[44] HOWARTH, *supra* n. 34, 332.
[45] A. NORVAL, *Deconstructing Apartheid Discourse* (London, 1996).
[46] L. RONIGER and M. SZNAJDER, *The Legacy of Human Rights Violations in the Southern Cone: Argentina, Uruguay and Chile* (Oxford, 1999).
[47] As in T. RISSE, S.C. ROPP and K. SIKKINK, *The Power of Human Rights: International Norms and Domestic Change* (Cambridge, 1999).
[48] As in the case of Chile in D. HAWKINS, *International Human Rights and Authoritarian Rule in Chile* (Lincoln, 2002).

Finally, the last two categories in the continuum (Columns VI and VII) share the same orientation toward providing universal knowledge claims and explanations for human rights violations based on deductive reasoning, while differing in their reliance on evidence. Most rationalist forms of analysis engage in a process of theorising, where assumptions about human nature are combined with a series of 'stylised facts' and then used to derive a set a propositions about social phenomena that can be observed. Approaches in the penultimate category (Column VI) involve deriving a set of propositions deductively from starting assumptions and then testing them with limited empirical evidence, which typically consists of confirmatory case studies. Thus, Mitchell[49] develops a rationalist model about the different relationships between principal's and agents (or leaders and followers) and how they explain the variation in atrocities across three different civil wars. In contrast, approaches in the final category (Column VII) deduce their propositions in exactly the same manner, but do not subject them to empirical testing. Wantchekon and Healy present an abstract and highly stylised set of strategic interactions between 'ideal type' torturers and victims to arrive at a set of deductive conclusions. Presenting such an analysis in abstract form only has led to such studies being criticised for providing 'inference without evidence',[50] since nowhere in the study is the theory of strategic interaction ever subjected to an empirical test.

This broad range of methodological approaches to studying human rights is a function of a general epistemological continuum that ranges from the more 'cloudlike' set of explanations at one extreme to their more 'clocklike' counterparts on the other extreme[51]; the variation in the use of inductive and deductive reasoning; the balance between pure evidence and pure inference, the nature of the of the knowledge claims; and the scope of geographical coverage in the collection and analysis of evidence on human rights problems. It is clear that extant and new studies located along this continuum ask different research questions or examine similar sets of questions differently, such that the universe of human rights issues and topics for research can be confronted by a plurality of methodological approaches. It is clear that a number of significant, valid, and recognised research traditions characterise the social sciences and that each of these traditions asks particular questions of its research material and applies different methods to its objects of inquiry.

---

[49]   N. MITCHELL, *Agents of Atrocity: Leaders, Followers, and the Violation of Human Rights in Civil War* (London, 2004).

[50]   G. ALMOMD, 'Political Science: The History of the Discipline', in R.E. GOODIN and H. KLINGEMANN (eds.), *The New Handbook of Political Science* (Oxford, 1996) 50-96, at 52.

[51]   K. POPPER, 'Of Clouds and Clocks: An Approach to the Problem of Rationality and Freedom in Man', in K. POPPER, *Objective Knowledge: An Evolutionary Approach* (Oxford, 1972); G. ALMOND S. GENCO, 'Clouds, Clocks and the Study of Politics,' 29 *World Politics* (1977) 489-522.

3.1.2. Cross-National Generalisations and Comparative Methods

Comparative methods provide ways in which to compare similarities and differences across countries to arrive at a series of generalizations about particular human rights problems. There are three general comparative methods available to social scientists of human rights: global comparisons, few-country comparisons, and single-case studies. The trade-offs associated with these methods involve the degree to which each can make broad ranging empirical generalizations at different levels of theoretical and conceptual abstraction.[52] Global comparisons tend to make broad ranging empirical generalizations using concepts and constructs at a fairly high level of abstraction. Few-country comparisons tend to limit their generalizations and lower the level the abstraction in analysing human rights problems across a selection of countries. Single-case analysis tends to limit further its empirical generalizations and concentrates on the contextual particularities of the single case under investigation, but can be constructed in such a way to contribute to larger theoretical and empirical problems. These three comparative methods and their associated strengths and weaknesses are considered in turn.

3.1.2.1. Global Comparative Analysis

Global comparative analysis typically involves the use of large and complex data sets comprised of variables that have been operationalised quantitatively (see below) and have been specified in such a way that they can be measured over time and across space. Rarely do such studies carry out their analysis using qualitative methods, which focuses more in-depth on particular features within countries and is therefore not possible with sample sizes that often exceed 100 countries. With such a large number of observations (typical time and space combinations exceed 4000 such observations), global comparisons make empirical generalizations about relationships between and among variables that have associated degrees of statistical significance. For this reason, such studies are known as 'variable-oriented' since their focus is on 'general dimensions of macro-social variation' and the relationship between variables at a global level of analysis.[53] The main strengths of this kind of analysis include statistical control to rule out rival explanations, extensive coverage of cases, the ability to make strong inferences, and the identification of 'deviant' cases or 'outliers'. For example, one typical finding from the extant global comparative literature on human rights suggests that 'personal integrity rights' violations are lower in countries that have high levels of economic wealth and democracy. The

---

[52] MAIR, *supra* n. 30; LANDMAN, *supra* n. 29; LANDMAN, *supra* n. 5, 2002; LANDMAN, *supra* n. 5, 2003; T. LANDMAN, *Protecting Human Rights: A Global Comparative Study* (Washington DC, 2005b).

[53] C. RAGIN, *Constructing Social Research: The Unity and Diversity of Method* (Thousand Oaks, 1994) 300.

fact that there are numerous wealthy countries and/or democracies that continue to violate human rights does not undermine this general finding. Rather, such countries become significant outliers to the general relationship that are need of further analysis to explain why their practices appear anomalous. For example, Saudi Arabia is a classic outlier that is wealthy and has significant problems with human rights violations, while Brazil and India are seen as consolidated democracies with exceptionally high levels of torture.[54]

Global analysis also has a number of weaknesses, including data availability, validity and reliability of rights and other measures, and its limited application to human rights problems. First, until very recently, there had been a dearth of cross-national data on human rights practices. There are still only five major sources of human rights measures available for global comparative analysis, all of which are limited ordinal 'standards-based' scales of human rights practices.[55] The 'political terror scale',[56] the Freedom House civil and political liberties scales,[57] and the torture scale[58] measure a narrowly defined set of civil and political rights, while the Cingranelli and Richards human rights data set[59] includes measures of civil, political and some economic rights. Second, there are serious questions remaining about the validity and reliability of these rights measures, which code qualitative information typically found in Amnesty International and/or US State Department human rights country reports into quantitative scales. Third, global comparative analysis cannot address a whole range of important research questions in the human rights field, since many such topics are not susceptible to quantitative methods. Even if they are, global quantitative analysis provides generalizations that need greater specification and in-depth research that can only be carried out on smaller samples of countries.[60]

---

[54]   LANDMAN, *supra* n. 53.

[55]   LANDMAN, *supra* n. 1, 2004.

[56]   C. MITCHELL, M. STOHL, D. CARLETON and G. LOPEZ, 'State Terrorism: Issues of Concept and Measurement', in M. STOHL and G. LOPEZ, *Government Violence and Repression: An Agenda for Research* (New York, 1986); S. POE and C.N. TATE, 'Repression of Human Rights to Personal Integrity in the 1980s: A Global Analysis', 88 *American Political Science Review* (1994) 853-872; M. GIBNEY and M. DALTON, 'The Political Terror Scale', in D.L. CINGRANELLI (ed.), *Human Rights and Developing Countries* (Greenwich, 1996) 73-84; M. GIBNEY and M. STOHL, 'Human Rights and US Refugee Policy', in M. GIBNEY (ed.), *Open Borders? Closed Societies?: The Ethical and Political Issues* (Westport, 1998); <http://www.politicalterrorscale.org>.

[57]   R.D. GASTIL, *Freedom in the World: Political Rights and Civil Liberties* (Boston, 1978); R.D. GASTIL, *Freedom in the World: Political Rights and Civil Liberties* (Westport, 1980); R.D. GASTIL, *Freedom in the World: Political and Civil Liberties, 1986-1987* (New York, 1988); R.D. GASTIL, *The Comparative Survey of Freedom: Experiences and Suggestions, 25 Studies in Comparative International Development* (1990) 25-50; <www.freedomhouse.org>.

[58]   O. HATHAWAY, 'Do Treaties Make a Difference? Human Rights Treaties and the Problem of Compliance', 111 *Yale Law Journal* (2002) 1932-2042; <www.todd-landman.com>.

[59]   <www.humanrightsdata.com>.

[60]   LANDMAN, *supra* n. 21.

3.1.2.2. Few-Country Comparisons

It is precisely because of the limitations and weaknesses of global comparative analysis that many human rights scholars carry out their analyses on a smaller selection of countries. Variously called the comparative method, the 'comparable cases strategy' 1975),[61] or 'focused comparison',[62] comparing few countries achieves control through the careful selection of cases that are analysed using a middle level of conceptual abstraction. Studies using this method are more *intensive* and less *extensive* since they encompass more of the nuances specific to each case. The outcomes that feature in this type of comparison are often seen to be 'configurative', i.e. the product of multiple causal factors acting together. In contrast to global comparative analysis, this type of comparison is referred to as 'case-oriented',[63] since the case is often the unit of analysis and the focus tends to be on the similarities and differences among cases rather than the analytical relationships between variables. Such comparisons tend to make generalizations that are less broad using concepts and constructs that have been analysed in greater depth across the countries that have been selected for analysis.

In order to make these generalizations, the comparison of the similarities and differences across a small number of countries is meant to uncover the empirical relationship between the presence of key explanatory factors (X1, X2, ... Xn) and the presence of an observed outcome (Y). The isolation of these explanatory factors and the determination of their relationship to the observed outcome can be achieved through adopting two distinct types of research design: 'most similar systems design' and 'most different systems design'.[64] Drawing on J. S. Mill's[65] 'method of difference', most similar systems design (MSSD) compares different outcomes across similar countries. Comparing countries that share a host of common features allows for the isolation of those factors that may account for an outcome. Typically, regional and area studies analysis compares countries that share similar history, language, religion, politics, and culture and then isolates the remaining factors that vary across the cases to see if that variation is related to the variation in the outcome that is to

---

[61]   A. LIJPHART, 'The Comparable Cases Strategy in Comparative Research', 8 *Comparative Political Studies* (1975) 158-177

[62]   R. HAGUE, M. HARROP and S. BRESLIN, *Political Science: A Comparative Introduction*, (New York, 1992).

[63]   C. RAGIN, *supra* n. 54.

[64]   A. PRZEWORSKI and H. TEUNE, *The Logic of Comparative Social Inquiry* (New York, 1970); T. SKOCPOL and M. SOMERS, 'The Uses of Comparative History in Macrosocial Inquiry', 22 *Comparative Studies in Society and History* (1980) 174-197; A.M. FAURE, 'Some Methodological Problems in Comparative Politics', 6 *Journal of Theoretical Politics* (1994) 307-322; LANDMAN, *supra* n. 29; LANDMAN, *supra* n. 5, 2002; LANDMAN, *supra* n. 5, 2003.

[65]   J.S. MILL, *A System of Logic* (London, 1843).

be explained. In this way, the common features are 'controlled', while the analysis focuses on the relationship between the explanatory factors and the outcome.

In contrast to MSSD, most different systems design (MDSD) compares similar outcomes across different countries. Drawing on Mill's[66] logic of agreement, MDSD compares countries that share very few features and then focuses on those factors common across the countries that may account for an outcome. In this way, selecting countries with the same outcome and matching that outcome to the presence of key explanatory factors allows the researcher to establish their empirical relationship. Comparative studies that focus on large historical events such as revolutions, military coups, transitions to democracy, or 'economic miracles' in newly industrialized countries[67] adopt this basic research design, where these types of outcomes are matched to the presence of key explanatory factors(s). For example, Hayner[68] compares the outcomes and impact of similar instances of truth commissions across countries in Latin America and Africa. Her comparisons reveal that ethnic, religious, and group conflict in Africa explains why reconciliation is less likely than in Latin America, where conflict was borne of an ideological struggle between forces on the political left and right. Thus the nature of conflict (X) is a key explanatory factor that accounts for the differences in impact of truth commissions (Y).

Both MSSD and MDSD seek to identify a relationship between explanatory factors and outcomes by comparing different outcomes across similar countries or similar outcomes across different countries. Of the two research designs, MSSD is slightly more robust, since it allows for the presence of different outcomes across the countries under investigation, such that the dependent variable is actually allowed to vary. In contrast, MDSD does not allow for the presence of different outcomes, and thus has no variance in the dependent variable (a form of selection bias). MDSD thus establishes a concomitance of explanatory factors and outcomes since it does not allow for 'negative' instances of the outcomes being examined.[69] Moreover, the number of outcomes that have actually occurred in the world limits the number of countries this framework of analysis can include in any one comparison (i.e. there are a finite number of outcomes of interest).

The comparison of few countries suffers from two major methodological weaknesses. First, such studies may identify a large number of explanatory variables

---

[66]   MILL, *supra* n. 66.

[67]   B. GEDDES, 'How the Cases You Choose Affect the Answers You Get: Selection Bias in Comparative Politics', 2 *Political Analysis* (1990) 131-150 at 134-141.

[68]   P.B. HAYNER, 'Fifteen Truth Commissions – 1974-1994: A Comparative Study, 16 *Human Rights Quarterly* (1994) 597-655; P.B. HAYNER, *Unspeakable Truths: Facing the Challenges of Truth Commissions* (New York, 2002).

[69]   J. MAHONEY and G. GOERTZ, 'The Possibility Principle: Choosing Negative Cases in Comparative Research,' 98 *American Political Science Review* (2004) 653-669.

whose full variation far exceeds the number of countries under investigation. This problem is commonly labelled 'too many variables, not enough countries',[70] or 'too many inferences and not enough observations'.[71] For example, a study that specifies three explanatory variables each with several categories (e.g. low, medium, and high) and outcome variable with as few as two categories (e.g. improvement in rights protection or not), and then analyses these variables across only three countries will never really be able to establish a relationship between the explanatory variables and the outcome. Solutions to this particular problem include raising the number of observations (include time, sub-national units, or more countries); resort to MSSD, which controls for the common features; or reduce the number of explanatory variables through adopting MDSD or through better theoretical specification.[72]

Second, the *intentional* selection of cases rather than a *random* selection can seriously undermine the types of inferences that can be drawn. This problem is known as selection bias, and occurs in comparative politics through the non-random choice of countries for comparison, or the deliberate selection by the comparativist.[73] Though selection of countries lies at the heart of comparison, selection without reflection may lead to serious problems of inference. The most blatant form of selection occurs when a study includes only those cases that support the theory. More subtle forms of selection bias, however, occur when the choice of countries relies on values of the dependent variable[74] and for qualitative studies, the use of certain historical sources that (un) wittingly support the theoretical perspective of the researcher.[75] As outlined above, MDSD suffers from selection bias relating to values of the dependent variable, where only those countries with the outcome of interest (e.g. democratic transition, military coup, revolution) have been selected. Relatedly, it is possible to construct a few-country comparison that contains an indeterminate research design by comparing different outcomes across different countries. For example, in the *Power of Human Rights,* Risse, Ropp and Sikkink[76] present five 'paired comparisons' (Kenya-Uganda, Tunisia-Morocco, Indonesia-Philippines, Chile-Guatemala, and Poland — the former Czechoslovakia) and one

---

[70] M. DOGAN and D. PELASSY, *How to Compare Nations: Strategies in Comparative Politics* (2nd ed.) (Chatham, 1990); D. COLLIER, 'New Perspectives on the Comparative Method', in D. A. RUSTOW and K. P. ERICKSON (eds.), *Comparative Political Dynamics: Global Research Perspectives* (New York, 1991) 7-31; HAGUE, HARROP and BRESLIN, *supra* n. 63.(King, Keohane, and Verba 1994).

[71] KING, KEOHANE and VERBA, *supra* n. 5.

[72] LANDMAN, *supra* n. 5, 2003, 40-41.

[73] D. COLLIER, 'Translating Quantitative Methods for Qualitative Researchers: The Case of Selection Bias', 89 *American Political Science Review* (1995) 461-466 at 462.

[74] GEDDES, *supra* n. 68; KING, KEHANE AND VERBA, *supra* n. 5; MAHONEY AND GOERTZ, *supra* n. 70.

[75] I. LUSTICK, 'History, Historiography, and Political Science: Multiple Historical Records and the Problem of Selection Bias', 90 *American Political Science Review* (1996) 605–618.

[76] RISSE, ROPP and SIKKINK, *supra* n. 48.

single-country analysis of South Africa to examine the transmission of international human rights norms. But the analysis reveals different outcomes across these different cases thereby limiting the types of inferences that are drawn.[77]

3.1.2.3. Single-Country Studies

The field of human rights research is full of single-country studies. By definition, they focus on countries with particularly problematic human rights records and include official reports from international governmental and non-governmental organizations, domestic commissions and NGOs, journalistic and descriptive accounts, and research monographs. The *Nunca Más*[78] report from Argentina and the *Nunca Mais*[79] report from Brazil are classic examples of such descriptive accounts of human rights abuse under conditions of authoritarianism, and as discussed above, truth commissions often publish their findings for the general public, such as the South African Truth and Reconciliation Commission and the *Comisión de Verdad y Reconciliación* in Peru (Truth and Reconciliation Commission, CVR). On balance, however, these descriptive accounts are not grounded in any one discipline, and they rarely make larger inferences from the intensive examination of the individual case. The descriptive accounts do, however, serve as the foundation for research monographs, which are grounded in one or more disciplines and tend to locate the country study in a broader set of theoretical and empirical questions relevant to the study of human rights.

Beyond their pure descriptive function, single-country studies can make significant and valuable contributions to the study of human rights, including establishing new classifications, the generation of hypotheses and their use as 'crucial cases' for testing hypotheses. There are several examples where the development of new classifications has advanced scholarship in describing, understanding, and explaining patterns of human rights abuse. Juan Linz's[80] development of the *authoritarian* regime type based on the case of Spain was extended by Gullermo O'Donnell[81] to classify the 'bureaucratic-authoritarian' regime based on the case of Argentina in the 1960s and 1970s, which was then applied to other Latin America regimes[82] as well as to those in Southeast Asia.[83] Patron-client relations and their permeation of state organization identified in Latin America have

---

[77]   LANDMAN, *supra* n. 5, 2003; LANDMAN *supra* n. 21.

[78]   CONADEP, *Nunca Más (Never Again): A Report by Argentina's National Commission on Disappeared People* (Buenos Aires, 1984).

[79]   J. DASSIN (ed.), *Torture in Brazil, A Report by the Archdiocese of São Paulo* (New York, 1986).

[80]   J.J. LINZ, 'An Authoritarian Regime: Spain', in E. ALLARDT and S. ROKKAN (eds.), *Mass Politics* (New York, 1964).

[81]   G. O'DONNELL, *Economic Modernization and Bureaucratic Authoritarianism* (Berkeley, 1973).

[82]   See also D. COLLIER (ed.), *The New Authoritarianism in Latin America* (Princeton, 1979).

[83]   GEDDES, *supra* n. 68.

been developed into models of neo-patrimonialism and predatory states in Africa.[84] Kaldor,[85] and Gilbert,[86] and Münkler[87] have specified new forms of warfare that move beyond more traditional understandings of conflict and that have grave consequences for human rights, and Payne[88] has developed the concept of 'uncivil' movements that can 'travel' for subsequent comparative studies.

Single-country studies are also useful for generating hypotheses for theories that have yet to be specified fully. As 'plausibility probes',[89] single-country studies explicitly (or implicitly) suggest that the generated hypothesis ought to be tested in a larger selection of countries.[90] For example, in their analysis of the effectiveness of international human rights pressure on the Argentine military regime, Weissbrodt and Bartolomei[91] conclude by arguing 'the lessons of this case study must be tested in cases involving other countries and time periods to determine whether more general lessons can be drawn from this single case'. In similar fashion, in his study of the relationship between international human rights pressure and the transformation of the Pinochet regime, Hawkins[92] tests the hypotheses generated in the Chilean case in the additional cases of Cuba and South Africa. His analysis of Chile shows that certain 'rule-oriented' factions within the Chilean military became influenced by outside human rights pressure, which ultimately led to gradual concessions by the regime and the transition to democracy. The further testing of his central hypothesis shows that a similar process took place in South Africa but not in Cuba, since there are not significant fissures in the ruling elite that would be susceptible to the influence of international human rights pressure.

Finally, single-country studies are useful if they act as 'crucial' cases drawn from theoretical expectations and propositions about the world. Such crucial case studies can confirm or infirm existing theories and are therefore conducted within the confines of extant generalizations.[93] There are two types of crucial case studies. 'most likely' and 'least likely'.[94] Least likely case studies select a country where theory

---

[84]   C. CLAPHAM (ed.), *Private Patronage and Public Power: Political Clientelism in the Modern State* (London, 1982); M. BRATTON AND N. VAN DE WALLE, *Democratic Experiments in Africa: Regime Transitions in Comparative Perspective* (Cambridge, 1997); J. HAYNES, *Politics in the Developing World: A Concise Introduction* (Malden, 2002).

[85]   M. KALDOR, *New and Old Wars: Organized Violence in a Global Era* (Cambridge, 1999).

[86]   P. GILBERT, *New Terror, New Wars* (Edinburgh, 2003).

[87]   H. MÜNKLER, *The New Wars* (Cambridge, 2005).

[88]   L. PAYNE, *Uncivil Movements: The Armed Right Wing and Democracy in Latin America* (Baltimore, 2000).

[89]   ECKSTEIN, *supra* n. 40, 108.

[90]   LIJPHART, *supra* n. 39, 692.

[91]   D. WEISSBRODT and M.L. BARTOLOMEI, 'The Effectiveness of International Human Rights Pressures: The Case of Argentina, 1976-1983', 75 *Minnesota Law Review* (1991) 1009-1035 at 1034.

[92]   HAWKINS, *supra* n. 49.

[93]   LIJPHART, *supra* n. 39, 692.

[94]   ECKSTEIN, *supra* n. 40, 118.

suggests an outcome is not likely to occur. If the outcome is observed, then the theory is infirmed, since it suggested such an outcome should not be obtained in that particular country. For example, in his analysis of democratic transition in South Africa, Howarth and Norval[95] argue that the South African case is the best example of a least likely case study since the longevity and strength of the Apartheid regime suggested that a democratic transition was highly unlikely. The fact that there was such a transition invites deeper analysis of the case itself and greater reflection on theories of democratization. Other 'least likely' candidates in this area of research include North Korea and Burma/Myanmar, which over the next coming years may undergo similar unexpected processes of democratic transition.

Most likely case studies apply a reverse logic to least likely studies by selecting countries where theory suggests the outcome is definitely meant to occur. If the outcome is not observed, then the theory is infirmed. For example, Brazil and the United States are seen to be most likely case studies that have confounded particular social theories that link socio-economic change to political outcomes. For the Brazilian case, many varieties of social theories suggest that Brazil has had all the objective economic conditions necessary for a social revolution and yet no attempt to organise a mass-based revolutionary force has ever been made. In similar fashion, despite its rapid pace of industrialization, expansion of its labour force, and constitutional protection for the rights to assembly and association, the United States has never had a strong socialist party. The task of the analyst is thus to explain these so-called 'non-events' in these particular cases through identifying those factors that have inhibited the development of a fully fledged revolutionary movement in Brazil or a strong socialist party in the United States. In this way, Brazil and the United States represent 'deviant' cases since they fail to fall in line with theoretical expectations. Thus, most likely case analysis provides the means to explain the presence of such deviant cases. Additional candidates for most likely case analysis include Cuba and China, which have failed to undergo processes of democratic transition despite the 'velvet revolutions' and the collapse of Communism in the Former Soviet Union.

Single-country studies thus serve larger comparative purposes if they lead to new classifications of social phenomena, generate new hypotheses about important empirical relationships, and provide critical tests of extant theories. Human rights abuses take place across a huge range of different social, economic, and political contexts, and single-country studies provide the richness of contextual description and the analysis of new institutional, cultural, and behaviour phenomena. Such studies should not be seen as 'merely precursory moments'[96] in the larger quest for

---

[95]   D. HOWARTH and A.J. NORVAL (eds.), *South Africa in Transition: New Theoretical Perspectives* (Basingstoke, 1998).
[96]   HOWARTH, *supra* n. 34, 332.

social scientific explanation, but as also having value in and of themselves. As we have seen, however, in making these new classification and analyses, single-country studies can generate important hypotheses to be tested in other countries and contexts. Moreover, crucial case studies, whether 'most likely' or 'least likely' do not definitively prove or disprove a theory in line with Popper's[97] notion of scientific falsification, but they do help *confirm* or *infirm* the applicability of social theories to all cases.[98] They are thus particularly useful in testing the robustness of theories and research programmes in the social sciences that make universal knowledge claims, such as those outlined in the first section of this contribution.

3.2. QUANTITATIVE AND QUALITATIVE EVIDENCE

The final methodological dimension in need of explicit attention is the difference between quantitative and qualitative evidence and its use in studying human rights problems. Quantitative methods seek to show differences in number between certain objects of analysis and qualitative methods seek to show differences in kind. Quantitative analysis answers the simple question, 'How many of them are there?',[99] where the 'them' represents any object of comparison that can either be counted or assigned a numerical value. Quantitative data can be official aggregate data published by governments on growth rates, revenues and expenditures, levels of agricultural and industrial production, crime rates and prison populations, or the number of hectares of land devoted to agrarian reform. Quantitative data can also be individual, such as that found in the numerous market research surveys and public opinion polls. In the field of human rights, it is possible to count human rights violations, convert subjective accounts of human rights practices into standardised scales, or to collect survey data on human rights practices from random samples of the population. Such measures of human rights can then be use for statistical analysis that describes and explains the nature, extent, pattern, and causes of human rights violations.

Quantitative methods are based on the distributions these data exhibit and the relationships that can be established between numeric variables using simple and advanced statistical methods. The common tools for estimating simple bivariate measures of association are correlation and cross-tabulation, where statistics help establish the magnitude, direction, and significance of the association between two variables. The common tool for estimating more complex and 'multivariate' relationships is some form of regression analysis, which determines the magnitude,

---

[97]   K. POPPER, *The Logic of Scientific Discovery* (London, 1959).

[98]   ECKSTEIN, *supra* n. 40; T. LANDMAN, 'Economic Development and Democracy: The View From Latin America', 47 *Political Studies* (1999).

[99]   W.L. MILLER, 'Quantitative Analysis', in: *Theories and Methods in Political Science* (London, 1995) 154-172, at 154.

direction, and significance of the independent relationships between the two or more explanatory variables and the outcome that is to be explained.[100] Multivariate analysis controls for these other factors to determine whether the original relationship is upheld. The results of this kind of analysis provide measures of association between all the explanatory variables and the outcome variable, which allows the analyst to determine their relative strength, magnitude, and statistical significance. If the original explanatory variable of interest maintains its significant relationship with the outcome variable in the presence of other explanatory variables, then it is possible to conclude that the original relationship has been upheld. The other explanatory variables are considered 'controls'.

Qualitative methods seek to identify and understand the attributes, characteristics, and traits of the objects of inquiry, as well as the meanings, processes, and context.[101] The nature of the method necessarily requires a focus on a small number of units of analysis, whether they are individuals, groups, sub-national regions, countries, or *supra*-national regions. As discussed across many of the examples above, qualitative methods include macro-historical comparison;[102] in-depth interviews and participant observation;[103] interpretivism, hermeneutics, and 'thick description';[104] and varieties of discourse analysis.[105] In none of these types of method is there an attempt to give numerical expression to the objects of inquiry, and in all of them, the goal is to provide well-rounded and complete discursive accounts. These more complete accounts are often referred to as 'ideographic' or 'configurative', since they seek to identify all the elements important in accounting for an outcome.

There has traditionally been a deep division in the social sciences between those who use quantitative methods and those who use qualitative methods; however, it seems that this division is a false one for several reasons. First, the strict separation between qualitative and qualitative methods is minimised if both methods adhere to the goal of making inferences from available evidence.[106] The same logic of inference and concerns over research design ought to apply equally to quantitative and

---

[100]   M.S. LEWIS-BECK, *Applied Regression: An Introduction* (London and Thousand Oaks, 1980); G.W. BOHRNSTEDT and D. KNOKE, *Statistics for Social Data Analysis* (Itasca, 1988); J. FOX, *Applied Regression Analysis, Linear Models, and Related Methods* (London, 1997).

[101]   DEVINE, *supra* n. 34; F. DEVINE and S. HEATH, *Sociological research methods in context* (London, 1999).

[102]   SKOCPOL AND SOMERS, *supra* n. 65; C. RAGIN and L. GRIFFIN (eds.), 'Formal Methods of Qualitative Analysis', 23 *Sociological Methods and Research* (1994) 4-21; J. MAHONEY and D. REUSCHEMEYER (eds.), *Comparative Historical Analysis in the Social Sciences* (Cambridge, 2003).

[103]   DEVINE, *supra* n. 34.

[104]   GEERTZ, *supra* n. 33; B. FAY, *Social Theory and Political Practice* (London, 1975).

[105]   D. HOWARTH, *Discourse* (Milton Keynes, 2000) ;TRAVERS, *supra* n. 34.

[106]   FOWERAKER and LANDMAN, *supra* n. 14, 48-49; TRAVERS, *supra* n. 34, 6-9.

qualitative studies that seek to move beyond pure description.[107] Second, the qualitative distinction made between and among categories in any attempt to classify social phenomena *necessarily precedes the process of quantification*.[108] In this sense, social science needs to know 'what kind' of object to count before counting it, and this qualitative step is vitally important in the quantification of human rights (for a general discussion see Goetz).[109] Third, and related to the first two points, there have been important and significant methodological developments in combining the strengths of qualitative and quantitative techniques by recognising that both methods are founded on the same logic of inference and linking qualitative distinctions to quantitative representation. These developments include 'qualitative comparative analysis'[110] and the use of Boolean algebraic techniques to identify necessary and sufficient conditions for outcomes; text and content analysis, which codes words into numbers;[111] and the quantitative deconstruction of victim testimonies to truth commissions.[112]

4. CONCLUSION: METHODS MATTER

In its analysis and discussion of the different methodological traditions and options in the social sciences, this contribution shows how and why method matters for the social scientific analysis of human rights problems. Methods link theory and evidence, provide the basic rules of inquiry, and provide the tools that maximise the kind of inferences that are drawn. The paper has argued that there is not one preferred method, since method is a function of the epistemological orientations of the researcher, the theoretical perspective that is adopted, the nature of the research question, as well as the available time and material resources with which to carry out any research project. It is clear that methods vary across the epistemological continuum from 'clouds' to 'clocks', the full range of comparative analysis from global comparative to single-country studies, and the degree to which qualitative, quantitative, or hybrid methods are adopted.

---

[107]   KING, KEOHANE and VERBA, *supra* n. 5; H.E. BRADY and D. COLLIER, *Rethinking Social Inquiry: Diverse Tools, Shared Standards* (New York, 2004).

[108]   SARTORI, *supra* n. 30; G. SARTORI, *Comparative Constitutional Engineering. An Inquiry into Structures, Incentives and Outcomes* (London, 1994).

[109]   G. GOERTZ, *Social Science Concepts: A User's Guide* (Princeton, 2006).

[110]   C. RAGIN, *The Comparative Method: Moving beyond Qualitative and Quantitative Strategies* (Berkeley, 1987); RAGIN, *supra* n. 54.

[111]   R. FRANZOSI, *From Words to Numbers: Narrative, Data and Social Science* (Cambridge, 2004).

[112]   B. BALL, H.F. SPIRER and L. SPIRER (eds.), *Making the case : Investigating Large Scale Human Rights Violations Using Information Systems and Data Analysis* (Washington DC, 2000); R.A. WILSON, 'Representing Human Rights Violations: Social Context and Subjectivities', in R.A. WILSON (ed.), *Human Rights, Culture, and Context: Anthropological Approaches* (London, 1997); R.A. WILSON, *The Politics of Truth and Reconciliation In South Africa: Legitimizing the Post-Apartheid State* (Cambridge, 2001).

The social sciences continue to address real-world problems and provide solutions and policy prescriptions based on the best evidence available. Ironically, at a time when world events call out most for unbiased, systematic, and rigorous social science analysis, there continues to be significant disagreement in some quarters of the about how social science can maintain its relevance. For example, in political science, the 'Perestroikan' movement primarily based in the United States, criticizes the discipline's overemphasis on method and mathematical sophistication, leading the profession to lose sight of political puzzles and problems and/or providing answers that are largely unintelligible to policymakers and practitioners.[113] The main charge of the movement is that the discipline has become highly 'technicist' and 'statistical', where method is given greater weight than substance.[114]

The movement and other like-minded proponents argue that more weight should be given to substance over method, effectively loosening the rules of inquiry and the logic of inference, while providing 'distinctive insights into substantive political questions'.[115] Flyvbjerg[116] proposes a way of recapturing the substance of politics and to make political science 'matter'. Flyvbjerg challenges fundamentally the desire and attempt within the social sciences to emulate the natural sciences (i.e. its appeal to observable events and the logic of inference advocated in King, Keohane and Verba).[117] He draws on a short passage in Aristotle's *Nichomachean Ethics* on the 'chief intellectual virtues' to build a framework for conducting more holistic social scientific analysis that pays greater attention to the rich complexity of context, while offering a deeper understanding of politics that moves beyond the narrow techno-rationalism of certain dominant strands in contemporary political science.

In particular, he uses Aristotle's virtues of knowledge (*episteme*), craft (*techné*), and practical wisdom (*phronesis*) to build what he sees is a more complete approach to studying social phenomena. Where *episteme* refers to abstract and universal knowledge (e.g. the rational individual) and *techné* to the specific 'know-how associated with practicing a craft' (e.g. multivariate regression analysis or the use of MDSD and MSSD), *phronesis* comes from an 'intimate familiarity with the contingencies and uncertainties of various forms of social practice embedded in

---

[113] S.E. BENNETT, "Perestroika' Lost: Why the Latest 'Reform' Movement in Political Science Should Fail', 35 *PS: Political Science and Politics* (2002) 177–179; R. SMITH, 'Putting the Substance Back in Political Science', (5 April) *Chronicle of Higher Education* (2002) B10–11; SCHRAM AND CATERINO, *supra* n. 28.

[114] BENNETT, *supra* n. 114; SMITH, *supra* n. 114.

[115] SMITH, *supra* n. 114, 10.

[116] FLYVBJERG, *supra* n. 28; B. FLYVBJERG, 'A Perestroikan Straw Man Answers Back: David Laitin and Phronetic Social Science', in S.F. SCHRAM AND B. CATERINO (eds.), *Making Political Science Matter: Debating Knowledge, Research, and Methods* (New York, 2006) 56-85.

[117] KING, KEOHANE and VERBA, *supra* n. 5.

complex social settings'.[118] *Phronesis* is thus 'situated practical reasoning'[119] and for Flyvbjerg, it ought to be at the centre of social science research. While he does not seek to displace *episteme* and *techné* altogether, which he sees as the essential features of the natural-science model of social inquiry, he does want to recapture *phronesis* and place it on an equal footing to these other two elements.

While not abandoning methodological concerns altogether, this proposition for social science and complementary arguments put forth more generally by the Perestroika movement suggest that social science research 'may not be methodologically innovative, unusually precise, or indeed mathematical, but [it must] nonetheless [provide] fresh empirical evidence and well-reasoned arguments sufficient to judge some positions on important issues to be more credible than others'.[120] In this sense, the movement is making a call to re-balance social science research away from an emphasis on *explanation* towards a greater emphasis on *understanding*. This duality between explanation and understanding, much like other dualities in the social sciences (e.g. universality and particularity, qualitative analysis — and quantitative analysis, nomothetic deductivism and hermeneutic interpretivism, methodological unity and methodological pluralism, value-free and value-laden political science, and method-driven and problem-driven political science research programmes) may be overdrawn for rhetorical purposes, and if taken to far, could steer social science in a dangerous and unhelpful direction.

It appears that there are three positions available to adopt. The first, which the Perestroikans charge is no longer tenable, is that method takes precedence over substance. The second, which many within the Perestroikan movement advocate, is that substance ought to take precedence over method. The third position, which this paper advocates, is that *method is the substance*.[121] Without careful specification of the research problem, the identification of observable implications of the theory, careful collection and presentation of the evidence, and logical drawing of inferences, social science research will never be more than speculation and conjecture. Research design, the strategy for collecting and analysing data, and setting up a research problem that provides the means with which to know if the propositions being tested are actually supported by the evidence are all part of sound social scientific research. As the human rights community seeks to make progress in the promotion and protection of human rights, it needs sound analysis and a systematic evidence base from which to make strong arguments that may lead to new international standards, concessions from rights-abusive governments, or humanitarian assistance, foreign aid, and other forms of human intervention on

---

[118] B. CATERINO and S.F. SCHRAM, *Making Political Science Matter: Debating Knowledge, Research and Method* (New York, 2006) 8.
[119] CATERINO and SCHRAM, *supra* n. 119, 8.
[120] SMITH, *supra* n. 114, B10.
[121] KING, KEOHANE and VERBA, *supra* n. 5, 9.

behalf of vulnerable peoples around the world. Social science method must be a cornerstone to this larger project. Analysing human rights problems with bad methods will lead to erroneous conclusions, bad policy advice, and failure to improve human rights conditions on the ground.

REDEFINING NORMATIVE LEGAL SCIENCE: TOWARDS AN ARGUMENTATIVE DISCIPLINE

Jan M. Smits*

1. INTRODUCTION

Legal scholars are increasingly interested in the proper methodology of their discipline. This debate is especially important in the United States and in the Netherlands,[1] but also in other countries the interest in the methodology of legal science is growing.[2] The interesting thing about this debate is that it seems to take on a new methodological perspective: no longer is it taken for granted that legal scholars make use of the same methods as practising lawyers. Instead, there is a search for scholarly methods that are specific to the *academic* study of law. In this contribution I develop a preliminary theory of what, in my view, is the core of academic legal scholarship and the methodology belonging to it. This theory will then be applied to one specific aspect of the human rights debate.

This paper is structured as follows. First (section 2), I will express concerns about the increasing reliance on *non-normative* perspectives in the law. This should make us think about what is actually the core of the *legal* approach towards questions arising in society or in academia. In section 3, I therefore attempt a redefinition of normative legal scholarship. The accompanying methodology is subsequently discussed in section 4. Section 5 looks at one example of this approach in the field of human rights, while section 6 contains some concluding remarks.

---

* This contribution is based on the lecture held at the Conference on Methods of Human Rights Research, Maastricht 23-24 November 2007. It is part of a larger research project co-funded by NWO (SARO-014-24-812).

[1] See, e.g. R. KOROBKIN, 'A Multi-Disciplinary Approach to Legal Scholarship: Economics, Behavioral Economics, and Evolutionary Psychology', *UCLA School of Law Research Paper 01-5* (2001); C.J.J.M. STOLKER, "Ja, geléérd zijn jullie wel!': over de status van de rechtswetenschap', 78 *Nederlands Juristenblad (*2003) 766-778; J.B.M. VRANKEN, *Exploring the Jurist's Frame of Mind* (Deventer, 2006) and the references listed below.

[2] Cf. for the United Kingdom, e.g. C. MCCRUDDEN, 'Legal Research and the Social Sciences', 122 *Law Quarterly Review* (2006) 632-650 and cf. for Germany J. IPSEN, 'Ranking juristischer Fakultäten in Deutschland', 60 *Juristenzeitung* (2005) 424-427.

There is one *caveat* for the reader: this paper is part of a larger research project on the aim and methodology of legal science. Some of the arguments used in this contribution will therefore be elaborated in future work.[3] This is particularly true for what is said in sections 3 and 4 about normative legal scholarship and its accompanying methodology: these sections sketch the contours of my approach, but do not discuss all relevant aspects of it.

2. FROM INTERNAL TO EXTERNAL APPROACHES OF LEGAL SCIENCE

Although criticism of the scholarly status of academic legal scholarship is not new,[4] it seems to have become particularly fierce over the last two decades. Paradigmatic is Becher's qualification of traditional work in British legal academia as 'narrow, conservative, illiberal, unrealistic and boring,' with too much attention on technical details and too little interest in the 'big' questions.[5] In other countries, similar criticism is expressed against the traditional academic approach towards law.[6]

What is this contested approach exactly? The usual criticism is mainly directed towards the black letter or 'doctrinal' approach, in which legal rules, principles and cases are studied from an internal perspective and in which the law is looked at as operating in a 'social, economic and political vacuum'.[7] The existing law in the form of statutes and case decisions is taken as a starting point and this law is further elaborated and criticized by legal scholars, leading to an intense inner relationship between legal scholarship and legal practice: scholars accept a large part of what the legislator and the courts produce as given, while legal practice can profit from the criticism and further systematization of the law by academia. The finding of *coherence* in the given materials is seen as an important, if not *the most* important, aspect of this type of scholarly work. Christopher McCrudden recently characterized this approach as a methodology that concentrates on the 'primacy of critical reasoning based around authoritative texts'.[8] Two aspects of this methodology are important. One is that it indeed centres around the authority of legislatures and courts: their statutes and decisions can be heavily criticized, but in the end their

---

[3]   Notably in a monograph on the status of legal science, to be published in 2009.

[4]   The reference to J. VON KIRCHMANN, *Die Wertlosigkeit der Jurisprudenz als Wissenschaft* (Darmstadt, 1848) should suffice.

[5]   See W. TWINING, *Blackstone's Tower: The English Law School* (London, 1994) 141.

[6]   See for the Netherlands, e.g. STOLKER, *supra*, n. 1 and for the United States the overview in, e.g. E.L. Rubin, 'The Practice and Discourse of Legal Scholarship', 86 *Michigan Law Review* (1988) 1835-1905.

[7]   See D. IBBETSON, 'Historical Research in Law', in: P. CANE and M. TUSHNET (eds.), *Oxford Handbook of Legal Studies* (Oxford, 2003) 863-879, at 864.

[8]   McCRUDDEN, *supra* n. 2, 633.

texts are seen as authoritative.[9] Another aspect is that this methodology is undoubtedly a legal one: even though it is not entirely clear what the legal methodology consists of exactly (it includes aspects of interpretation and systematization and certain argumentation techniques)[10], it is beyond doubt that it is seen as an *autonomous* one: it does not have to include other perspectives than the legal approach. Reference to its own sources is traditionally seen as sufficient in legal studies.

This classical academic approach towards law is now under pressure. I leave aside the reasons for this[11] and limit myself to summarizing what others have said about this 'crisis' in legal scholarship. There is — not for the first time in history — a clear tendency towards the view that the only 'real' knowledge is not based on making conceptual constructions, finding coherence or developing abstract theories (important methods in the 'internal' approach towards law), but on empirical investigation of natural phenomena.[12] It is the view expressed well by the famous physicist Richard Feynman who said that 'the test of all knowledge is experiment. Experiment is the sole judge of scientific truth.'[13] Even though this debate is not new at all (it has been around since the scientific revolution of the seventeenth century), it seems as if the law is now affected by it with much more rigour than in the past.

The most important development in this respect is that the internal perspective towards law is increasingly replaced by an external one. The esteem of critical legal studies, behavioural and empirical analysis of law, law and economics and other 'law and...' approaches are now much higher than traditional doctrinal analysis. This is certainly true in the United States,[14] but to a lesser extent also for an increasing number of European countries. In short: doctrinal analysis is out; external legal research is in. This also means that law has become the domain of other scholars than just lawyers (philosophers, economists, psychologists, sociologists and others) and the tendency seems to be that in matters such as competing for research funds, the representatives of these other disciplines are more successful than lawyers. Thomas Ulen put it like this: 'legal scholarship is on the verge of a dramatically different manner of doing routine legal investigation. Put in a nutshell, that change

---

9   Cf. R.A. POSNER, *The Problems of Jurisprudence* (Cambridge, 1990) 83: 'To be blunt, the *ultimate ratio* of law is indeed force' and the classical statement in T. HOBBES, *A Dialogue Between a Philosopher and A Student of the Common Law of England* (1681), ed. CROPSEY 1971, 55: 'It is not wisdom, but authority that makes a law.'

10   Cf. R.A. POSNER, 'Legal Scholarship Today', 115 *Harvard Law Review* (2002) 1314-1326 at 1316.

11   It is likely that shifts in the way research is funded and universities are organized are to some extent responsible for this.

12   Cf. MCCRUDDEN, *supra* n. 2, 633.

13   R. FEYNMAN, *The Feynman Lectures on Physics* (Reading, 1964).

14   The *locus classicus* is probably R.A. POSNER, 'The Decline of Law as an Autonomous Discipline 1962-1987', 100 *Harvard Law Review* (1987) 761-780.

is to make law much like the other disciplines in the university that believe themselves to be practising 'science' (...)'.[15]

What should one think of this development? I consider it a dangerous one. Of course, there is little doubt that law can profit from taking into account other perspectives than the strictly legal one. But this does not mean we should give up on the *legal* approach towards law. In particular in the present time, the core question in the debate should not be so much how *other* disciplines and methodologies can help us to make the academic study of law more 'scholarly',[16] but how the legal approach *itself* can be made more consistent and match better the expectations one has about a truly scholarly discipline of law. It seems to me there is every reason to 'rediscover' this legal approach towards law. The next section therefore tries to define the contours of that approach.

3. TOWARDS A REDEFINITION OF NORMATIVE LEGAL SCHOLARSHIP: THE *HOMO JURIDICUS*

How to redefine the core of the 'legal' approach towards law? It is in a way surprising that there is not so much debate about what the core of this legal scholarship is. This may have to do with the fact that there are many different areas of law and different approaches towards it. Still, I think it is possible to define the goal and methods of legal scholarship in a relatively uncomplicated way. However, before we do so it may be useful to consider in more detail what is characteristic for scholarly disciplines in general: what are the requirements they should meet?

Although the natural sciences, social sciences and *Geisteswissenschaften* are very different disciplines, they seem to have several things in common. First, they all seek the *systematization* of knowledge: they are not satisfied with just a loose collection of data but try to describe, evaluate and explain these by reference to an existing body of knowledge.[17] Second, the existing knowledge must be the result of some generally accepted *research method*: knowledge has to be obtained in a way that is accepted by the relevant academic community. A third characteristic of most scholarly disciplines is that these are *international*: knowledge achieved through the required method is not local, but is of a universal nature and can therefore transcend

---

[15] T.S. ULEN, 'A Nobel Prize in Legal Science: Theory, Empirical Work, and the Scientific Method in the Study of Law', *Illinois Law and Economics Working Papers* Series LE03-008 (2002), 2. Also see McCRUDDEN, *supra* n. 2, 641: '(...) the growth of an approach to law that may challenge the idea of legal scholarship as a separate craft'.

[16] As many authors in the debate suggest. See, e.g. STOLKER, *supra* n. 1 and R.A.J. VAN GESTEL and J.B.M. VRANKEN, 'Rechtswetenschappelijke artikelen: naar criteria voor methodologische verantwoording', 82 *Nederlands Juristenblad* (2007) 1448-1461.

[17] *Cf.* the German idea of Wissenschaft as any systematic body of enquiry and not to be equated with science in the Anglo-American sense of the word.

national boundaries. As we will see later on, there is little doubt that legal science has the potential to fulfil these three requirements as well — even though the way in which large parts of legal academia operate at the moment seems to contradict this.

This leads me to ask what the ultimate research question in legal scholarship is. At the heart of almost all academic disciplines, there are one or two such core questions. In physics, it is how to understand the natural world, in (micro) economics it is how agents (individuals and firms) behave, and in biology it is how living things function, grow and evolve. But what is the core of legal scholarship? In my view, legal science tries to answer the normative question *what ought to be*. Legal scholars try to establish what it is that individuals, firms, states or other organizations should do or not do as a matter of law. While economists consider the behaviour of the *homo economicus* (trying to explain human conduct from the economic perspective), legal scholars look at a question that precedes this behaviour: what is it that people *should* do as a matter of law? It is this 'prescriptive voice'[18] that makes legal science distinct from other disciplines. 'Should the death penalty be imposed?', 'When is war justified?', 'May we steal from others?', 'Should constitutional review be allowed?' and 'Should we allow positive discrimination?' are only some of these specific 'legal' questions that spring to mind. These are normative issues we should clearly separate from description and explanation (the main activities in, for example, physics and the social sciences) and from interpretation (such as in literary and cultural sciences).[19] The core of legal science is the behaviour of the *homo juridicus*.[20]

One may object that this emphasis on the normative is not a very revolutionary view. It seems a matter of course that legal scholars are ultimately interested in normative questions. And one may even state this is not only true for legal scholars, but also for practising lawyers and that there is no fundamental difference with the traditional 'internal' approach. I believe this criticism is mistaken. The type of question practitioners and positivist legal scholars are usually interested in, is what *positive* law (law as it exists here and now, as apparent from national legislation and case law) says. It may happen that this positive law is not entirely clear and in such a case the question arises how 'the law' should read. This question is then answered on the basis of the existing legal system, often by way of interpretation of the existing sources. There is nothing wrong with practitioners approaching a legal problem in

---

[18]   RUBIN, *supra* n. 6, 1847.

[19]   Cf. G.H. VON WRIGHT, *Explanation and Understanding* (London, 1971). To avoid any misunderstanding: description, explanation and interpretation are certainly also tasks of legal science, but they do not belong to the normative core of it.

[20]   The term was used before, but in other contexts. See, e.g. D.G. RENGERS HORA SICCAMA, 'Homo iuridicus', *Verspreide geschriften* (Zwolle, 1954) 448 and A. SUPIOT, *Homo juridicus: essai sur la fonction anthropologique du droit* (Paris, 2005).

this way. But if academics do the same thing, they make use of the internal approach towards the law that is now so much under pressure. In my view, the main business of academics should be with what the law *should* say and this cannot be decided primarily by reference to national statutes and court decisions. We therefore have to make a difference between the question what the *binding* law says (which is always a matter of looking at authoritative sources) and how the law should read from the purely normative viewpoint. Put another way and perhaps somewhat paradoxically: legal scholars should adopt an *external* normative approach.

This prompts the question what this approach consists of: what is the methodology of finding what normatively belongs? If we cannot fall back on the authority of the state institutions, and the democratic decision process embedded therein, how can we find out what the law should say? This question is discussed in the next section.

4. THE METHODOLOGY OF NORMATIVE LEGAL SCHOLARSHIP

4.1. LAW AS THE SCIENCE OF COMPETING ARGUMENTS

What research methodology belongs to an outright normative view of legal scholarship? It is clear from the outset that the traditional method of establishing what the law says in a national legal system cannot be decisive. In national jurisdictions, the law is based on the authoritative decisions of legislators and courts: their choices are partly based on a democratic decision process and partly on assumptions about what is the 'right' answer to a legal problem in the society involved. The main task of these State institutions is to make binding law and academics writing about such State law not able do so but from the perspective of the authoritative text, directing themselves at least implicitly towards the legislator, court or policy maker.

I believe the question about the proper methodology of normative legal scholarship can only be answered by reference to the core of the normative approach. This core is that, in finding what normatively belongs, there is not one objective truth. As Rubin puts it: 'the conflict of norms is the essence of normatively-based scholarship'.[21] Law is about conflicting normative positions: if law is regulating society and opinions on how to do this differ — which is necessarily the case — there also have to be differing opinions about what the law should say. The academic-legal method must reflect this important characteristic of law. It means

---

[21]   RUBIN, *supra* n. 6, 1893.

that law is about ideas and arguments,[22] turning legal science into an argumentative discipline in which the various arguments in favour of, or against, certain rules or outcomes should be identified and thought through. What normative legal science should therefore do, is carefully consider the arguments behind certain rules and their consequences. Even when there seems to be consensus about a rule, it is the task of legal scholarship to uncover the conflicting arguments behind it. It would be the end of legal scholarship if the debate ends in case of normative agreement.[23] Matthew Arnold puts it like this:[24]

> 'That is what I call living by ideas: when one side of a question has long had your earnest support, when all your feelings are engaged, when you hear all round you no language but one, when your party talks this language like a steam-engine and can imagine no other, — still to be able to think, still to be irresistibly carried, if so it be, by the current of thought to the opposite side of the question (...)'.

The examples given in section 3 are mostly issues that receive different answers in different places and at different times. Some countries accept the death penalty, while others do not. Some countries allow constitutional review; others do not. There was a time when positive discrimination was not allowed; today it is often accepted. But the mere fact that no consensus can be found on the right answer does not turn legal science into a non-academic discipline. This is because the 'universal' character of the legal discipline does not lie in establishing similar rules or outcomes for various jurisdictions, but in identifying the relevant arguments for and against these rules or outcomes.

4.2. HOW CAN THE BETTER ARGUMENTS BE FOUND?

If the core of legal scholarship lies indeed in discussion about conflicting normative positions and arguments, what does this mean for the day-to-day method of legal scholars? It means nothing less than a change of paradigm: until now, legal scholars usually look at existing legal systems because they want to know what the law says within this system.[25] But existing jurisdictions can also be considered as *empirical material* of how conflicting normative positions are being reconciled. If one's research question is not what the law says but what it *should* say, this empirical

---

[22] Cf. C.W. COLLIER, 'The Use and Abuse of Humanistic Theory in Law: Reexamining the Assumption of Interdisciplinary Legal Scholarship,' 41 *Duke Law Journal* (1991) 191-272 at 271: 'the true realm and *métier* of legal scholarship (...) is the world of ideas'.

[23] Cf. RUBIN, *supra* n. 6, 1893. It gives me great pleasure to quote the professional motto of the Tilburg law professor Herman Schoordijk (born 1926) that as academics 'we should not unnecessarily disagree'.

[24] M. ARNOLD, *The Function of Criticism at the Present Time* (1864), cited by COLLIER, *supra* n. 22.

[25] Which is true for both scholars of one specific jurisdiction and for comparative lawyers.

material can be used to test whether some idea or argument was already used elsewhere and how it was received in that other jurisdiction.

In my view, the most important research method to evaluate arguments is therefore the *comparative* one. Comparison with other jurisdictions and even with other normative systems (such as morality and systems of social norms)[26] can unveil whether solutions adopted elsewhere function or not. Other jurisdictions should in this respect be seen as — to borrow from the famous judicial opinion of Brandeis — 'experimenting laboratories':[27] the experiment elsewhere can set a good or a bad example for one's own jurisdiction.[28] This may mean that the factual situation elsewhere — a certain rule fulfils a useful role in the other jurisdiction — can lead to the normative judgment that this rule should be accepted as the right one. Comparative law is thus an important method of normative reasoning beyond state law.[29]

But this is not all. If legal science is indeed involved with finding what people should do, making an inventory of arguments for and against certain behaviour cannot be enough. This leads us to the important question whether there is some criterion to decide which rule or argument[30] is the *better* one. It is clear that the test cannot be the acceptance by some authority.[31] I have more doubts about academic consensus (academics accepting that some rule is the best one to adopt), but even such consensus cannot be the decisive factor as it should always rest on other reasons.[32] Yet another — now popular — approach is to find the criterion in some external goal or policy. It regards law as a means to an end:[33] law is an instrument with which to attain a certain external goal (like efficiency) and if the rule in question does not help in doing so, it should be abolished. This approach is equally problematic because it misjudges the function of law: any policy or public end is in the end based on (democratic) consensus, while the law should offer a counterweight against the majority view.[34] But, more importantly, to look at law as

---

[26] E.A. POSNER, *Law and Social Norms* (Cambridge, 2000).

[27] Louis Brandeis, in: *New State Ice Co. v. Liebmann*, 285 U.S. 262: 'To stay experimentation in things social and economic is a grave responsibility. Denial of the right to experiment may be fraught with serious consequences to the Nation. It is one of the happy incidents of the federal system that a single courageous State may, if its citizens choose, serve as a laboratory; and try novel social and economic experiments without risk to the rest of the country'.

[28] F.A. HAYEK, 'Der Wettbewerb als Entdeckungsverfahren', 56 *Kieler Vorträge N.F.* (Kiel, 1968).

[29] H.P. GLENN, 'A Transnational Concept of Law', in P. CANE and M. TUSHNET (eds.), *The Oxford Handbook of Legal Studies* (Oxford, 2003) 839-862, at 844.

[30] Or the outcome of a case. In the remainder of this contribution, I use the term 'rule' to indicate any normative statement about the law.

[31] See for a different view: S. FISH, 'Fish v. Fish', 36 *Stanford Law Review* (1984) 1325-1347 at 1342.

[32] Cf. RUBIN, *supra* n. 6, 1850.

[33] B.Z. TAMANAHA, *Law as a Means to an End* (Cambridge, 2006).

[34] Cf. A. WATSON, *The Shame of American Legal Education* (Lake Mary, 2006) 212-213.

fulfilling some external function is wrong because it is not a *normative* approach: it replaces the law for something else. As Weinrib says:[35]

> 'Because the functionalist goals are justifiable independently and the law's purpose is to reflect them, the study of the law becomes parasitic on the study of the non-legal disciplines (economics, political theory, and moral philosophy (...)) that might validate these goals. (...) Law provides only the authoritative form into which the conclusions of non-legal thinking are translated. The governing presupposition is that the content of law cannot be comprehended in and of itself, simply as law'.

Of course, this does not mean that if a rule explicitly seeks to establish a certain goal (e.g. make traffic more safe, protect weaker parties or prevent crime), the rule cannot *also* be evaluated on the basis of the extent to which it fulfils this role, taking into account empirical evidence. The only thing is that, in a normative view of law, this cannot be the decisive factor.

But how then should we establish what is the better argument? In my view, the question whether one argument is better than another one can only be answered in a specific normative setting. If opinions on what is right do differ, the answer must be found in the normative presuppositions underlying the acceptance of an argument. Whether the law should intervene in the case of a grossly unfair contract or to what extent consumers should be protected against professional parties, are questions to which an answer can only be given in such a specific normative setting. This is why the answers to these questions often differ from one country to another and is, even within one country, dependent on one's political position. This leads some authors[36] to assert that the only foundation for accepting an argument is the articulation of this specific normative (liberal, socio-democratic, etc.) position: it depends on one's view of politics and society whether an argument should be accepted or not and academics should therefore make their own values more explicit. I believe this view makes the acceptance of an argument too dependent on the individual scholar's political views.

My normative setting — and framework to evaluate the importance of an argument — is another one. I agree that each argument can only be assessed within a certain normative framework. But in doing so, we should not forget that in many jurisdictions there is already such a framework available in the form of a doctrinal system. Each jurisdiction has its own 'internal morality'[37] as a reflection of the prevailing normative views within that jurisdiction. It is no coincidence[38] that,

---

[35]   E.J. WEINRIB, *The Idea of Private Law* (Cambridge, 1995) 6.
[36]   Notably RUBIN, *supra* n. 6, 1893 ff. and M.W. HESSELINK (forthcoming 2008), A European legal science?
[37]   For this term: L. FULLER, *The Morality of Law* (New Haven, 1969) 33.
[38]   As remarked before by S.D. SMITH, 'In Defense of Traditional Legal Scholarship: A Comment on Schlegel, Weisberg and Dan-Cohen', 63 *University of Colorado Law Review* (1992) 629: 'Indeed, to

despite fierce attacks from different angles,[39] doctrinal thinking has survived over the ages. The doctrinal system not only ensures that requirements as to coherence, clarity, objectivity and transparency are met; it also reflects the prevailing normative view within this system. The well-known criticism on legal formalism that it refers to only a technical and indeterminate system which covers up the underlying controversies[40] is therefore not entirely correct. The legal system usually[41] offers the framework to decide whether an argument should be adopted: arguments always have to pass the test of the system.[42]

This view of legal methodology implies that each normative scholarly exercise consists of two steps. The first is to identify the relevant arguments in favour of and against a certain solution. Several methods can be used to do this, including empirical and functional approaches, but in the end the comparative method is the most promising one. The second step is to see whether these arguments fit into an already existing normative setting.[43] As this setting may differ from one jurisdiction to another, it is difficult to say in the abstract if the fit will be there. What is considered as the prevailing argument in American law may be outweighed by another argument in German law.

4.3. THREE CONSEQUENCES

Adoption of the view set out in the above has several consequences relating directly to the present debate about legal science. It seems useful to touch upon some of these consequences without discussing them in any detail. One consequence is that the place of non-legal approaches towards the law can be better defined. Economic analysis and behavioural analysis can play a role in establishing whether an argument is the right one, but in the end they always have to pass the test of the system in which they are applied. This is the inevitable consequence of the approach adopted in this article: any other view would replace the normative perspective with something else.

---

suggest that legal scholarship should be less obsessed with doctrine would be like suggesting that historians should not spend so much effort studying things that happened in the distant past, or that astronomers ought to worry more about earthly concerns instead of concentrating so exclusively on remote heavenly bodies'.

[39] Apart from the present 'doctrinal crisis' by Legal Realism and by Critical Legal Studies.

[40] Cf. R.M. UNGER, *The Critical Legal Studies Movement* (Cambridge, 1986) and D. KENNEDY, 'Form and Substance in Private Law Adjudication', 89 *Harvard Law Review* (1976) 1685.

[41] There are some exceptions: see the book announced *supra* n. 3.

[42] Often, they did so already. See POSNER, *supra*, n. 9, 112, who emphasizes the importance of the 'test of time': the longer a widespread belief persists (...) the likelier it is to be correct' because 'you can't fool all of the people all of the time'.

[43] Once more, I refer to H.C.F. SCHOORDIJK, *Het algemeen gedeelte van het verbintenissenrecht naar het Nieuw Burgerlijk Wetboek* (Deventer, 1979) 453, who emphasizes the importance of 'feeling out' ('aftasten') the system.

Second, a normative view of law no longer takes the *existing* norm (often derived from the national legislature or court) as a starting point for analysis. Instead, the scholarly discussion takes place at the level of arguments. This implies that instead of a focus on the *substance* of law, the *method* towards finding what belongs is given pride of place. It also means that the traditional focus on legal sources must be amended: legal decision-making already takes on new forms in which reference to foreign sources takes place more frequently.[44] Philosophical thinking along the lines of Kelsen's *Grundnorm*[45] and Hart's rule of recognition[46] no longer seems to reflect this practice.

Third, this approach makes clear it is wrong to look at legal science as accumulating knowledge in the way this is done in the natural sciences. In law, there is an ongoing debate about which argument is the right one and it may well be that arguments once discarded as not useful will receive a reappraisal at a later stage.

5. TWO EXAMPLES: FUNDAMENTAL RIGHTS IN RELATIONSHIPS BETWEEN PRIVATE PARTIES

It is now time to briefly illustrate this rather abstract plea with some concrete examples from the field of human rights. These examples are taken from the debate about the so-called 'constitutionalization' of private law. This term refers to the increasing influence of fundamental rights in relationships between private parties.[47] Although these cases can be used to illustrate several of the things discussed in the above, I will use them[48] to answer the question whether fundamental rights offer any real 'normative' guidance to decide disputes between private parties and whether a different approach is not more helpful. This also illustrates why normative legal research should rely on the comparative method.

The first example concerns the fundamental 'right' to human dignity as applied in the well-known wrongful birth cases. Human dignity is laid down in several national constitutions,[49] but the way in which it is applied differs from one country

---

[44] See the references infra, n. 58.
[45] H. KELSEN, *Reine Rechtslehre* (2. Auflage) (Wien 1960, Nachdruck 2000).
[46] H.L.A. HART, *The Concept of Law* (2nd ed.) (Oxford, 1997).
[47] See, e.g. O. CHEREDNYCHENKO, *Fundamental Rights, Contract Law and the Protection of the Weaker Party* (München, 2007); C. MAK, *Fundamental Rights in European Contract Law* (Alphen aan den Rijn, 2008); G. BRÜGGEMEIER, A. COLOMBI CIACCHI and G. COMANDÉ et al (eds.), *Fundamental Rights and Private Law in the European Union* (Cambridge, 2008).
[48] I used them before in J.M. SMITS, 'Contract Law in the European Union: Convergence or Not?', in: *Proceedings of the 4th European Jurists' Forum* (Vienna, 2008 - forthcoming).
[49] Art. 1 s. 1: 'Die Würde des Menschen ist unantastbar. Sie zu achten und zu schützen ist Verpflichtung aller staatlichen Gewalt.' Human dignity is also codified in the constitutions of Belgium (Article 23) and South Africa (Articles 1 and 10). Also see Article 1 of the European Union Charter of Fundamental Rights.

to another and even *within* jurisdictions. Thus, even though the highest courts of the United Kingdom, Germany and the Netherlands all referred to the argument of human dignity in relation to the general personality right of the healthy child in deciding whether the parents had a claim for damages, it is far from it that this provided the court with a criterion to decide the case. Since 1980, the German *Bundesgerichtshof* has allowed claims for damages for raising a child.[50] The first senate of the *Bundesverfassungsgericht* is of the same opinion,[51] but the second senate of the same court has, in a case on abortion,[52] held that to regard the existence of a child as a ground for damages is contrary to human dignity and therefore a violation of Article 1 of the German constitution. Apparently, there is uncertainty about what human dignity requires. This is also clear from a comparison of the Dutch and English wrongful birth cases. While the Dutch *Hoge Raad* allowed the claim for damages on basis of the argument that it is not the child itself that is being regarded as damages but only the costs of raising that child,[53] the House of Lords expressed the opposite view. In *MacFarlane*, Lord Steyn held:[54]

'Instinctively, the traveller on the Underground would consider that the law of torts has no business to provide legal remedies consequent upon the birth of a healthy child, which all of us regard as a valuable and good thing. (...) Relying on principles of distributive justice I am persuaded that our tort law does not permit parents of a healthy unwanted child to claim the cost of bringing up the child from a health authority or a doctor. (...)'.

The opinion of Lord Millet in the later case of *Darlington Memorial Hospital v. Rees*[55] reveals the fact that one can think differently about this, stressing the autonomy of a party:

'I still regard the proper outcome in all these cases is to award the parents a modest conventional sum by way of general damages, not for the birth of the child, but for the denial of an important aspect of their personal autonomy, viz the right to limit the size of their family. This is an important aspect of human dignity, which is increasingly being regarded as an important human right which should be protected by law'.

These are clearly normative statements about the law. The courts use human dignity to come to a normative conclusion. These cases also illustrate the existence of competing notions of human dignity: one that is based on 'respect' for the child and

---

[50] Bundesgerichtshof, *NJW* 1980, 1450.
[51] Bundesverfassungsgericht 96, 375, *NJW* 1998, 519 (*Sterilization*).
[52] Bundesverfassungsgericht 88, 203, *NJW* 1993, 1751 (*Schwangerschaftsabbruch II*).
[53] Hoge Raad 21 February 1997, NJ 1999, 145.
[54] *MacFarlane and Another v. Tayside Health Board*, [1999] 4 All ER 963.
[55] [2004] 1 AC 309.

one that is based on the personal autonomy of the parents. My point is that such a normative debate should not take place on the basis of vague notions like human dignity, but on the basis of other arguments. Legal scholars should try to identify and evaluate these arguments pro and contra the claim for compensation. In doing so, the comparative method plays an important role, not only to find the (explicit or implicit) arguments used by the national courts to allow or refuse such a claim, but also to see how the chosen outcome is received in the country involved.

The second example concerns a conflict between the fundamental rights of freedom of the press and privacy. In this respect, a similar case was decided in Germany and in the Netherlands. In both cases, a criminal was convicted to a long sentence. At the time of the crime and the conviction, the case received a lot of publicity and pictures of the criminal were published in the national newspapers. A few years after the conviction, the question arose whether it would infringe the criminal's privacy to publish these pictures again. The Dutch *Hoge Raad* decided this conflict between privacy and freedom of the press by holding that the criminal's privacy should prevail.[56] The German *Bundesverfassungsgericht* on the other hand found, making use of the same arguments but weighing them in a different way, the freedom of the press to be superior.[57] My point is, again, that the different outcomes of these cases do not matter. Behind the balancing of fundamental rights in private law cases, there are arguments to let one of these rights prevail. The normative method should consist of identifying these arguments on the basis of comparative law research. A universal legal science seeks convergence at this level of argumentation. Subsequently, it is left to a specific normative framework (e.g. of a national jurisdiction) to decide which argument should prevail.

6. CONCLUSIONS: LEGAL SCIENCE AS A SCHOLARLY DISCIPLINE

In the above (section 3), three requirements for an academic discipline were identified. First, knowledge must be systematized, evaluated and explained by reference to an existing body of knowledge. Second, this knowledge must be the result of a generally accepted research method. Third, the discipline must try to create knowledge that is to some extent universal (being of importance beyond the national level). Legal science as an argumentative discipline can fulfil these three requirements.

First, it does so if it widens the existing body of knowledge from the national 'system' to more universal sets of arguments. At the moment, the body of legal knowledge in many areas of law is to a large extent based on national legislation and

---

[56]   Hoge Raad 21 January 1994, *Nederlandse Jurisprudentie* 1994, 473 (*Ferdi E./Spaarnestad*).
[57]   Bundesverfassungsgericht 35, 202.

court decisions. But there is no reason why the materials this body consists of should be confined to only national sources. In private law, there once was such an international system, namely before national codifications were enacted in the nineteenth century. Present Europeanization and globalization of law prompt us to extend this national body of knowledge in the way described in the above: by identifying the arguments in favour of and against specific rules. Highest courts already increasingly refer to foreign law and doctrine to justify their decisions.[58]

Second, the accompanying research method focuses on whether these arguments function or not in the respective jurisdictions in which they are used. This puts the comparative method at the core of legal scholarship. The paradigm shift is this: do not look at binding court decisions and legislation as telling us what the national law says (there can be relative certainty about this), but as informing us about the strength of a normative viewpoint. Law should not be considered a binding system (with a focus on the sources of law, as in traditional scholarship) or as a functional system (focusing on the question whether the law realizes some goal), but a normative system (what is it we should do?).

Third, the focus on arguments used across national borders implies that legal science is no longer dependent on national law, but has the potential to become a truly international discipline. It would be wrong to find this universal character of legal science at the level of rules — as is being done in projects like the drafting of a Common Frame of Reference for European private law.[59] This mistakenly assumes that there is a shared understanding of what these rules mean at the European level. The best thing we can hope for is that an argumentative practice about the arguments behind the rules will evolve.

---

[58] See, e.g. *Roper v. Simmons*, 543 U.S. 551 (2005), B. MARKESINIS and J. FEDTKE, *Judicial Recourse to Foreign Law: A New Source of Inspiration?* (London, 2006) and the special issue of 3 *Utrecht Law Review* (2007), 1 devoted to Adjudication in a Globalizing Context.

[59] CHR. VON BAR, E. CLIVE and H. SCHULTE-NÖLKE (eds.), *Principles, Definitions and Model Rules of European Private Law: Draft Common Frame of Reference, Interim Outline Edition* (München, 2008).

HUMAN RIGHTS STUDIES: ON THE DANGERS OF LEGALISTIC ASSUMPTIONS

DAVID P. FORSYTHE

1. INTRODUCTION

Human rights is by nature an interdisciplinary subject, and the study of it can entail numerous approaches. Most fundamentally, human rights centres on a moral argument that cannot be empirically proven and thus is accepted (or not) mostly on faith — namely, that individuals, and perhaps some of their associations, have human rights. (This formulation of course refers to the on-going debate as to whether collectivities in addition to individuals should be seen as having fundamental rights.) One can empirically study the *results* of belief. That is, one can look for evidence that societies which accept and practice the notion of human rights are more peaceful, or prosperous, or stable, or free, or that their residents are more satisfied, or whatever. But while moral philosophers and normative political theorists have reasoned about why one should approve of the notion of human rights (or why not) this process is different from proving the existence of those personal rights in the first place.

It is more than interesting that first so much of the Western world, and then so much of the rest of the world, has constructed the state, which is a political-legal system of decision-making, on an idea that amounts to a secular religion, that is a system of belief. For liberals, human rights is a moral assumption, that human beings *should be viewed* as possessing fundamental rights, also known as entitlements, which public authorities are duty bound to respect. There are various forms of liberal reasoning in behalf of human rights, but no proof of their independent existence apart from these arguments. One might recall the observation, attributed to Jacques Maritain, regarding those who supported the 1948 Universal Declaration of Human Rights: we are all in favor of human rights as long as no one asks why (meaning where they come from).

Perhaps no philosopher has been more important in the West concerning human rights than John Locke, with his assumptions about the individual being born into a dangerous state of nature, and about how this individual enters into a social contract with the state to get out of this state of nature, on condition that the state, in providing order and security, respect his/her human rights. But this is a fictional if influential account, because none of us were born into a state of nature, territorial states or other public authority already being in existence, and no one ever asked us if we signed the social contract, metaphorically speaking, or not, or if we wanted to opt out. Moreover, all sorts of other Western thinkers denied precisely what Locke asserted, from Edmund Burke through Jeremy Bentham to Alasdair MacIntyre.

Ironically enough, while human rights is most fundamentally a matter of social construction or moral argument about what 'should be' in order to produce various individual and collective 'goods,' moral philosophy or normative political theory is not all that crucial for accepting the idea of human rights. As Michael Ignatieff has argued, to understand fundamental personal rights it is more important to read history than philosophy.[1] Enlightenment thinkers invented human rights in eighteenth century Europe, and political activists in North America and France then put those ideas into political practice from roughly 1776 and 1789 – the Americans more consistently, in a limited way, than the French. What all these philosophers and political leaders were doing was reacting to history. They looked at the tyrannies and intolerances so evident in particularly European history and devised an ideational and institutional scheme to minimize them in the future. U.S. founding fathers were driven by the perceived injustices under the British monarch George III, and the French revolutionaries by those of Louis XVI and his supporters in the nobility and Catholic clergy. In short, they looked at historical wrongs in the immediate and more distant past and devised human rights to forestall their reappearance.

So while human rights is fundamentally a matter of moral social construction, historical analysis is crucial. It is thus more than strange that historians have come so late to the study of human rights, although at least in the United States human rights is emerging as a recognized sub-field of historical studies, that study being originally led by philosophers and law professors, with social scientists trailing-- but not as far behind as the historians.[2]

Political scientists, sociologists, anthropologists, and now even some economists increasingly bring their disciplinary perspectives to the study of human rights. This is also true of some of those in the humanities who focus on film studies, painting, and literature. Journalism can be involved as well. So we do not lack for a variety of

---

[1]   M. IGNATIEFF, *Human Rights as Politics and Idolatry* (Princeton, 2003).

[2]   L.A. HUNT, *Inventing Human Rights: a history* (New York, 2007). This is an important comparison of the French and American revolutions in relation to human rights. Hunt is a former president of the American Historical Association. See also J. HEUER, 'The French Revolution', and also A. KOHEN, 'The American Revolution', both forthcoming in D. FORSYTHE (ed.), *The Human Rights Encyclopedia* (Oxford, 2009).

perspectives on how we might understand the different dimensions of human rights – those personal rights seen as crucially fundamental to a life with human dignity and/or to other 'goods' such as peace and prosperity. (Thus, human rights can be seen as fundamental to individual welfare, but also fundamental to broader societal goals.) The contribution by Todd Landman in this volume is a very good summary of the variety of studies that can exist in the social sciences.

This having been said, law has remained central to the notion of human rights. That is because, whatever the underlying theoretical arguments (which is not the same as empirical proof), it is law that authoritatively defines a society's understanding of what are human rights at a given point in time. Or, on the other side of the coin, it is law, as in Nazi Germany or Myanmar today, that indicates the absence of human rights as a national and positivistic matter. Thus in the contemporary world, when we speak of universal human rights, it is international law that defines them in a positivistic sense, for better or worse. And it is national (municipal) law that either does or does not incorporate that universal conception into more local legal codes. To complicate matters, there are now regional conceptions of human rights law in Europe, the Americas, and Africa, mediating presumably between the global and the national legal norms.

Now one may very well say, and accurately from a certain moral assumption, that Nelson Mandela had certain human rights whatever the law might have been in apartheid South Africa. At the same time, one of the positivist tests of whether or not human rights *practically* exist in a particular context is whether an individual can go to an independent court, or other authoritative body, and successfully demand that public authorities respect his or her human rights. Mandela may have had human rights, but he did not have *effective* human rights because South African law did not recognize them. Hence the legislation and adjudication of human rights law, or the lack thereof, retains a prominent place in human rights studies – globally, regionally, and locally.

I therefore take as my central concern in the pages that follow a consideration of certain legal approaches to the study of human rights. In doing so I bring to bear my disciplinary training in the study of politics, which emphasizes power and policy. In the study of politics, law can be seen as not just a technical and perhaps even scientific field but a matter of formalized public policy, which is the result of a certain type of policy making process. And the policy making process, as well as matters of implementation quite often, entail power relations. It is an approach that looks at more than legal text and legal reasoning. The approach from political studies emphasizes a broad range of factors relevant to understanding law, entailing above all an awareness of power relations and policy evaluation.

2. LEGALISTIC STUDIES

Some legal approaches can be legalistic rather than just legal. Legal of course refers to legal rules; what is legal is what is in accord with legal rules. Legalistic refers to an *excessive* or *unrealistic* interest in, or reliance on, legal rules.

There is also great confusion between the words legal and legitimate. What may be seen as legitimate is not always legal. Many in the West saw the NATO bombing of Serbia in 1999 as legitimate, even if not clearly legal, at least at the start. Here I refer to the fact that Russia, in proposing a condemnation of NATO's action in the UN Security Council, and in losing that vote, in a process of reverse logic might have conferred some legality on the bombing. That is, since the Council formally refused to condemn the bombing, it must have been legal, or at least not clearly illegal. Also, the fact that the UN Security Council accepted the outcome of the bombing, by creating a field mission to supervise and consolidate and try to make manageable the results, again seemed to confer some legality on the bombing ex post facto. But a focus on legitimacy, and whether such matters as the NATO bombing were correct, meaning appropriate in context, would require a lengthy analysis, best left for another time and place.

Suffice it to say here that the notion of legitimacy is a highly subjective concept that can vary, and often does, among policy makers and their observers. It is an idea that should be used sparingly in analysis, and with great care, given its often contested status. Legitimacy should certainly not be considered a perfect synonym for legality. To act in accord with legal rules is supposed to create some legitimacy, some sense of correctness, but it is often the case that actors find reason to violate law while claiming legitimacy on other grounds.[3]

Lest I digress too far, we should return to the main point, namely that human rights studies are often legalistic. This view suggests that some human rights analysts, who, I maintain, are often those trained in law, frequently place too much emphasis on legal wording and legal obligation, to the exclusion of other, highly relevant factors in understanding the fate of human rights. So I think we have a strong moral-legal tradition in human rights scholarship that could benefit from a more critical approach.

The crux of this view is that many human rights lawyers are often too uncritical about international human rights law, too focused on treaty language and court cases, and not appreciative enough about soft law and extra-legal factors that affect policy and behavior related to human rights. The contribution by Eva Brems in this volume shows clearly that many of those trained in law are not very careful about

---

[3]   For a discussion of the various sources of legitimacy, of which fidelity to law is only one, see D.P. FORSYTHE, *Human Rights and Peace: International and National Perspectives* (Lincoln, 1993).

how they set up their analysis of human rights and do not consider questions of approach and method. Let me begin to specify my argument.

2.1. GENERAL OVERVIEW

One is hard pressed to recall very many publications by a human rights lawyer suggesting that the human rights discourse is only one route to human dignity, and that other progressive discourses exist – religious, humanitarian, feminist, economic, moral, diplomatic, political, etc. In fact, there are very few such publications at all, and almost none, in so far as I am aware, by a law professor specializing in human rights. In general, this record suggests that human rights lawyers do not acknowledge different paths to protecting or advancing human dignity – a life worth living, a life with social justice. In short, they do not compare the rights discourse with the others.

In a way this gap in thinking is understandable. Since human rights are defined by law, as a positivistic matter, as a means to human dignity, one might indeed assume that great attention to human rights law is a good thing, and that relying on the human rights legal discourse must necessarily lead to desirable outcomes. But such thinking merits close analysis.

Relevant is the book *The Dark Side of Virtue*, by the American lawyer David Kennedy at Harvard, which argues that lawyers in general are too focused on legal process to the exclusion of other important factors affecting order and virtue. He argues that lawyers often forget to inquire about the impact or result of process. That is, love of legal process diverts from what should be primary – namely, a focus on the results or impact of process. (I will come back to this.)

He also argues that much international human rights law and international humanitarian law (IHL) codify state interests rather than human interests. Up to a point he is correct in this analysis. One can note IHL and notions of military necessity. That body of international law is a product of both: humanitarian concern and conceptions of military necessity.[4] For example, some prisoners in international armed conflict can be denied visits by the International Committee of the Red Cross for (undefined) reasons of military necessity, as least for a time. (As stipulated in the 1949 Geneva Convention number Three, the POW convention.) One can also note international refugee law and the exclusion of internally displaced persons from the legal protections of the 1951 Refugee Convention (extended by the 1967 Protocol). Or, with regard to the same Convention, note that refugee status, and thus entitlement to temporary asylum, is codified in the law as granted by states, not by the UN Office of the High Commissioner for Refugees. So international refugee law

---

[4]   See particularly J.F. HUTCHINSON, *Champions of Charity: War and the History of the Red Cross* (Boulder, 1989).

codifies much state interest that can be detrimental to the human dignity of uprooted people. One can also note the six or seven major UN human rights treaties and their monitoring mechanisms. These UN diplomatic, and not judicial, processes, supposedly to guarantee the implementation of treaty provisions, have, by all accounts, resulted in the lack of significant change in state behavior from that process — at least in the short term. (I will come back to this subject in particular). States negotiate human rights treaties, which many then ratify, but they are careful to keep implementation measures weak. This human rights law actually codifies weak international authority, and strong state authority, which can be, and often is, detrimental to human rights — states being one of the principal violators of those rights.

So Kennedy appropriately reminds us that international human rights and humanitarian law may entail some negatives for human dignity, and that perhaps a more political or diplomatic approach might do just as well if not better, at least sometimes. While I am not persuaded by all of his argument, and have said so in a published review, I do commend him for a questioning, skeptical look at international human rights, humanitarian, and refugee law.[5] At least he raises the 'so what' question: does it matter for human welfare and human dignity if we have this or that treaty, this or that legally codified review process? Does the law do as much damage as good?

Also relevant is another book by another American lawyer, *Atrocity, Punishment, and International Law* by Mark Drumbl.[6] He asks, with regard to international criminal justice, who are the trials for and what are their purposes. He suggests that if the trials are for society, to promote reconciliation among protagonists and a rights protective society in the future, then the courts that have been created thus far are not likely to achieve their stated aspirations. Like some others, he believes the courts, with their complicated rules of procedure and standards of evidence, are not well suited for what he calls 'expressive purposes' — namely, to get a general population to express faith in the law. So whereas some legal analysts, who are thrilled to have increased court cases about individual responsibility for war crimes, crimes against humanity, and genocide, are content to analyze the jurisprudence of various international and internationalized courts, Drumbl steps back and examines questions about purpose and accomplishment.

In addition to Kennedy and Drumbl, one might cite a book chapter arguing that a feminist ethic of caring would produce better results than the discourse of human rights, at least re socio-economic rights. While one might not be persuaded by the

---

5   See my book review of D. KENNEDY, 'The Dark Side of Virtue: Reassessing International Humanitarianism', 99 *American Journal of International Law* (2005) 736-740.
6   M.A. DRUMBL, *Atrocity, Punishment, and International Law* (Cambridge, 2007).

argument, it is at least an explicit comparison of a rights approach with a non legal, feminist, essentialist approach.[7]

One can recall a debate in Foreign Policy magazine between Aryeh Neier, arguing for an absolute commitment to human rights, especially via war crimes trials and other judicial processes, and Jeffrey Garten, arguing for a delay in attention to particularly labor rights because of the need to pursue economic growth. According to the latter argument, expanding the economic pie would lead to more human dignity than restricting growth in an effort to protect labor rights in the contemporary context among developing countries. At least the comparison was explicit re how best to achieve human dignity, with there being, on the part of Garten at least, no automatic support for the rights discourse as a preferred means to human dignity broadly defined.[8]

These kinds of debates about how to advance human dignity almost never involve human rights lawyers, who assume — but do not critically examine — the superiority of the rights approach. (Drumbl is among the exceptions, since he served for a time on the staff of the ICTY.) So while it has been said of Americans that 1) they comprise a litigious society that tries to turn every dispute into a court case, and 2) in foreign policy they have a moralistic-legalistic tradition, [9] my view is that in current times it is more likely to be human rights lawyers who prioritize and emphasize a legalistic approach to world affairs.

Now this automatic assumption by many human rights lawyers about the inherent superiority of the human rights discourse, particularly in the form of hard law or adjudicated law, is a bit strange, because there is rather obvious evidence from real world observation that we should not make this assumption.[10] That is, there is ample evidence we should not assume the superiority in all situations and at

---

[7] See T. EVANS (ed.), *Human Rights Fifty Years On: A Reappraisal* (Manchester, 1998).

[8] See the exchange between A. NEIER, 'The New Double Standard', and J.E. GARTEN, 'Comment: The Need for Pragmatism', both in 105 *Foreign Policy* (1996-1997) 91-101, 103-106.

[9] For a classic argument along these lines see G.F. KENNAN, *American Diplomacy 1900-1950* (Chicago, 1985).

[10] There has never been agreement on the widely used terms soft and hard law. In my view hard law is adjudicated law — that is, law that is specified and made concrete in court cases. For me soft law comes in two forms: treaties that are by definition law but do not get adjudicated in court; and certain other international documents or instruments that become an authoritative statement of proper guideline, but lack the formal status of positivistic law. An example of non-adjudicated treaties that have effect by political decision, at least in the U.S., is the UN Charter. An example of influential non-law is the UN Declaration of Human Rights (excepting the possibility that some court might hold that parts of it have become customary international law subject to court interpretation).

all times of the legal-rights approach, with a strong emphasis on court decisions which I have labeled judicial romanticism.[11]

Consider the Rome Statute of the International Criminal Court, and its acknowledgment that sometimes one should not prosecute for criminal behavior but rather engage in the granting of amnesties and other political/diplomatic measures. The Statute authorizes the UN Security Council to postpone criminal prosecutions for up to a year, renewable indefinitely, which codifies the notion that in some situations one might not want to prosecute for war crimes, crimes against humanity, and/or genocide, in the interest of advancing human dignity broadly and politically defined. In other words, the Statute's authors wanted to allow for the possibility that avoiding human rights adjudication might be a wise and appropriate policy in certain contexts.

This provision of the ICC Statute reminds us of the recent practice of offering amnesty, *de facto* or *de jure*, so as to end dictatorships and presumably advance the prospects of liberal democracy, which means rights-protective polities, without great bloodshed. George W. Bush offered Saddam Hussein safe sanctuary out of Iraq in early 2003, which, had Saddam accepted, would have saved the lives of perhaps 150,000 Iraqis (the number is contested), and of more than 3,000 U.S. military personnel killed in the subsequent invasion, occupation, and transitional situation in Iraq. The subsequent national trial of Saddam did little to offset the appalling human and societal destruction that occurred in the wake of the U.S. invasion. In the name of ending tyranny, hundreds of thousands of Iraqis were killed, wounded, or displaced.

General Cedras, on the other hand, did avail himself of the U.S. offer of safe passage out of Haiti in 1994, which, while it did not permanently pacify and liberalize that impoverished country, at least avoided another U.S. invasion, perhaps similar to the one in Panama in 1989, which led to many deaths (the number has never been definitively established). In El Salvador in 1991, progress was made in improving human dignity in the wake of a murderous civil war by various non-legal measures, such as the transfer of various Salvadoran military officials abroad, the encouragement of others to retire abroad, as well as an agreement not to pursue those who authorized and/or carried out atrocities by means of criminal prosecutions.[12] For a time, Nigeria offered Charles Taylor, rapacious head of Liberia,

---

[11] See my *Human Rights in International Relations* (2nd ed.) (Cambridge, 2006), where I accuse classical liberals of judicial romanticism, or of expecting too much from courts, by contrast to pragmatic liberals who acknowledge different roads to advancing human dignity.

[12] It is only fair to note that avoiding criminal responsibility for gross violations of human rights in El Salvador, as in South Africa, has not satisfied all. Some relatives of victims have brought civil suits against former Salvadoran civilian and military officials who retired to Florida (and where encouraged to so retire by Salvadoran and U.S. officials). State Department officials refused to testify for plaintiffs, given past U.S. policy of encouraging an advance in human dignity in El Salvador, which has occurred there in relative terms, by political arrangements rather than criminal trials.

safe haven, which at least encouraged beneficial change not only in Liberia but also Sierra Leone. Of course Taylor finally found himself before an internationalized criminal tribunal sitting at the Hague, which indicates that the timing of developments may properly play a very large role in decisions about the best course of action.[13] Rather than automatic and generalized assumptions, one needs particular contextual analysis. While I believe there are universal human rights, their implementation should be contextualized.

In a different category of policy making, but demonstrating the same point, there is the diplomacy of the ICRC, which sometimes eschews legal discussion, at least in public, while pursuing practical humanitarian objectives in the field or on the ground. Take the case of Kuwait under Iraqi occupation during 1990-1991. While the entire international community regarded the situation as one that should be legally regulated primarily by 1949 Geneva Convention number four, the ICRC made no headway with the Saddam regime in emphasizing this correct interpretation of the law. Therefore the ICRC eschewed the legal discourse and sought access to those suffering under Iraqi occupation by reference to the ICRC traditional offer of humanitarian services of an a-legal nature. The ICRC never got into occupied Kuwait, but it did manifest the right approach in context, trying a-legal diplomacy as compared to futile legal argument.

Something similar (with more positive results) transpired at the Guantanamo prison facility, where the United States refused, until a Supreme Court ruling in 2006, to apply any part of the 1949 Geneva Conventions to prisoners there, they being presumably linked to the so-called U.S. war on terrorism, but did permit the ICRC to exercise its traditional prison visits from early 2002. A focus on IHL was actually detrimental to the exercise of ICRC efforts to gain access for visits, so the Geneva headquarters once again employed the discourse of a-legal humanitarianism, even as it continued a quiet dialogue with U.S. officials about legal issues. In effect, the ICRC succeeded in separating the legal arguments from the practical matter of detainee treatment 'on the ground.'

Certain decisions were also similar in the Middle East, where the ICRC had been engaged in prison visits and other activities from 1967, after earlier involvements in the late 1940s and 1956, even though Israel disagreed with the ICRC and other parties about the applicability of all parts of the 1949 Fourth Geneva Convention to seized new territory. For the ICRC, the key to its operations in the field was often

---

[13] Hence I argue that in 1995 it was correct not to seek criminal prosecution of Slobodan Milosevic at that time because of the need to enlist his support for the diplomatic end to atrocities, as per the Dayton peace agreement, which worked; and also correct to indict and try him later in the ICTY, given that a relative calm had taken hold in Bosnia and Croatia. (He was sent to The Hague in June, 2001). In 1995, Milosevic was both the chief arsonist and the chief firefighter regarding Bosnia, and a black and white, criminal law approach to affairs would have been legalistic and contrary to an interest in advancing human dignity.

the avoidance, at least for a time, of legal interpretations, and the preference for searching for humanitarian cooperation that was more moral than legal. Indeed, the head of the ICRC delegation in Israel was rebuked by the ICRC President at one point when he publicly characterized certain Israeli actions related to the West Bank and Gaza as constituting war crimes, since the organization generally tried to leave such clear designations of major violations of IHL to others. In other words, the ICRC often found that staking a clear legal position impeded what it could do through its practical diplomacy to improve the human dignity of victims of war. Even if one found the ICRC headquarters sometimes making reference to the fourth Geneva Convention from 1949, the organization did not confuse legal interpretation with working out practical, a-legal arrangements on the ground for the benefit of victims of war and politics. Thus the ICRC walked a tightrope or high wire between the diplomatic and legal discourses.

This pattern has many manifestations. The ICRC bypassed the legal characterization of the situation in Northern Ireland at the peak of 'The Troubles'. Since the United Kingdom objected to the idea that the situation was an armed conflict, which at a minimum would have triggered the application of Common Article 3 of the 1949 Geneva Conventions, and would have thereby brought increased status to those opposing its policies there, once again the ICRC proceeded with prison visits to detained IRA suspects on the basis of a-legal or diplomatic humanitarianism. So sometimes the ICRC finds it useful to distance its practical humanitarian diplomacy from a strictly legal-rights approach.[14]

Sometimes a focus on human rights law and criminal justice not only impedes progress towards human dignity; it also can create a sizable negative backlash that does considerable damage to liberal and humane concerns. In Somalia in the early 1990s, the decision was taken in international circles to characterize Mohamed Farah Aidid, then resisting U.S. and UN plans for state and nation-building after widespread anarchy and starvation, as a criminal. His arrest was sought. Key results of this policy decision involved increased conflict between UN and U.S. forces on the one hand, and certain Somalia militia on the other. This in turn led to a firefight in 1993 that cost 18 American military lives and an untold higher number of Somalia lives. And this in turn led to both a winding down of international involvement in Somalia, without an increase in order, much less liberal order, and, worst of all, U.S. reluctance to support muscular UN intervention in the Rwandan genocide of 1994

---

[14] Regarding these and other examples drawn from ICRC history, see D.P. FORSYTHE, *The Humanitarians: The International Committee of the Red Cross* (New York, 2005). Complicating analysis is the fact that ICRC prison visits in legally uncertain or contested situations, under its offer of humanitarian services, can be very similar to, if not identical with, prison visits in international armed conflict as called for in 1949 Geneva Conventions III and IV. So when the ICRC proceeds diplomatically by ad hoc agreement with the detaining authority, there may be no loss, or almost no loss, of substantive legal standards as found in IHL.

for fear of another costly and unsuccessful involvement. With the benefit of hindsight, we see in this tragic series of events the hell of good intentions, and the inescapable conclusion that it would have been better not to try to criminalize Aidid's behavior in the first place.

So the idea that we should always emphasize human rights law as the preferred means to human dignity, and we should always prosecute those who violate that law, needs careful examination. My own view is that while the liberal rule of law and the ending of impunity for egregious human rights violations is a worthwhile objective, along the pursuit of that goal we need to be aware of the hell of good intentions, which means recognizing that in some situations human dignity is better served by a temporary and exceptional waiving of the emphasis on rights discourse. (Recall Somalia in particular.) The ultimate goal is to establish a rights protective rule of law, but exceptions need to be recognized. Unfortunately, the well considered exceptions may turn out to be rather numerous, given the distribution of power in certain situations. After all, many situations of atrocity are ameliorated by negotiated agreements rather than total defeat of 'the bad guys,' the latter, quite often, being found on all sides of a conflict situation. Dayton is a good example of this dilemma.

My view is that we need to keep a broad, comparative perspective in mind, and be aware of contextual factors that would suggest a non-legalistic approach in fashioning a response to atrocities, as part of a policy to advance human dignity in the future. Easier said than done, but thus far we are discussing general approaches and the desirability of suspending automatic assumptions in behalf of emphasis on the law, in favor of contextual analysis and flexible choice of approach.

To be more specific, the situation in Uganda demonstrates the difficulty of choice. At the request of the Ugandan government, the Prosecutor of the ICC, Luis Moreno Ocampo, has opened an investigation into whether the leadership of the Lord's Resistance Army, particularly, a brutal opposition militia, has committed various violations of IHL, some of which might also constitute crimes against humanity. Subsequently not only did that leadership, particularly Joseph Kony, indicate a possible willingness to suspend violent operations if the legal charges were dropped, but also other Ugandan circles advocated local and traditional measures of reconciliation in place of international or national criminal justice. Complicating debate were assertions that the government side, too, had committed various war crimes. The matter was still evolving at the time of writing.

However the Ugandan situation plays out, my central point thus far is that we should not assume that the best course of action is always to emphasize rights and to prosecute under the law. We have to recognize that sometimes a political or diplomatic approach to a problem, based on morality in context, can be progressive, can advance the cause of human dignity, more so than a focus on particular criminal justice tied to human rights.

2.2. A FOCUS ON IMPACT

Let me use the now late-but-not-much-lamented UN Human Rights Commission to further discuss one specific problem identified by Kennedy and others. In certain legal journals one can find a regular summary of Commission resolutions and debates. Nowhere in these quite reputable journals, which have a strong legal orientation, can one find an analytical overview of the Commission demonstrating with empirical evidence that the debates and resolutions and decisions in the Commission have had virtually no demonstrable short term impact on structural, by which I mean systematic and fundamental, violation of internationally recognized human rights in targeted states. The most important point about the Commission is that it was almost always ineffective in the short term amelioration of human rights violations in UN member states, but one would never know this by reading most legal analyses of the Commission. One has to look at social science analysis outside of legally oriented publications to find this point clearly documented.

There were several analytical overviews of the Commission. The only analytical book was done by Howard Tolley in 1987. The most recent penetrating article was by James H. Lebovic and Erick Voeten in 2006. Both showed, by careful examination of empirical evidence, among other conclusions, that the various measures used by the Commission were ineffective in fundamentally changing governmental violation of rights in the short to medium term.[15]

For Leboic and Voeten, they identified 4 steps in the Commission (I will simplify their analysis a bit): discussion of a state, creation of a special procedure affecting a state, a presidential statement criticizing a state, and a formal resolution of censure by the Commission. They found that these four measures, when studied as a composite independent variable, had no significant impact on repressive states that had violated (mostly civil and political) human rights.

This type of research places in proper context the lawyerly debate about Commission special procedures and their continuation in the new UN Human Rights Council. Whatever the ultimate fate of the special procedures, meaning the creation of independent experts (viz., rapporteurs and working groups) to focus further on certain states or themes affecting states, the debate about their continuation has so far mostly obscured the fact that they do not have major, timely, and clear impact on a situation of rights violation. If they have other value, and they might, the special procedures as discussed by mainly lawyers has mostly obscured the fact that they are not very effective in advancing human dignity in the short run.

---

[15]   H.B. TOLLEY, *The UN Commission on Human Rights* (Boulder, 1987), and J.H. LEBOBIC and E. VOETEN, 'The Politics of Shame: The Condemnation of Country Human Rights Practices in the UNCHR', 50 *International Studies Quarterly* (2006) 861-888.

In short, the debate about special procedures has blown the subject out of proper proportion.[16]

It is social scientists who have rescued the main point from oblivion. By a careful review of the evidence, they have shown that one cannot much rely on the special procedures, or other Commission measures, to ameliorate state repression. In fact, in particularly treatments of the Commission by those trained in law, one often finds a description of this or that new development, but without attention to impact or effectiveness at all. It is as if lawyers were uncomfortable with analysis of impact, believing it the domain of others. Procedural new developments are duly noted, sometimes at length, but effectiveness and impact are rarely addressed. Some lengthy studies of the Commission explicitly and intentionally exclude coverage of impact, as if legal and diplomatic process were an end in itself.[17]

2.3. A FOCUS ON LEGAL OBLIGATION

Oona Hathaway, an American law professor, has demonstrated that many states that consent to the UN Convention against Torture continue to practice, or allow the practice of, torture.[18] Here we find a careful and mathematical examination of empirical evidence. Her study, now widely reprinted, raised fundamental questions about the value of core human rights treaties in advancing human dignity, even before the storm broke about U.S. interrogation policies from 2002 linked to its so-called war on terror.

The United States is, as is now widely known, a party to the UN Convention Against Torture which also prohibits lesser forms of mistreatment, the International Covenant on Civil and Political Rights which also prohibits torture and mistreatment, and the 1949 Geneva Conventions, which equally prohibits torture, along with humiliating and degrading treatment. It is generally now concluded, on the basis of media reports and other sources, that particularly in the CIA run 'Black Sites,' as well as in other places, the United States has employed 'water boarding' and other harsh interrogation techniques, long considered torture, and certainly at the upper end of the scale of mistreatment, against an unknown number of suspected

---

[16] In two follow-on studies, extending the Lebovic and Voeten study, I discuss the merits and demerits of the Commission and Council. While there is more to these bodies than just short term protection through their own actions, one should definitely not be Pollyanish about their utility for the advancement of human dignity. See D.P. FORSYTHE, 'Turbulent Transition', in S. KAUFMAN and T.A. WARTERS (eds.), *The United Nations: Past, Present, Future* (Nova Science, 2009); D.P. FORSYTHE, 'The Changing of the Guard', in *Human Rights Law Review* (forthcoming).

[17] See M. LEMPINEN, *The United Nations Commission on Human Rights and the different treatment of governments : an inseparable part of promoting and encouraging respect for human rights?* (Turku, 2005).

[18] O. HATHAWAY, 'Do Human Rights Treaties Make a Difference?', 111 *Yale Law Journal* (2002) 1935-2042.

enemy prisoners. The fundamental point here is that a U.S. sense of legal obligation under various legal instruments, has not been sufficient to block abusive interrogation deemed necessary in the name of national security. In certain U.S. circles, as was also the case in certain British, French, and Israeli circles of policy making in the past, moral consequentialism prevailed: it is not moral to avoid torture and mistreatment, if the result is significant amount of death of civilians and destruction of civilian property at the hands of enemies.

Therefore, as Hathaway showed in general with regard to the torture treaty, and as can be shown in particular with regard to U.S. policy after 9/11, the effectiveness of legal obligation under international treaties (and U.S. law for that matter) can be greatly overstated.

Furthermore, James Morrow, an American social scientist, demonstrates in an issue of the American Political Science Review, through a statistical review of much data, that some parts of IHL fare better than others across time.[19] In particular, he shows that protection of civilians, a fundamental rule of IHL, is the least well respected, whereas rules on chemical and biological warfare are the best respected. Surprisingly, treatment of POWS does not fare very well, ranking rather low on his hierarchy of compliance.

Now one can very well question this data set. We are not sure about the extent of attacks on civilians in Iraq since 2003, and exactly who caused exactly what number of killed and wounded. It is therefore suspect to use exact numbers for civilians killed and wounded in various wars over considerable time, especially in the past when reporting on these points was not very good. Nevertheless, especially since the coders of the data set in this study are aware of the problem and try to control for it, it may still turn out to be the case that imprecise numbers can lead to valid generalizations. The numbers may be slightly off, but the comparative conclusions may still hold.

My central point about the Morrow study is that legal obligation per se explains very little about why fighting parties do or do not respect this or that part of IHL. All states have consented to the 1949 Geneva Conventions. All states now have the same legal obligation. But it is a careful study of such factors as type of ratifying state, self-interest, reciprocity, and capability to violate that appears to explain what part of the law works and what does not — not legal obligation per se. So in this example, our understanding of IHL is enhanced by a broad social or political analysis, based on quantitative analysis of coded information, which gives us a picture that traditional legal analysis cannot.

Let me add two anecdotes about the weakness of a sense of obligation under international law. First, the UN Charter is quite clear that the regular or

---

[19]   J.D. MORROW, 'When Do States Follow the Laws of War', 101 *American Political Science Review* (2007) 559-572.

headquarters or administrative budget is to be set by the General Assembly. There is no provision for state withholding of its assessed dues (which are set according to a formula determined by a sub-committee of the Assembly). These Charter Article 17 provisions, reinforced by Charter Article 19 provisions, allowing for loss of vote in the Assembly for states falling the equivalent of two years behind in their assessed payments, make no provision for state withholding of dues by unilateral decision. All of this legal wording has not stopped the United States from withholding of some parts of assessed payments for political reasons — e.g., opposition to this or that UN expenditure. (France and the Soviet Union did the same in the past.)

At one point the chair of the International Relations Committee in the House of Representatives, Dante Fascell (D., FL), and by no means the most parochial or obstructionist member of the U.S. Congress, when faced with State Department legal arguments about the U.S. obligation to pay, simply said: these legal arguments will not persuade Congress to authorize the contested money. Arguments about legal obligation are going to be dismissed by many MCs, starting with members of my Committee, so find some different arguments.[20]

Second, I myself have participated in meetings with a number of lawyers who were outraged by various U.S. policy decisions, whether about not fully paying U.N. dues, or ignoring the judgment of the International Court of Justice in the Nicaragua case,[21] or abusing prisoners after 9/11. They continually referred to this or that provision of this or that treaty or document, as if the repetition of legal wording would convince Washington to change this or that policy. It was a completely unrealistic approach to the problem.

If we take the latter example — U.S. policy toward presumed enemy prisoners after 9/11— as a matter of fact opposition to the policies of forced disappearance, indefinite detention, and harsh interrogation crystallized on two different grounds: 1) self-interest, namely that the Bush policies did more harm than good; and 2) culture, namely that Americans should not do that sort of thing. Legal obligation played a very small role in American debates about prisoner policy, and when it did arise it was linked most often to self-interest — properly implementing IHL now (and the Convention Against Torture) would protect U.S. military personnel when captured by others in the future. Arguments about legal obligation per se were relatively unimportant.[22]

---

[20]   D.P. FORSYTHE, *The Politics of International Law: U.S. Foreign Policy Reconsidered* (Boulder, 1990).

[21]   When the ICJ ruled in 1986 that the United States was liable for certain damages inflicted by its de jure or de facto agents in Central America, Washington, having already objected to the Court's accepting jurisdiction in the first place, then turned its back on the substantive judgment as politically biased. Neither the Reagan Administration nor the Congress, including the MCs from the Democratic Party, rose to the defense of the ICJ.

[22]   See further D.P. FORSYTHE, 'U.S. Policy toward Enemy Detainees in the 'War on Terrorism'', 28 *Human Rights Quarterly* (2006) 465-491; D.P. FORSYTHE, 'U.S. Treatment of Enemy Prisoners', in

David P. Forsythe

I should not like to be misunderstood about the role of legal obligation, especially in the form of ratification of treaties. I think this legal factor can have significance at times. It made a difference in World War II that both Nazi Germany and the Allied Powers were obligated to respect the 1929 Geneva Convention for the Protection of Prisoners of War, whereas Nazi Germany was not so bound vis-à-vis the Soviet Union, the latter not having accepted it. Nazi treatment of Allied POWs was infinitely superior to Nazi treatment of Soviet POWs (not that Soviet care of Nazi POWs was any better). Given a curious German sensitivity to certain legal issues, which obtained even in the Nazi era, the 1929 Convention made a difference. However, it made a difference because of reciprocity (self-interest) and culture, not because of the power of legal obligation by itself.

And certainly when we get to hard law in liberal democratic states, we find that judicial determination of legal obligation under human rights and humanitarian treaties can make a difference. A recent example concerns the 2006 Hamdan judgment by US Supreme Court, holding that Common Article 3 of the 1949 Geneva Conventions did apply to prisoners at Guantanamo. That judgment about legal obligation did affect subsequent U.S. policies both pertaining to the use of military commissions to try those accused of illegal behavior and pertaining to interrogation measures — at least in military facilities (we are not sure about the CIA).

In general, however, and especially keeping in mind that much international law, especially on human rights and humanitarian affairs, never gets adjudicated in courts, and certainly so outside of Europe, the role of legal obligation per se remains often a weak reed on which to lean. Non-legal factors such as perceptions of self-interest, including the notion of reciprocity, and culturally established notions like self-image, are often more important. This is precisely what the Morrow study in the APSR shows, as well as my own studies of U.S. policy toward enemy detainees.

3. CONCLUSION

Whether or not some human rights lawyers are more legalistic than some social scientists is, of course, not the central point in my remarks above. Areyh Neier, a judicial romantic, was not legally trained. Howard Tolley was trained both in law and in political science. David Kennedy and Mark Drumbl, who raised penetrating issues about law's purpose and effectiveness, were legally trained. I have used a stereotype of some human rights lawyers, no doubt a contested generalization, to launch the discussion. I do believe that much legal training, however, when it is

---

D.P. FORSYTHE, et al (eds.), *American Foreign Policy in a Globalized World* (New York, 2006); and D.P. FORSYTHE, 'The Politics of Protecting Enemy Detainees', in A. BRYSK and G. SHAFIR (eds.), *Democracies Debate Counter Terrorism* (Berkeley, 2007).

traditional and technical, is not conducive to an appropriately broad focus, including studies of impact.

My essential points are these: 1) Human rights is an interdisciplinary subject, and there are many ways to address it, not just by a focus on legal wording, legal obligation, and court cases. 2) One should never forget the 'so what' question: does the law and the implementation processes make any difference re public policy and human behavior. One should be prepared to conclude, on the basis of careful research, that human rights law is misguided or not working, and perhaps that diplomatic or economic approaches, inter alia, would be more beneficial for the advance of human dignity, at least in some situations. Human rights are a means to human dignity; as means, they should not be confused with the desired end. 3) Analysts should be contrarian, willing to challenge conventional wisdom, and willing to examine unexamined assumptions.

METHODS IN LEGAL
HUMAN RIGHTS RESEARCH

Eva Brems

1. INTRODUCTION

When the editors of this book invited me to reflect on this topic, I hesitated. I am convinced that the topic is a very important one and I have personally been feeling the need to discuss methodology in legal human rights research for some time. But one way may wonder whether I have anything particular to contribute to such discussions. I have been involved in human rights research since 1992, on a wide variety of topics. But I have never researched or taught methodology and I have not experimented with any special or innovative methods. Hence I am discussing a topic in which I do not consider myself to be expert. At the same time, I do not know who the experts are — possibly all legal human rights scholars are equally non-expert in this field.

In this paper, I try to turn this weakness into a strength, by doing two things at once: while I present my findings on method in legal human rights research, I'll take the reader with me on the methodological journey of this paper, being entirely transparent about what I have done and what I have not done and about the reasons for those choices.

2. RESEARCH QUESTION(S) AND METHOD

2.1. RESEARCH QUESTIONS

- The topic for this paper was provided by the conference organizers. The research questions I derived from their background paper include empirical and normative questions. They are quite basic and straightforward. Some research questions are empirical:
- How much attention is paid to method in legal human rights research?
- Which research methods are used in legal human rights research?

Others are normative:

-   What would good practice look like?

How can current practice be improved to approach good practice?

2.2. METHOD

I decided on the method of this small research project on the basis of criteria that are not likely to be considered good practice:
I decided *not* to do a study of the literature on methodology on the basis of:

-   Considerations of expertise: I would not know where to start looking for this literature.
-   Time constraints: I wanted to use other methods as well and I knew I had limited time available for this paper.
-   Considerations of motivation: I did not feel like doing this; I thought it would be boring.

Hence I decided to draw normative conclusions only from my own reflection on the results of empirical research. For lack of theoretical background, my evaluative framework for the normative conclusions is a simple one, based on common sense. I will consider an approach to methodology as good to the extent that it furthers the quality of the research results and that it allows others to assess that quality.

In order to answer the empirical questions, I could think of two approaches: asking researchers and looking at the research. I decided to do both:

-   On the basis of a vague intuition (it would be an overstatement to call it a thought-through methodological principle) that combining insider (subjective) information with outsider (objective) information would give me more information (quantitative argument) and also more complete and more balanced information (qualitative argument).
-   Because both seemed fun to do, so why choose?

2.2.1. Examining the attitudes and practice of researchers

How should I ask the researchers? I could think of two techniques: interviews and a questionnaire. Initially, I wanted to do both: first send out a questionnaire and then follow up on some of them with interviews. Due to time constraints, I only did the questionnaire. I had never done a questionnaire before and yet I did not consult any literature or any experts on this matter. I included the questions that in my opinion were suitable for gathering information to answer the research questions. The questionnaire is copied below.

a) Questionnaire

Questionnaire 'Methods of legal human rights research'

Please add your answers in this Word document. Feel free to add as much explanation as needed. Return to eva.brems@ugent.be before 15 October 2007.
Dutch and French speakers, please feel free to answer in your own language.

What is meant by 'research method'?

- how to gather information (which sources to use, how to get the information from the sources)
- how to organize and interpret the information:
  - hierarchy of sources
  - theoretical framework
  - level of analysis: micro/macro
  - comparison or not
  - ...

THE QUESTIONNAIRE APPLIES ONLY TO YOUR HUMAN RIGHTS RESEARCH

1. How many years have you been active in legal human rights research?

2. Is human rights law your main field of research?

  - If not, what is your main field?
  - What are your other fields of research, besides legal human rights research, if any?

3. Is your research related to:

  - United Nations mechanisms
  - Regional mechanisms (which?)
  - Domestic law in my own country
  - Domestic law of another country/other countries
  - Theory
  - Other?

4. To what extent do you consider your research as:

- o normative?
- o empirical?

5. When starting work on a new research topic, do you always take time to reflect on the most appropriate research method? (If you do this sometimes, but not always, what are the determining factors for doing so?)

6. When starting work on a new research topic, do you take time to reflect on the relationship of this research to earlier research?

7. When reporting your research (in a paper, book, etc.) do you as a rule include information on the research methods that were used? If you do, it would be nice if you could add an example (as an attachment).

8. Please describe your research method(s).

9. Do you always use the same research method(s)? If not, what factors determine the choice of method?

10. Do you have any experience with interdisciplinary research in the field of human rights? If you do, describe briefly your experience (with an emphasis on method).

11. Do you make statements in your work about what is the correct interpretation of a particular human rights norm (in a particular context)? If you do, what is the basis on which you make such statements?

12. In your research, do you sometimes/generally work on the (tacit) assumption that your research should contribute to a better protection and promotion of human rights?

13. How/when were you trained in research methods?

14. Have you ever experienced a need for more training or guidance with respect to research methods? If you have, under what circumstances?

15. Any other comments?

Thank you very much!

b) Comment

I thought it would be necessary to report on the kind of researchers from whom I had obtained the information. I already knew their affiliation, but included three questions (1 to 3) to situate them as researchers. Three questions (8, 9 and 10) asked the researchers about the methods they use. Three questions (5, 6 and 7) asked about the importance that the researchers attach to method. An implicit assumption here was that many may do not attach much importance to this. Three questions (4, 11 and 12) focused on the normative character of legal human rights research. There are also implicit assumptions here, which are made explicit in the background paper of the conference organizers, namely that most legal human rights research is normative in character and that the basis of normative statements may not always be clear. Finally I enquire after their training in methodology (13 and 14) and leave room for additional comments (15).

In making this questionnaire, I was aware of the risk of ambiguity of some of the questions: what we understand as 'method', 'empirical' or 'better human rights protection' may differ from one person to another. I did not think it necessary to define or explain much, working on the assumption that the differences in understanding certain concepts would be among the information I was looking for; in other words that I would be gathering information from the answers to my questions not only directly but also indirectly. Yet I did think it would be necessary to give some guidance as to what the questionnaire was looking for and therefore included an introductory paragraph on 'what is meant by research method'. This is based on the background paper of the conference and on my own thinking. Yet it leaves room (…) for other conceptions.

c) Addressees

How should I identify the relevant people to whom to send this questionnaire? I selected 65 people from my address book. These are people for whom I know that at least some of their research is legal human rights research. Why this method of selection? Because it is easy and fast; I already had the addresses and I knew the people were relevant for this research. How did I select these people within my address book? There were basically two criteria:

- All addressees were people whom I dare ask for their cooperation in this matter either because they owe me something or because I know them to be friendly and helpful (this is related to a definite uncertainty about not having done such research before, and an awareness of the imperfections in my questionnaire and in the logic underlying it).
- Three diversity criteria.
  o Postdoc/predoc (43/22)

o   Affiliation to a Flemish/Dutch/other university (25/16/24)
o   Women/men (27/38)

The first two seemed relevant in the light of the representative character of the results. The final one is a matter of principle to me at all times. I did not set targets; the feeling that the questionnaire was sufficiently balanced was purely subjective and intuitive.

I sent the questionnaires by e-mail and after a few weeks I sent one reminder. Out of 65 questionnaires I received 28 useful responses. The diversity spread was as follows:

- Postdoc/predoc: 17/9
- Flemish/Dutch/other university: 9/7/12

(The 'other' are: 2 from Walloon universities, and 1 each from the UK, France, Germany, Switzerland, Sweden, the Czech Republic, Israel, the US, South Africa and New Zealand.)

- Women/men: 11/17

2.2.2. Examining the Research Output

How should I examine the research itself? Ideally one would monitor the entire research process, but due to time constraints I looked only at the research output. I decided to take the 2006 volume (the most recent complete volume) of a number of journals specializing in human rights law. I identified the journals on the basis of those that are available in the Ghent University library, either in paper or electronic form. I selected those that announce themselves as dealing with human rights law or that I knew to be adopting a predominantly legal perspective. Interdisciplinary journals were not included. This explains why *Human Rights Quarterly*, possibly the most influential journal in the field, was left out.[1] The journals I selected were the following:

- *Revue Trimestrielle des Droits de l'Homme*
- *NJCM* (Dutch Lawyers' Committee on HR) *Bulletin*
- *European Human Rights Law Review*
- *Netherlands Quarterly of Human Rights*

---

[1]   Cf. H-O. Sano and H. Thelle, 'The Need of Evidence Based Human Rights Research', in the present volume, who rely on an analysis of data used in the Human Rights Quarterly and the Netherlands Quarterly of Human Rights.

- *Human Rights Law Review*
- *Columbia Human Rights Law Review*
- *Buffalo Human Rights Law Review*

I looked at all the articles in the 2006 volumes of these journals and I eliminated a number of categories: editorials or opinions, tributes, case law comments, case law chronicles, purely informative contributions, brief updates on recent developments, articles that were not really dealing with human rights and articles that were clearly not legal (but instead sociological, philosophical, political or historical) as well one article written by myself.

This left me with a corpus of 90 papers that I read through, looking for information on the method used by the author. This included both direct information and indirect information (mainly looking in the text and the footnotes to see what kinds of sources were used).

3. RESULTS OF THE EMPIRICAL RESEARCH

3.1. QUESTIONNAIRE

3.1.1. Who?

The 28 academics who filled out the questionnaire, have 3 to 30 years of experience in legal human rights research. One third of these reported 3 to 6 years of experience, another third 7 to 13 years of experience and another third 15 to 30 years. A total of 22 out of 28 reported that human rights law is their main field of research. Within their human rights research, 22 reported that they had done research on the Council of Europe mechanism, 22 reported their work was on domestic law in their own country, 19 investigated theory, 18 were concerned with UN mechanisms and 15 examined the domestic law of countries other than their own.

3.1.2. The Importance of Methodology

Asked whether they always take time to reflect on the most appropriate research method when starting work on a new research topic, 13 said 'yes', nine said 'no' and five said 'sometimes'. Among the 13 yeses, two added that they considered this as 'crucial' or 'very important', two others added apologetic words in the sense 'well, I do some reflection on how to deal with an issue but maybe this is not explicitly on method'. Among the nine no's, two specified that they first start gathering information and afterwards try to organize it. People answering that they 'sometimes' reflect on method were asked to specify what were the determining factors of doing so. Two mentioned the topic, two gave the framework (project funding and interdisciplinary project), one stated the type of article (substantive articles yes; smaller ones no), and one said that it depended on prior knowledge. To the question 'do you take time to reflect on the relationship of new research to earlier research?' 26 out of 28 replied 'yes'.

It is one thing to use a method, it is another thing to reflect upon it and it is yet another thing to report on the method you used in your published research. On the question 'do you as a rule include information on the research methods you used in your published work?' only three respondents replied 'yes'. 15 said no, and ten gave a mixed answer. Among these mixed answers, four said 'only in my doctoral thesis', one said 'only in books', one said 'only in longer articles, but in my home country journals accept only short papers so I have to leave out this information', two said they include brief references to method, e.g. saying that there has been comparative research or indicating that particular information was obtained in an interview. One person said: 'I don't do this in my work but I have written a specific paper on methodology'. I received four samples of reporting on methodology in respondents' published work. Two of these were around a half page, one was 1.5 pages and the fourth was 25 pages. The long one explains an interdisciplinary method. The other ones describe the sources used, one case describes a research hypothesis and one other case, concerning a comment on a treaty provision, described the hierarchy among the sources used to interpret that provision.

3.1.3. Training and Guidance

I asked people how and when they were trained in research methods. Fourteen stated that there had been no training: they had learned by doing. Eight persons referred to limited training at bachelor's level during their legal studies. Two mentioned training as a doctoral candidate, one person enjoyed an explicit course on research methods at university and one person had learned through personal reading on the issue. I also asked about the need for more training or guidance with respect to research methods. Only three persons stated they felt no such need. One person said that he had felt this need in the past but no longer today. Ten persons answered that they feel this need when they engage in interdisciplinary or multidisciplinary research, either because they want to learn the methods of non-legal disciplines or because in an interdisciplinary context they feel challenged with respect to legal methods. Other contexts in which respondents felt the need for guidance with respect to method were: when conducting empirical studies (1) and when filling out forms for research grants (1). Respondents expressed their wish for a formal course on human rights research methods (1), or a guide on human rights research (2) more methodology in legal training in general (2), peer groups or seminars of researchers sharing methods (1), more discussion of method and theory (3) or a more generally accepted human rights law research method (1).

3.1.4. Methods Used

A central question in the questionnaire was number 8: 'please describe your research method(s)'. One respondent wrote 'This is where things really start to look bad for me. I can't actually describe any particular 'method''. Others tried to describe what they do in plain words. For some this came more or less down to 'I find as much information as I can. I read and digest this information. I write up the article'. Still others have some jargon they can mobilize, such as 'desktop research', 'primary and secondary sources', 'inductive method', 'meso-level' or 'functional comparative method'.

One clear outcome of this question was that most respondents exclusively use desktop research. Six mentioned occasional use of other methods: surveys (2), interviews (4), focus groups (1) and workshops (1) or discussions (1) with relevant actors. Beyond that, the replies did not enlighten me much: I got some feedback on the different issues I suggested as falling within the definition of 'method': 12 people reported on the types of sources they use, but only three stated where they find them and two mentioned the hierarchy of sources. Six respondents stated that they usually use a comparative method; two of them specified that they prefer the functional method of comparison. Three respondents referred to a theoretical framework of analysis. Among the terms used to describe research methods, I noted two references to working with hypotheses, one mentioning the 'inductive method' ('discovering patterns and inconsistencies in the output of monitoring bodies', and one referred to 'qualitative methods' as opposed to quantitative methods, the example of the latter referring to the caseload of judicial bodies.

Nine out of 28 respondents stated that they always use the same research method.

Seven persons stated that they had no experience with interdisciplinary research on human rights. The experience of the others in this field can be subdivided into three types:

- Type 1 was called 'passive interdisciplinarity' by one respondent: the human rights lawyer reads materials from other disciplines, possibly discusses them with colleagues from those disciplines and integrates the information to some extent in her own writing. Six respondents referred to this type of experience.
- Type 2 is the use of a multidisciplinary approach in the human rights lawyer's own work. Six respondents referred to this type of experience, with two stating explicitly that it was challenging.

- Type 3 is the participation in an interdisciplinary project with colleagues from other disciplines. Ten respondents mentioned this type of experience. Concretely, people referred to a joint book project, in which each author contributes from his/her own discipline to co-author a paper and to a joint research project in which agreement has to be reached on a common methodology.

3.1.5. Empirical vs. Normative Research

Asked to what extent they consider their research normative or empirical, 16 respondents stated that it was mainly or exclusively normative, two stated that it was mainly or exclusively empirical and nine stated that it was both. From the answers it was clear that there was some lack of clarity as to what exactly counts as empirical research for a legal scholar in the human rights field. Doubts were expressed as to whether case law analysis or comparative study is empirical or not.

I asked respondents whether they make statements in their work about what is the correct interpretation of a particular human rights norm (in a particular context) and on what basis they do this. A total of 22 answered 'yes' and five respondents stated that they did something different than claiming one correct interpretation, for example criticizing the norm, not its interpretation, or indicating agreement or disagreement with interpretations of others, or giving indications as to the correct interpretation. Nobody claimed that they did not make normative statements. As the basis of their normative statements, three respondents referred to theoretical or philosophical views, four referred to comparisons, two referred to the rules of interpretation in general international law (Articles 31-33 of the Vienna Convention on the Law of Treaties) and four mentioned authority of other authors in addition to other sources. One respondent was honest enough to say that 'wishful thinking' was among the bases of normative statements.

I also asked respondents whether they sometimes or generally work on the tacit assumption that their research should contribute to a better protection and promotion of human rights. A total of 24 answered in the affirmative, with accompanying statements expressing feelings of pride (5) or hope (2) or on the other hand a sense that this may be problematic or a need to make their motives clear (4). Two respondents answered in the negative and two gave a mixed answer. Both of these clarified the fact that they did not always promote the most expansive interpretation of human rights norms, but that the latter is not necessarily synonymous with 'better protection of human rights'.

3.1.6. Some Conclusions from the Questionnaire

Even though the large majority of respondents state that their choice of method varies from one research project to another, only half make it a habit to reflect on method before starting work on a new topic. Reporting on method is even less widespread. This may be linked to the fact that most have not been trained in research methods. The need for more support on methods is felt mostly in an interdisciplinary context. Cooperating with colleagues from other disciplines forces human rights lawyers to reflect on their methods. Externally sponsored research, even if it is strictly legal, may have the same effect. There appears to be a lack of agreed-upon language to describe methods. As a result of that, experienced scholars show themselves to be inarticulate when faced with questions about the methods they use. Moreover, all legal human rights scholars make normative statements in their work, yet there is no agreed way of framing or legitimizing such statements. There was no meaningful link between types of answers and personal criteria such as gender, number of years of research experience or country of affiliation.

3.2. EXAMINATION OF THE CORPUS

The examination of 90 published papers confirms the finding from the questionnaire that explicit reporting on method is not the rule.

Two papers are special cases: one concerns a comment on another paper and hence a debate between two authors who disagree in particular on an aspect of methodology, i.e. the correct interpretation of human rights treaties and in particular the role of a general comment. The other is a paper that explains and promotes a particular method of evaluating human rights performance. Hence, while these papers do not explain the methodology of the paper as such, they have method as their main topic. In each case, two authors are involved. It is remarkable to find that all four are Australians.

Only two of the 90 papers contain a separate section on 'methodology' or 'methodological considerations'. Both papers happen to be authored by female Swiss academics and published in the Human Rights Law Review.[2]

The large majority of the papers contain at least some direct information as to the method used. I used a very low-threshold standard here: even half a sentence

---

[2]   I have deliberately stayed out of the delicate issue of ranking the journals that were included in the corpus with respect to the degree to which they pay attention to method. However, the reader may like to know that American journals do not appear to perform clearly better in this field than European journals or vice versa. Some journals clearly give fewer guidelines to their contributing authors than others; yet from the analysis it appears very unlikely that any of the journals consider reporting on method as a requirement for publication. Hence the extent to which information on method is included in a paper depends entirely on the author, rather than on the journal.

clarifying that the research question would be addressed 'through the analysis of the case law of the European Court of Human Rights' would count. Yet in 22 out of 90 papers (almost 1 in 4) no direct information on method was found. In most cases I experienced this as problematic; I found I had to read almost the entire paper before even knowing what kind of paper I was dealing with: authors put forward a topic or research question in the title or the introduction and do not even make it clear whether they are going to address this on the basis of scholarly literature or case law analysis, or even whether they are addressing the matter in the context of domestic or international law. Those papers that do include information on method, include this:

- in the title of the piece (35);
- in a footnote (11);
- in the introduction (30);
- in the main body of the text (7).

Information on method in the title is necessarily brief, but may enlighten the reader on the forum in which the topic will be studied (domestic law, international law, etc.), the use of a comparative method, the analysis of the case law of a particular body or the analysis of a treaty 'in the light of the travaux préparatoires'. It may also make reference to a theoretical framework (e.g. 'postcolonial theory') and it may reveal a normative tendency of the research ('redefining', 'an appraisal' or 'a case for').

Information included in a footnote mostly refers to the broader research in which the paper is to be situated or the sources that were used (e.g. 'thanks to a grant from X, I was able to interview this type of people in country Y').

In the introduction as well as in the main body of the text, information on method is generally intertwined with information on the outline of the paper. Authors describe what they have studied and incidentally some information on how they have done this comes along. Yet this mostly remains very general and incomplete.

Taken together, the direct and indirect information on method allows the reader to know the forum and level of the analysis, the use of comparative method or case studies, theoretical reference points and at least part of the sources on which the author relies. In this respect, I noted significant use of sources outside the classical legal ones, in particular NGO reports and press reports. Another thing I noted was the very limited use of other methods than desk research. Among the 90 papers, two mentioned interviews and one mentioned a questionnaire as well as workshop discussions with relevant actors.

Yet due to the scarcity of direct information on method, there are clear shortcomings. I noted widespread (nearly generalized) omission of information on the following:

- Selection criteria for the corpus on which case law analysis is performed. Take the example of the European Court of Human Rights. Authors do not specify whether they have examined the whole body of judgments; they do not even mention whether they have included decisions of inadmissibility in addition to judgments on the merits. As a result the reader cannot assess the validity of the conclusions. Especially in a strongly normative paper, it is important to know whether the author has selected from among the case law those judgments that prove her point ignoring those that disprove it or whether she has based her conclusions on an examination of all the case law.

- Selection criteria for the jurisdictions included in a comparative research and for case studies. As a result the reader cannot assess the scope of the conclusions. It seems important to enable the reader at least to assess to what extent the conclusions drawn from a specific analysis have a more general breadth.

- Explicit mention of the benchmarks or criteria that will be used in a normative assessment. This may result in an impression that the normative assessments in the conclusion or throughout the text are subjective or random. For example, an author may state that a particular legal arrangement is not appropriate because it is 'too complex', yet without any further indication as to why simplicity is an indicator of appropriateness in the matter at hand or what degree of complexity might be acceptable.

4. NORMATIVE CONCLUSIONS

What can we learn from the results of this small research project and from my own clumsy efforts at innovating my research methods in the context of this paper?

One respondent noted: 'the fact that we do not report on method in our publications does not mean that we do not have a valid method'. True. But I would suggest that the following two statements are equally true:

1. Because we do not report on method, no claims can be made about the validity of our methods and this includes the claim that our method is valid. This makes our research vulnerable to criticism. When our research results are contested, do we have solid ground to stand on or does our defence resemble a subjective viewpoint rather than scientific findings? The risk is even stronger as many human rights topics touch upon highly debated and contested issues that are sensitive from a political or ethical viewpoint, and because many of us are also human rights activists and are known as such in our respective societies.

2.   In combination with the finding that most of us do not reflect on method at the start of a research project, the practice of not reporting on method may threaten the quality of our research. In this paper I have behaved atypically, in the sense that I have reported honestly on the reasons for the methodological choices I have made. Some of these were manifestly detrimental to the quality of the research. I can guarantee that I would never report on such deficiencies in any other type of article. But I cannot guarantee that I would never make (or have never made) a methodological choice only because of time constraints, laziness or subjective preferences.

As human rights lawyers, surely we do not need to be persuaded that reporting mechanisms are useful to improve practice? Remember Philip Alston's report on UN human rights reporting mechanisms:[3] among the benefits of such mechanisms he cites a monitoring function, a policy formulation function, a public scrutiny function, an evaluation function and a function of acknowledging problems.

My hypothesis (not yet confirmed by empirical research though) is that more reporting by human rights lawyers on their research methods would be beneficial, as it would stimulate reflection on these methods, which in turn would lead to improved methods. A first step to this is the development of common jargon to describe current methodologies. Other steps may include a stronger emphasis on method in human rights education and/or in legal education in general, and the sensibilization of peer reviewers to pay increased attention to reporting on method in their assessment of papers that are submitted for publication.

---

[3]   P. Alston, Effective functioning of bodies established pursuant to United Nations human rights instruments: Final report on enhancing the long-term effectiveness of the United Nations human rights treaty system, UN Doc. E/CN.4/1997/74.

THE NEED FOR EVIDENCE-BASED HUMAN RIGHTS RESEARCH

HANS-OTTO SANO and HATLA THELLE

1. INTRODUCTION

This paper makes an argument for evidence-based human rights research. In referring to evidence-based research, we refer to the use of empirical data, whether qualitative, quantitative, administrative or events-based, which illustrates and documents the respect for and implementation of human rights including how rights-holders are deprived of their rights or alternatively how duty-bearers make efforts to fulfil human rights obligations.

This is a crude description of what evidence-based data could entail. The point is not to detail all aspects of evidence, but rather to make the observation that too little empirical evidence enters into human rights research. The consequence of this shortcoming is that 'people' are not sufficiently present in human rights research and that institutional processes are under-researched. Perhaps a consequence is also that human rights researchers know too little about the reality of human rights implementation — or lack of it.

There are three reasons why this could be an argument to consider: First, much human rights research is about normative, legal and philosophical interpretation. Thus, human rights sources for research have typically been legal and or quasi-legal documents based on court rulings or on administrative regulation. Philosophical texts are often employed to back up arguments about the legitimacy of human rights law and about its normative foundation. Human rights studies have addressed the political and social implications of legal norms, but people — individuals and groups — have often entered as shadow images where the real actors have been lawmakers, judges, politicians, bureaucrats and organizations.

Second, the indivisibility and interdependence of rights has increasingly led to a growing concern with social rights. This means that new subjects manifest themselves in human rights studies, the distance between legal norms and the plight of the majority of the world's population in terms of poverty, marginalization, discrimination, and oppression which become ever more relevant. There is a lot of interest in indicators, and this may be useful enough, but what seems more important is to get data[1] which illustrates a broader range of domains and issues than usually covered by indicators. The subject of indicators cannot cover the need for evidence. With a growing interest in rights-based approaches especially in transitional and developing contexts, there is a strong need to document how rights-holders address issues of rights-deprivation and how duty-bearers respond. Human rights research aiming to analyze macro-trends must use competences that are not the traditional domain of human rights training. Such competences are, however, needed in order to undertake comparative analysis of, e.g. human rights violations, in order to examine data describing social contexts relevant in human rights analysis, and in order to generate broader thinking and hypotheses about the behaviour of actors and institutions.[2]

Third, human rights studies have entered into domestic policies in many countries as a perennial domain of politics. This means that human rights activists and research institutions are challenged on a growing number of fronts, simply because politicians, at least in some countries, cannot live with claims that they do not live up to their human rights obligations. A case in point is the ECRI report on discrimination in Denmark published in 2006.[3] The recommendations of the report as regards a number of discrimination-related issues such as the incorporation of specific human rights treaties, citizenship law and administration, promotion of anti-racism legislation, and promulgation of new criminal law were rejected by the government claiming that the recommendations were either based on insufficient or wrong evidence, were politically biased or were unfounded as issues were effectively dealt with by other government institutions than the ones mentioned in the report. One professor backed up the government arguing that:

'It is not acceptable to argue in a public debate that one's analysis is not a real one. The analysis will be evaluated on the basis of whether the allegations promoted are substantiated. Peter Dahler-Larsen [professor at University of Southern Denmark] characterizes it as problematic that ECRI has not documented the allegations concerning whether Denmark has become more xenophobic. I think that ECRI has taken for granted that we all think that racism is terrible. ECRI has circulated impressions of impressions. But the Committee has failed to realize that we disagree

---

[1] A distinction between indicators and data is emphasized. Indicators are defined by institutions and researchers as purposive tools of measurement used for measuring specific phenomena of change or to document specific situations. Empirical data is a broader category which relates to all aspects of social reality irrespective of whether these are used as indicators. Indicators are linked to institutional ownership or to specific measurements. See E. A. ANDERSEN, and H-O. SANO, *Indicators at the Programme and Project Level: Guidelines for Indicator Definition, Monitoring and Evaluation* (Copenhagen, 2006).

[2] See T. LANDMAN, *Studying Human Rights* (London 2006). See chapter 5 in particular.

[3] ECRI, *Third Report on Denmark. Adopted 16 December 2005* (Strasbourg, 2006).

fundamentally about this in Denmark... He encourages ECRI to a more systematic account of methods and a more critical scrutiny of the sources."[4]

Thus, the report was discredited as it was too easy for its opponents to point to errors and to document the fact that the evidence was not solid enough. This example can serve to illustrate some of the difficulties of externally based monitoring of human rights. Such monitoring must either be based on the government's own reporting like for instance is happening in the treaty bodies, or be founded on solid quantitative or qualitative evidence, eventually cross-checked by other sources.

The present article will focus on human rights research and data, especially as regards transitional contexts and developing contexts. An underlying premise of the paper is that human rights research follows the general laws and criteria for sound and reliable research such as the validity and representativeness of the data used, clarification of basic premises and possibly relating to a body of theoretical literature or to other literature in the domain of research. And, as in other research, the crux of the matter is that the methodology used should provide appropriate answers to the research questions. This may sound self-evident, but in practice a researcher time and again can face a situation, where she has a substantive amount of data, but finds out that it does not exactly answer the question she had in mind. Then one has to go back again, adjust the methods and collect new material. This back-and-forth process is often halted because of time or money constraints. But human rights research is special in the relatively long distance and complicated interplay between international standards and lived lives, making it easy to stop at the stage of the legal measures and institutional description. However, these methods are seldom sufficient to answer the question of whether a certain right is effectively protected or not. Neither will a social science analysis be able to pass the ultimately legal judgment concerning whether violations occur or not, but by investigating material conditions and the context around individual and group protection including social perceptions of protection, a social science study will be able to point to areas where violations might occur, and where it is therefore important to undertake further investigations.[5]

The paper will reflect generally about the use of evidence in human rights research. It will depart from an analysis of sources used in articles of the most recent volumes of *Human Rights Quarterly* and in the *Netherlands Quarterly of Human Rights* — assuming that choice of sources inform about the methodology of the

---

[4]   <http://www.dr.dk/Nyheder/Indland/2006/05/16/125939.htm?rss=true>.

[5]   Perception analyses are increasingly undertaken within the field of good governance and human rights. Megatora, the OECD-based initiative sought during 2005-07 to establish an Inventory of local research initiatives globally which attempted to measure human rights, good governance and democracy. An important part of the local initiatives were sample surveys investigating perceptions about security, human rights atrocities and corruption. See <www.metagora.org>.

research in question. We distinguish between different categories of data classified below. The point is that human rights research rarely bases itself on other sources than administrative, judicial and secondary literature sources. Evidence which analyzes institutional decision-making processes concerning, e.g. compliance or which illustrate the struggles by marginalized groups for realization of their rights or which examine the effectiveness of human rights implementation enter rarely into the analyses.[6] The employment of data categories indicates methodological choices, but it also alerts us to subjects which are seldom covered in human rights research. However, a more detailed scrutiny of subjects selected in human rights research might complement the present analysis.

Finally, the article will discuss the need for specific competences as regards quantitative as well as qualitative methods in the human rights field. Both qualitative and quantitative research methods are relevant when examining how local struggles, poverty and marginalization relate to human rights subjects, but the competences required relate also to the research of institutional processes and decision-making. Such methodology of elite-based interviews may be understood as part of a qualitative methodology, but it deserves some further methodological consideration. In order to understand how decision makers alter policies from non-compliance to compliance, institutional analyses are required, but such analyses are rarely undertaken in human rights studies.

We begin by four assumptions and hypotheses about human rights research:

a. Human rights research tends to focus on legislation and on policy, but less on the practice except when individual cases or law suits are addressed. This means that system performance as regards human rights implementation is mostly addressed in individual cases or as matters of principled discussions.[7]

b. Human rights research does not easily address institutional matters, partly because institutional and organizational theory is unfamiliar[8] to most

---

[6] A Mexican saying (Mentándose al ajo — Plunging into the garlic) is used to describe a challenging situation in which one throws oneself in at the deep end in order to acquire a profound understanding of complexity. This saying may illustrate part of what may increasingly be needed in human rights research interested in implementation issues. This type of research may be characterized too little by efforts to "plunge into the garlic". See G. TORRES, 'Plunging into the garlic', in N. LONG and A. LONG (eds.), *Battlefields of Knowledge* (London 1992) 85-115.

[7] N. Luhmann categorizing the law sub-system according to a binary code: legal or non-legal, Law as a Social System (Oxford, 2004). This dichotomous code has been criticized by several scholars. However, irrespective of whether it is correct or not, it may capture the core of what is legal science, i.e. the assessment of validity by a criterion of legality. As such, the criterion may imply that much energy in legal research is devoted to the assessment of legal validity.

[8] A highly interesting contribution though is B.M. FRISCHMANN, 'A Dynamic Institutional Theory of International Law', 51 *Buffalo Law Review* (2003) 679-805.

human rights scholars, partly because system performance is an issue which is not frequently addressed. In this respect, there is quite a lot of complementarity between governance research on the one hand and human rights research on the other.[9]

c. Human rights research does not easily deal with social conditions and situations as a matter of a rights discourse. The processes of implementation from law to policies, to decentralized implementation including resource allocation to social impact among the poorest section of the population is unexplored territory to a significant degree. The China case in this paper illustrates what we have in mind in this regard. This implies that it is a challenge to build theories of implementation.

d. Human rights research has begun to interest itself for measurement and impact assessment, but what tends to be measured and assessed are laws and policies, while neither institutional practices nor social impact in terms of exclusion, marginalization and remedies have been adequately addressed in debates about monitoring and impact assessment although the situation is improving as regards an emerging theoretical consensus on how to measure it.

Below we address, albeit not conclusively, how these issues are addressed in recent human rights research.

2. THE SOURCES OF HUMAN RIGHTS RESEARCH

On what sources is human rights research based? We raise this question to a discipline which is in the process of developing into an interdisciplinary subject existing on a par with other disciplines like development studies or environmental research. As a departure for the work, we examine two interdisciplinary human rights research journals, Human Rights Quarterly and Netherlands Quarterly of Human Rights. They have been chosen as they are among the most respected human rights journals which publish interdisciplinary articles.

---

[9] A. EIDE, 'Good Governance, Human Rights and the Rights of Minorities and Indigenous Peoples', in H-O. SANO AND G. ALFREDSSON (eds.), *Human Rights and Good Governance: Building Bridges* (The Hague, 2002).

Table 1. The References Quoted in the *Human Rights Quarterly* and the *Netherlands Quarterly of Human Rights* 2005-07

	2005	2006	2007
Organizational reports, total	153 / 8.9%	399 / 22.3%	333 / 17.4%
UN	85 /4.9%	288 / 16.1%	106/ 5.5%
Other int. organizations	19 /1.1%	22 / 1.2%	183/ 9.6%
NGOs	38 /2.2%	52 / 2.9%	22/ 1.1%
Research Institutions	11 /0.6%	37 / 2.1%	22/ 1.1%
Administrative doc., total	238 /13.8%	354 / 19.8%	94/ 4.9%
Legal documents, total	449 /26.0%	252 / 14.0%	217 / 11.3%
Core Conventions	131 /7.6%	82 / 4.6%	106/ 5.5%
Reg. conventions	76 /4.4%		20 / 1.0%
Other conventions	2 /0.1%	2 / 0.1%	28 / 1.5%
National Laws	26 /1.5%	93 / 5.2%	50 / 2.6%
Domestic courts	57 /3.3%	28 / 1.6%	9 / 0.5%
Int. courts	4 0.2%	47 / 2.6%	4 / 0.2%
Quasi-legal, total	54 /3.1%	49 / 2.7%	110 / 5.7%
Treaty-bodies	48 /2.8%	22 / 1.2%	99 / 5.2%
Ombudsman	4 /0.2%		
National Institutions	2 /0.1%	27 / 1.5%	11 / 0.6%
Secondary sources, total	722 /41.8%	681 /38.1%	1029 / 53.8%
Books	292 /16.9%	467 / 26.1%	461/24.1%
Periodicals	430 /24.9%	214 / 12.0%	568/29.7%
Internet sources, total	89 /5.2%	49 / 2.7%	98 / 5.1%
Quantitative data, total	2 /0.1%	0 / 0%	1 / 0.1%
Surveys	2 /0.1%		1 / 0.1%
Perception surveys			
Expert-based			
Quantitative organizational data			
Qualitative data, total	4 /0.2%	2 / 0.1%	29/ 1.5%
Events-based data, total	17/ 1.0%	3 / 0.2%	3/ 0.2%
Total references	N=1728/100.0%	N=1789/100.0%	N=1914/100.0%

Table 1 shows the number of references quoted in these journals disaggregated by the number of categories: Organizational reports, legal and quasi-legal documents, administrative documents, secondary and internet sources, quantitative and survey-based data, qualitative data, and events-based evidence.[10] It appears that on average

---

[10] The following categories form the basis for the classification:

Organization reports: reports published by the organizations indicated;

Administrative documents: unpublished documentary evidence from government or other agencies and corporations;

Legal documents: conventions and declarations, domestic laws, court rulings, whether domestic or international;

Quasi-legal documents: treaty-bodies, ombudsman and national human rights institutions' statements;

Secondary sources: book publications, articles in books and periodicals, scientific or non-scientific;

Internet sources: sources only available on the internet, if available as a government or organization published report they are attributed to this category;

Quantitative data: data created and/or collected by researchers, primary evidence. This category includes a number of sub-categories such as surveys, e.g. quantitative household or individual data,

46% of the sources for scholarly articles in the quoted journals during these three years were respectively organizational reports, administrative or legal documents while on average 45% of the references quoted were secondary literature. The remaining references (9%) were almost equally distributed between quasi-legal and internet sources. Virtually none fall into our category of quantitative or qualitative data.

A number of preliminary observations can be drawn from this table:

- Human rights research seems to be based to a high degree on secondary literature.
- Human rights research draws to a large degree on core conventions, and on UN and other organizational reports, including administrative documents.
- Human rights research does not to any important degree base itself on primary qualitative or quantitative research.
- The data reveals a surprisingly modest quotation of court cases. If the journals quoted were regional in scope, e.g. European or American, a much higher degree of court cases could be expected to underpin researchers' arguments. Treaty body interpretations together with reference to conventions may fill in similar perspectives in the international journals.

What are the implications which should be highlighted based on this situation? It must be stressed that we are *not* making any arguments about the relevance of the research topics selected. That would require an altogether different approach. We are rather making arguments about the relevance of topics that are not selected, but we do this on the basis of the sources quoted, i.e. on the basis of a somewhat crude analysis. In most cases, however, there is a narrow connection between the research question posed, the analytical work undertaken and the data quoted. To the extent that this logic is vindicated, human rights research is characterized by not asking a number of relevant questions about the interplay between power and rights, about decentralization, and about local rights struggles.

The data of table 1 can be used as a starting point for making reflections about issues and topics which do not seem to be covered sufficiently in human rights

---

perception surveys, i.e. surveys soliciting perceptions by the informants, expert-based quantitative assessments, i.e. experts assessing, e.g. numbers or levels of human rights violations, and quantitative organizations data, for instance lists or registrations of numbers of, e.g. prisoners, collected by government or private organizations;

Qualitative data: evidence collected by researchers as part of qualitative interviews or anthropological observation;

Events-based data: descriptive and quantitative recoding of events and situations often undertaken by human rights organizations in connection with atrocities and systematic or gross human rights violations.

research. We shall make these reflections on the basis of perceived ambitions of human rights research.

- There is an ambition to analyze the implementation of human rights. This ambition was espoused during the 1990s, and even during the present decade, yet theory-building and general lessons learnt are vague and rarely address a level of generality that allows for summaries of lessons learnt. The literature tends to focus on how human rights law can be enacted and implemented to enhance protection of marginalized groups. The perspective is supply-led rather than demand-led in the sense that the point of departure is in law and in institutional out-reach. However, the point of assessment is rarely how well law and institutions address the rights-deficits that marginalized groups have.[11] The case study on access to justice in China at the end of this paper illustrates the complexities involved in examining access to justice from below.

- A dimension of the discussion on implementation is improvements of human rights compliance, i.e. dealing directly with specific human rights obligations, while the broader debate on human rights implementation may relate to the prevalence of a culture of human rights and to issues such as access to rights redress and access to institutions and public authorities. However, the discussion on compliance relates partly to the debate about measurement.[12] Progress has been achieved in this field as regards the methods of measurement.[13] This is in itself an achievement, especially when the methods agreed upon are taken up by treaty-bodies. However, it is one thing to monitor compliance and another to institutionalize it. Hence, there are additional dimensions of compliance which need consideration. It can be argued that the mechanisms by which perpetrating institutions are

---

[11]   A book on human rights implementation was published at the Danish Institute for Human Rights during 2007. See R.F. JØRGENSEN and K. SLAVENSKY (eds.), *Implementing Human Rights: Essays in Honour of Morten Kjærum* (Copenhagen, 2007). Yet, despite the involvement of distinguished human rights scholars, many of the articles of the book focus on institutions and institutional policies and on a number of relevant normative and legal issues. The point is that few articles depart in struggles and dilemmas where local groups are actors, and too few articles take as a point of departure that the international human rights regime is not a very effective one.

[12]   See T. LANDMAN, 'Measuring Human Rights: Principle, Practice and Policy', 26 *Human Rights Quarterly* (2004) 906-931; T. LANDMAN, 'Comparative Politics and Human Rights', 24 *Human Rights Quarterly* (2002) 890-923; H-O. SANO, 'Implementing Human Rights: What kind of record?', in R.F. JØRGENSEN and K. SLAVENSKY (eds.), *Implementing Human Rights: Essays in Honour of Morten Kjærum* (Copenhagen, 2007).

[13]   A methodology of measurement has been agreed by the UN inter-committee meeting during June 2006, see OHCHR, Fifth inter-committee meeting of the UN treaty bodies, 2006a. *Report on Indicators for Monitoring Compliance with International Human Rights Instruments*, UN Document HRI/MC/2006/7.

changing their practices are not understood well enough. One hypothesis deriving from studies on police training and torture prevention is that significant changes occur when commitment from the top of institutions are combined with a drive from within the institutions for reform, and when both these processes are monitored by actors from outside the institutions. A key thinking in this hypothesis is that institutional reforms are vital, but the implication of this is that knowledge about how institutions operate is also vital.

- Finally, there is an ambition to address rights-based development and to put human rights in the lead of development efforts. Such ambitions are rather policy than knowledge-based.[14] Rights-based approaches are highly interesting from the point of view of human rights implementation because of the focus on rights-holders as well as duty-bearers. But the research data for underpinning rights-based analysis is barely available. Decisions to apply rights-based strategies are hardly undertaken on the basis of a careful analysis of the value added by the approach. This is hardly surprising. However, the point is that implementing rights-based approaches will require critical research on the impact and implications of the strategy in terms of its potential for improving people's livelihood and for improving governance performance.[15] For instance, to what degree do marginal groups manage to claim their rights, what are the modalities of claiming? Does this happen via the activities of local organizations? How do duty-bearers respond — and what is the actual outcome for poor people of these processes of empowerment and accountability?

Given these ambitions, it can be argued that there is some mismatch between what is actually researched in human rights and the ambitions and that there is also a failing correspondence between the ambitions and the professional capacities that human rights researchers are traditionally endowed with.

It should be stressed that this is not necessarily a plea for more statistical research, but rather for the kind of social science research which can examine institutional and social actors operating in diverse contexts, especially the

---

14 See the UN STAMFORD DECLARATION 2003. 'Human rights standards contained in, and principles derived from, the Universal Declaration of Human Rights and other international human rights instruments guide all development cooperation in all sectors and in all phases of the programming process', *The Human Rights Based Approach to Development Cooperation: Towards a Common Understanding among the UN Agencies*.

15 For an assessment, see H-O. SANO, 'Does Human Rights-Based Development Make a Difference', in M. SOLOMON, A. TOSTENSEN and W. VANDENHOLE (eds.), *Casting the Net Wider: Human Rights, Development and New Duty-Bearers* (Antwerp, 2007).

performance of institutions,[16] and the role of communities, social movements and civil society. What is also needed is a kind of research which can make realistic assessments of how the rights discourse can be an instrument in poverty reduction and in furthering human agency.

Excellent articles have been written about how statistics can be used in human rights research.[17] However, there is some tendency that these articles either focus on human rights indicators, or on event-based data, counting gross human rights violations and atrocities. Such data is crucial. Similarly, perception surveys are important not least when they give a voice to groups who are otherwise excluded.[18]

However, apart from perception surveys, there is a wider field of quantitative data which is required such as survey data on households whose rights protection is very insecure, not least in terms of discrimination. Such data is vital because it may help in defining how the rights discourse can contribute to alleviating or reducing poverty. For example in China poverty alleviation policies stipulate that poor counties are selected and these receive government subsidies, while other counties, which also house poor people, do not receive anything, because they are not designated as poor.[19] Quantitative research may show how equally poor people receive very different support because of the design of state intervention and the data can reveal how many people living under the poverty line are not receiving any support at all.

The point is also that data should not be only quantitative. Research on institutional practices will not necessarily be based on quantitative methodology. Qualitative research and elite-based interviews are important instruments when addressing governance and human rights accountability. Moreover, it can be argued that such methodology is underexploited in human rights research.

In the text below, we provide two cases, one illustrating the different contexts within which rights-based development approaches are implemented. The prospect of improving development performance by applying a rights-based approach to development (RBA) is often taken for granted by the UN[20] or by NGOs. However, the value added by the approach must be documented and efforts in that direction

---

[16]   S. MCINERNEY-LANKFORD, 'Human Rights and Development: Some Institutional Perspectives', 25 *Netherlands Quarterly of Human Rights* (2007).

[17]   See for instance R. P. CLAUDE, *Science in the Service of Human Rights* (Philadelphia, 2002).

[18]   DIAL (Développment Institutions et Analyses de Long Terme), J. HERRERA, M. RAZAFINDRAKO and F. ROBAUD, *Governance, Democracy and Poverty Reduction: Lessons Drawn from household Surveys in sub-Saharan Africa and Latin America* (Paris, 2005).

[19]   R. TAO and M. LIU, 'Poverty reduction, Decentralization, and Local Governance in China', in D. YANG (ed.), *Discontended Miracle: Growth, Conflict, and Institutional Adaptations in China* (New Jersey, 2007) 193-221.

[20]   See the UN Stamford Declaration 2003, *supra* n. 14; ECRI, *supra* n. 3.

have been undertaken by only a few NGOs[21] and generally not by researchers yet.[22] In the examples from respectively Malawi and India below, we try to illustrate briefly the importance of the socio-political context in making the effective generation of tangible results for the target groups a probable outcome. Thus processes of empowerment seem to start from very different points of departure: in one case the prospects of making claims and raising demands from the marginalized groups are not very far-fetched: the organizational structures are in place, and the chances of obtaining substantial results for the groups seem realistic, not least because some progress as has already been achieved. In another case the distance between the ideal scenario of RBA in terms of advocacy and transformative strategies and the reality on the ground seem much more distant as the authorities are vested with little capacity to respond to claims and as the rights-holders are endowed with little initial organizational power and muscle. In the case on China we analyze the complexities involved in assessing human rights protection, even when empirical data is used.

3. EMPOWERMENT AND MAKING CLAIMS — TWO DIFFERENT CONTEXTS

According to the tenets of rights-based strategies, the capacities of rights-holders should be reinforced in order that they are able to address claims of rights realization to the duty-bearers.[23] The notion of advocacy and goals of structural change are inherent in the rights-based thinking. Thus RBA is based on notions of empowerment of rights-holders and of invoking duty-bearers to respond in accordance with their legal obligations. Empowerment is defined in various ways, but the mobilization and capacity-building of rights-holders to claim justice and rights realization are central components of RBA.

Two short examples may illustrate the substantial contextual differences in socio-political departures on which to base RBA strategy: in Malawi, a baseline study on RBA programming in a HIV/AIDS programme undertaken by one of the authors

---

21 During late 2007, UK INTERAGENCY GROUP ON HUMAN RIGHTS-BASED APPROACHES issued a report on *The Impact of Rights-Based Approaches to Development: Evaluation/Learning Process, Bangladesh, Malawi and Peru*. The research makes a comparison between rights-based and non-rights-based programmes. The report also illustrates the difficulties of working within a comparative framework and provides well justified ideas about the need to measure not only processes, but tangible results. However, due, e.g. to the general lack of baseline data, the degree to which the report provides firm evidence on actual results is somewhat in question.

22 The book edited by P. GREADY and J. ENSOR, *Reinventing Development? Translating Rights-Based Approaches from Theory into Practice* (London, 2006) provides good insight, but the articles are not based on very solid research — rather on evaluation-based documentation.

23 OHCHR, Frequently Asked Questions on a Human Rights-Based Approach to Development Cooperation (OHCHR, 2006) 15.

indicated that processes of empowerment were not really strongly experienced in the communities visited. The conclusion at the end of the baseline study was:

'the prevailing situation is one of disempowerment, i.e., of very restricted and confined processes of change. The situation as it prevails in these poor communities is one of lack of confidence in institutionalizing change and one where resource constraints are integral in every situation or event.

This does not mean, however, that empowerment is impossible, but rather that it starts from a very low level. In terms of rights-based empowerment: knowing your rights, acting on them and holding duty-bearers to account, there is a lot of 'mileage which has to be covered'. I.e., awareness and knowledge on rights must be improved, disadvantaged groups must be made confident that action is not theoretical, duty-bearers must know what responsibilities they have and they must have access to resources to deal with them, and a clear strategy of implementation on matters of decentralization, prevention and reaching out to communities will certainly facilitate the processes of empowerment from below.'[24]

The baseline research in Malawi revealed that the rural rights-holders (smallholder peasants, pieceworkers and fishermen) were barely confident to make claims beyond their community. This was not necessarily because of fear, but because of low expectations as regards the structures of local governance. The capacity and willingness of district authorities to respond to such claims were deemed to be weak or non-existent by communities; hence, they tended to see efforts of claim making as a futile effort. The opportunities of meaningful exchange required duty-bearers to be responsible. Where duty-bearers did respond in a more positive way, this happened when NGOs facilitated their outreach or facilitated linkages between communities and district authorities. Given the level from which RBA strategy departs, questions thus remain in the Malawian context what can be achieved in terms of substantial benefits for the rights-holders, in this case the rural poor and the HIV/AIDS infected. The value added is not rejected by this research, but it still has to be proven in terms of the tangible results for the marginal rights-holders.[25]

This is not the case in India as regards the rights-based approach. In the latter context, benefits have already accrued to rights-holders and the latter are not so dependent on the international NGOs to promote their claims. They might not even need local NGOs to facilitate exchange and claims with duty-bearers. In the Indian context, important legislation has been enacted which has allowed rural poor to claim at least 100 days of work at a minimum wage per year. Subsidized food is also provided to households below the poverty line on the basis of ration cards. An

---

[24]   H-O. SANO, *Malawi Baseline Data* (2006), <http://www.humanrights.dk/research/research+projects>.

[25]   See also H. ENGLUND, *Prisoners of Freedom: Human Rights and the African Poor* (Berkeley, 2006).

Informant Act allows freedom of information which provides powerful tools for local organizations to seek information and to claim transparency with local governance structures. A warm midday meal has to be provided to school children irrespective of social background.

Such legislation and legal directives are being used by Dalits and by Adivasis (tribals) in the rural areas in Rajasthan, but also in other regions of India with the result that marginalized groups are interpreting that power balances are changing in their favour in certain respects, and with the result that officials claim that corruption has decreased. In the Indian context, emerging evidence points to the merits of RBA. The Indian data indicated firstly that strong rights-based organizational efforts had emerged within the communities supported by local, regional or international NGOs. The organizational experiences within these communities date much further back than to the current efforts, but these experiences are now employed in efforts where constitutional rights and court orders form the departure of campaigns and advocacy. The organizations directed part of their activities towards reinforcement of access by marginalized households to the subsidized food to which they were entitled. Other activities focus on struggles to prevent land from being grabbed from Dalits or other groups and to retain entitlements to access to forest land and resources in the hands of tribal groups. In both of these endeavours there have been some successes. Achievements have also been made in securing access of Dalits to potable water resources. Discriminatory practices in village councils are also becoming less pronounced as it has become increasingly difficult for privileged groups to uphold former discriminatory practices.[26] These achievements are the result of a combination of rights-based advocacy, social mobilization and assertiveness, and cultural change.

As baseline studies, these examples do not provide concluding evidence on the value added by RBA, but they point to conditions under which the strategy may hold a high development potential and where the potential seems to be less clear. What is important to underline in the context of this article is that applied and action human rights research is needed for at least three different purposes: first, qualified documentation of the value added by a rights-based strategy which is being promoted quite dogmatically by some organizations must be brought forward. Second, the universal applicability of RBA as a means to achieve development must be examined critically. The way in which a rights-based strategy can contribute to empowerment deserves some attention - especially it would seem, in localities where the concept of rights is not a well-known category. Moreover, Englund's research from Malawi on the application of rights-based approaches by some organizations brings reminiscences of imposition and on the wide gap between the

---

[26] H-O. SANO (2008), Baseline study from Rajasthan, Action Research, DanChurchAid, <http://www.humanrights.dk/research/research+projects>.

aspirations of local NGOs and the rural poor. His research prompts some caution as regards how human rights strategies are applied. Third, solid human rights research beyond evaluation research and beyond NGO investigations are needed to clarify how law, power and governance interact locally in localities where the most marginalized live.[27]

4. EVIDENCE-BASED RESEARCH: AN EXAMPLE OF THE COMPLEXITIES INVOLVED

The following case is discussed to point to the need for a whole range of different methods to be involved if one is to get closer to understanding whether certain rights are effectively protected. A strict legal analysis can hint at whether they are respected and protected, but when we come to the question of fulfilment (facilitate and provide) knowledge of the legal framework has to be supplemented by knowledge obtained by methods belonging to different social sciences. To facilitate and provide protection of human rights, the state has to design and establish institutions with certain mandates and decision-making structures. People have to know where and how they can claim their rights and inform the authorities of violations and they have to believe that competent authorities are in place to address these matters. These are just a few of the many conditions for compliance and they will not easily be revealed by an analysis of the legal framework or a report from an international body.

The case is about conflict resolutions mechanisms in China, in broader wording the access to justice for poor Chinese citizens. The right to a fair trial, enshrined in Article 14 of the International Covenant on Civil and Political Rights (ICCPR) is one part of the complex of issues pertaining to access to justice, but other rights are also at play, notably most social rights, underpinned by the general right to participation included in Article 25c of ICCPR as the right to access to public service but also as appearing in many other human rights instruments.[28] The case illustrates three points: 1. How legislation in itself can be construed in a way that is detrimental to fulfilling the goal of the endeavour. Thus, legislation must always be analyzed in relation to the purpose of the regulation. At least this is very important in administrative regulations, designed to implement social policies. 2. Statistics are important but they also cannot stand alone. They always have to be broken down into smaller elements, but they are certainly very important in raising questions for further research. 3. It is imperative to find a way to judge 'quality' of legislation and policies and this can only be done by using qualitative data.

---

[27]   See ENGLUND, *supra* n. 25.
[28]   A. EIDE, et al. (eds.), *Economic, Social and Cultural Rights: A Textbook* (Dordrecht, 2001) 380.

A poor Chinese citizen with a social and/or legal problem will have a whole range of roads to walk fanning out in different directions in order to reach a solution and get redress or compensation for damage or protection against authorities or civil actors.[29] The ways to solve a specific problem are at hand as mechanisms, institutions, groups or individuals, supported by the state to varying degrees. In this situation traditional and modern mechanisms co-exist, collide or support each other. In a transition process as huge as the Chinese, former legal, economic and social structures will inevitably persist and shape and be shaped by the newly introduced structures and the outcome will reflect of special mix of tradition and modernity. Basically there are today four kinds of dispute resolution mechanisms in China: consultation, mediation, arbitration and litigation and they are in principle all open to disadvantaged groups of people under certain conditions. Different institutions and organs solve conflicts and/or help people choose between the different forms of dispute resolution and guide them to act in a relevant way vis-à-vis each other or a state organ with which they perceive a conflict. They represent a spectrum from small independent groupings of a grass-root nature over commercial law firms to established academic institutions close to the political level.

Given this web of avenues, how is it possible to evaluate whether access to justice is guaranteed? One place to look will naturally be *legislation*. The spearhead of legislative efforts to introduce 'modern' guarantees has been the development of a nationwide legal aid system since 1994.[30] An administrative regulation was adopted in 2003 stipulating that a system of legal aid institutions shall be set up to provide poor people with the 'necessary' legal services to protect their rights and the Lawyers Law from 1997 oblige all registered lawyers in China to take a small number of pro-bono cases a year. In short the state obligations have been transferred to a certain group of individuals, who are ordered to work for free! Furthermore the burden of financing the system have been de-centralized to the local level and there are no indications of how much money shall be allocated except that there has to be a special budget line for legal aid. The new system is being used in official sources (*inter alia* in the frequently published 'white papers'[31] on the human rights situation in China) to prove that an improvement in the rights protection and statistics show that the number of cases being solved through legal aid centres is rising by up to 50% in some years.[32]

---

[29]   The case is part of a Nordic research project on law implementation in China. See furthermore J. CHEN, Y. LI and J.M. OTTO (eds.), *Implementation of Law in the People's Republic of China* (The Hague, 2002).

[30]   See 'Legal Aid Chronicle of Events', Renmin Ribao, 8 September 2004. For development of the legal profession and legal services for the poor before the mid-1990s, see B.L. LIEBMAN, 'Legal Aid and Public Interest Law in China', 34 *Texas International Law Journal* (1999) 215-219.

[31]   IOSC (Information Office of the State Council of the People's Republic of China), *Progress in China's Human Rights Cause in 2003*, March 2004.

[32]   *Law Yearbook of China 2005* (in Chinese), (Beijing, 2005) 228 ff.

Another place to search will be the *statistics* on how many people can benefit from the measures. The legal aid centres under the Ministry of Justice discussed above in reality only help a small proportion of the population, but their services are exclusively for poor people and they just began publishing detailed figures in a yearbook of 2005, which enable us to analyze local variations.[33] The data has been compared at the provincial level as to expenses per person, expenses per case and the number of cases per staff member. At the outset one would expect to find low investment and low quality services in poor regions and the opposite in richer areas. The expectations are only partly fulfilled. Not surprisingly, the big cities contribute most with a budget of more than 0.3 yuan per person, while poor provinces provide less than 0.1 yuan per person. But there are strange differences, unrelated to economy, which show us that the money can be used more or less effectively; the same amount of money or the same workload can yield very different results, i.e. produce a different number of cases. The expense for one case is highest in rich Beijing and Shanghai, but the cost in poor Tibet is just as high. Besides, the expense is - not surprisingly - low in many poor provinces, but it is also low in some richer places. Concerning the number of cases per staff of the legal aid centres we should find fewer cases per staff members in the affluent areas and more in the poor areas. But in Beijing each staff member has 44 cases, while the number is 8 in a poor province like Qinghai. All in all there are huge differences when one looks at the regional figures and based on these statistics, there is really no basis for claiming that the richer provinces have better legal aid services.

Table 2: Indicators of legal aid services (RMB)

Province	GDP per capita[34]	Expense p.p.[35]	Expense per case	No cases per staff
Beijing	22.460	0,7	2.075	44
Tianjin	17.993	0,25	1.263	31
Hebei	7.663	0,05	463	14
Shanxi	5.137	0,08	376	17
Shanghai	34.547	0,8	2.305	47
Hubei	7.188	0,1	975	18
Hunan	5.639	0,1	850	21
Guangdong	12.885	0,4	1.309	44
Guangxi	4.319	0,1	946	25
Yunnan	4.637	0,2	642	-
Xizang (Tibet)	4.559	0,2	2.025	8

[33]   *Yearbook of Legal Aid in China 2005* (in Chinese), (Beijing, 2005).
[34]   China Statistical Yearbook 2001
[35]   Investment per capita, *i.e.* how much money is spent on legal aid in relation to the population of the area in question.

Shaanxi	4.549	0,03	288	12
Qinghai	5.087	0,2	767	8
Ningxia	4.839	0,3	571	23
Xinjiang	7.470	0,2	720	23
Average	9.931	0,24	1.197	22

Source: Yearbook of Legal Aid in China 2005

The discussion above relates to a very fragile set of data, if the intention is to judge the protection of civil and social rights in this Chinese setting. One can identify the economic investment, the number of staff and the number of cases this staff can handle. The most interesting finding is that money alone is no guarantee for the number of cases, which will be handled in each locality. This knowledge is useful in order to address the argument that the state does not have the economic resources to shoulder a certain task. Without these figures we would not be able to point out the fact that the same investment can produce very different results, in terms of number of cases. But this is only a short step towards the goal of judging state compliance with a certain standard. What we do not know, but must ask for, is the quality of the solution of each single case and how many people in need actually can get help under this specific regulatory system, just to mention a few of the existing problems. The qualities of solutions in the places where they solve many cases are maybe very bad because the cases are solved too quickly. So one needs qualitative interviews to explore this aspect. And maybe only a small fraction of vulnerable people get the support they need. Here we must study the composition of the population in the area, the crime rate, social conditions, etc. and also do comparative studies to reach a rough estimate of what the need actually is.

In the above analysis, statistics can be used to point to a fact of local variation where coverage differs from province to province, which results in turn could inspire one to search for the reasons behind these variations. Other methods will tell us about a range of different *institutional problems* in reaching the goal of ensuring 'necessary legal services' to citizens with financial difficulties through implementation of the Legal Aid Regulations. These are discussed in the Chinese and Western literature[36] and appear from *interviews and case material.* Some concern weaknesses in legislation as such, i.e. in the content of the regulations; others relate to implementation of the existing regulations. These two aspects are inter-related in the way that some implementation problems perhaps are not directly caused by the

---

[36] J. ZHU, *Report of Law and Development in China* (in Chinese), (Beijing, 2007); J. LI, *China Legal Aid System* (in Chinese), (Beijing, 2004); F. REGAN, 'Legal Aid in China: an Analysis of the Development of Policy', 24 *Civil Justice Quarterly* (2004) 169-186; N. DIAMANT, S. LUBMAN and K.J. O'BRIEN (eds.), *Engaging the Law in China* (Stanford, 2005); K. O'BRIEN and L. LI (eds.), *Rightful Resistance in Rural China* (Cambridge, 2005); E. MICHELSON, 'The Practice of Law as an Obstacle to Justice: Chinese Lawyers at Work', 40 *Law & Society Review* (2006).

wording of the legislation but point back to weaknesses in the basic thinking or 'ideology' behind the legislation.

First of all the funding issue is important. The regulations on the one hand demand that local authorities shall earmark funds for legal aid activities; on the other hand they do not set a lower limit for the amount of money, neither in absolute nor relative terms. And there are no direct sanctions imposed on local governments who do not set funds aside. Secondly it is also a problem that legal aid centres are set up and funded by the local governments. The staff and funding of a district or county LAC are controlled by the local people's congress. So they will tend to take mostly easy cases and cases where they do not risk coming into conflict with powerful local interests. A third problem connected to the economy is that the conditions for getting legal aid are very strict. The regulations stipulate that economic hardship is defined by the provincial authorities. The normal practice is to determine a low standard. People with higher income can easily have problems hiring a lawyer at their own expense. The grounds for applying for legal aid are also narrow, confined to few kinds of cases: seeking state compensation, missing pensions, etc. As a last, but very important point, the whole system rests on the basis of the willingness and capacity of one professional group — lawyers — to work for free. To force an obligation on lawyers does not ensure commitment and work of good quality. Debates on the legal aid system are often focused on the morale of lawyers being low and ethical codes of lawyers have been adopted by the bar association, including demands on lawyers to sacrifice themselves for justice. But still most good lawyers are not willing to work for free and choose the lucrative business of taking only commercial cases and buying the fulfilment of their obligation from less qualified colleagues.

The above short summary of the problems related to the protection of Chinese citizens' rights are derived from a set of different channels: legislation was studied in documentary research; statistics found in published material; interviews with staff in the Legal Aid Centres provided information on the criteria for getting a case accepted at all, and for the methods by which the legal aid centres allocate lawyers to handle cases; the institutional problems were mentioned in interviews and articles in professional journals.

5. CONCLUSION

This paper serves different purposes. One aim has been to point to what we perceive as a weakness in the current human rights research tradition, i.e. a lack of attention to the economic and social realities in which vulnerable groups of people live their lives and in which their rights are least protected. A study of selected literature in two important human rights journals for the years 2005-2007 shows that secondary sources, institutional and administrative reports and documents together with core conventions and legal documents are by far the overriding sources of the articles in the journals. The data sources quoted in these journals are used as a crude indicator of how the human rights research investigated tends not to confront the deeper constraints of human rights implementation - those associated with power, poverty and capacity. This methodology is of course in itself open to discussion and critical assessment. Further research is needed in order to assess whether the conclusion that we arrive at concerning the need for more evidence-based human rights research is correct.

The article also makes a call for more human rights research which relates the complexities involved in studying what here with reservations is called 'real life' and especially to assess whether individuals are duly protected in respect of their rights. Socio-economic field research is required to understand in depth how a rights discourse may be difficult to implement in certain contexts and how vulnerable groups may be reluctant to raise rights claims either out of risk perceptions or because of lack of faith in the state apparatus. To human rights groups, there may be a risk of imposing a rights discourse in a way which is not in tune with the notions of the local and vulnerable groups.

Socio-political data is also warranted, partly in order to explore how states fulfil their rights obligations, partly in order to understand the processes of decision-making within institutions. What are the processes involved when a situation of non-compliance is gradually shifted to one of compliance? What sort of interaction exists in the power and rights nexus? These issues are necessary to address for theoretical reasons, but also in order to provide learning on the major problems of human rights implementation. However, even with the collation of empirical evidence, a challenge exists in designing sufficiently precise research which can answer questions about the scope of human rights protection. Our three cases from Malawi, India and China have been used to illustrate some of these complexities.

A third aim has been to argue that legal research methods can hardly stand alone if the objective of the research is to study the actual problems of human rights implementation. In the case examples above, one would get a misleading interpretation when only looking at the legislation or using the data on the formal institutional setup. 'Plunging into the garlic', i.e. studying social, political and economic reality implies the use of a variety of methods and a commitment and capacity to create such data where it does not exist.

Finally, these arguments rest on an observation implying that human rights research has broadened its scope for the simple reason that human rights implementation has become increasingly relevant both locally and globally. With this development, there is a need to develop the competences of human rights scholars. Thus, one major implication of the arguments forwarded in the article is that it seems that more social science research is needed that addresses human rights subjects, but also that opportunities are provided for interdisciplinary training.

MEASURE FOR MEASURE: UTILIZING LEGAL NORMS AND HEALTH DATA IN MEASURING THE RIGHT TO HEALTH

DABNEY EVANS and MEGAN PRICE

1. INTRODUCTION

'The health of a population is a measure of whether, in the end,
that population is benefiting as the result of a set of its social arrangements.'[1]

Over the past 50 years major strides have been made in reducing preventable morbidity and mortality including the eradication and near elimination of several diseases.[2] Despite these advances, global health remains a major concern for reasons of both personal security in the form of both infectious diseases such as SARS, as well as national security, as in the potential threat of bioterrorism. Both within and between states inequalities across health indicators are vast. Inequalities at the domestic level are reflective of the same phenomena responsible for inequalities on the international stage, namely differential availability of and access to quality health care services. While this study presents data from both the international and national levels, these data are merely illustrative. More important than the specific data presented in this paper are the methods by which the authors suggest that states, individually and collectively, may address global inequalities specific to health. These methods are based on a novel theoretical approach which combines human rights discourse with traditional public health data analyses. This paper describes the foundations for this new theoretical model, the proposed epidemiological analysis and some illustrative data in order to demonstrate the potential utility of this approach. The paper begins with an overview of the relationships between health and human rights and the right to health under international law which provide the foundations for a new theoretical model, the synergistic approach. Following the presentation of the model, the methods utilized to select and analyze data relating to the right to health are presented including

---

[1] M. MARMOT, 'Social determinants of health inequalities', 365 *The Lancet* (2005a) 1099.
[2] WORLD HEALTH ORGANIZATION, *The World Health Report*, <http://www.who.int/whr/previous/en/index.html>.

some descriptive examples. Finally the advantages and challenges facing this approach are discussed.

2. GLOBAL HEALTH INEQUALITIES BETWEEN STATES

In many states health has been commodified and treated as any other good available for purchase rather than as a universal and inalienable human right. The reasons for this are many including the historical split between civil and political rights on the one hand and economic, social and cultural rights on the other. Falling in the latter category has meant that the right to health is subject to progressive realization and therefore highly sensitive to the accessibility of resources impacting the availability of and access to quality health care services. Wide disparities in State resources may be illustrated by a number of variables including Gross Domestic Product (GDP). For example, there is a 70-fold difference in income between Tanzania's GDP at $470 per year compared to Luxembourg's $32,902.[3] Figure A demonstrates Gross Domestic Product (in billions) weighted by Purchasing Power Parity (the value of the dollar in the local economy) where State territories are re-sized according GDP/PPP.

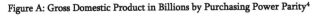

Figure A: Gross Domestic Product in Billions by Purchasing Power Parity[4]

These economic differences often translate into differences in health outcomes as in the case of global life expectancy rates which range across the span of over four

---

[3]   Data available from THE KAROLINSKA INSTITUTE, *World Health Chart,* <http://www.whc.ki.se/index.php> or <http://gapminder.org>.

[4]   <http://www.worldmapper.org/display.php?selected=170>.

decades, from 79 years in Japan to a mere 37 years in Sierra Leone.[5] Similarly, there is a 100-fold difference across child survival rates across states. Under-five mortality ranges from 3 per 1,000 in Iceland to 296 per 1,000 live births in Sierra Leone.[6] Figure B displays State territories re-sized according to their under-five mortality rates.

Figure B: Under-Five Mortality Rates[7]

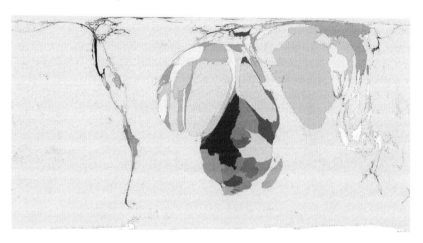

At the macro-level individuals within developed states generally enjoy increased availability of and access to health care services resulting in improved health status as compared to less developed states. However even in developed states health status is not homogeneous. Health inequalities exist across racial, gender, age, socio-economic status and other such categories of demographic vulnerability.[8] For example, in the United States (US) racial minority populations such as African Americans have a health status more closely resembling that of a developing nation rather than that of a developed State.[9]

The treatment of health as a good for purchase and the subsequent inequalities in health that exist as a result are contrary to the ethos of human rights which is based

---

5   World Health Organization, *Core Health Indicators: Life Expectancy at Birth (Years) Males*, <http://www.who.int/whosis/database/core/core_select_process.cfm>.

6   WORLD HEALTH ORGANIZATION, *World Health Report 2006: Working together for health*, Annex Table 1 Basic indicators for all Member States, <http://www.who.int/whr/2006/annex/06_annex1_en.pdf>.

7   WORLDMAPPER, *supra* n. 4.

8   See for example, M. MARMOT, *The Status Syndrome: How social standing affects our health and longevity* (New York, 2005b).

9   WORLD HEALTH ORGANIZATION, *WHO Issues New Healthy Life Expectancy Rankings*, <http://www.who.int/inf-pr-2000/en/pr2000-life.html>.

on principles of equality and non-discrimination. Under the current paradigm, macro-level vulnerabilities such as country of origin, as well as individual vulnerabilities such as race largely contribute to one's health status and enjoyment or more often non-fulfillment of the right to health. Therefore, an approach which capitalizes on the existing human rights corpus in order address health inequalities at both the international and national levels is warranted.

The following section provides an overview of the contemporary view of the right to health under international law which serves as the basis for the theoretical and methodological approaches presented in this paper.

3. ESTABLISHMENT OF RIGHT TO HEALTH UNDER INTERNATIONAL HUMAN RIGHTS LAW

Health is both defined and asserted as a right in the preamble of the Constitution of the World Health Organization which states that:

'Health is a state of complete physical, mental and social well-being and not merely the absence of disease or infirmity. The enjoyment of the attainment of the highest attainable standard of health is one of the fundamental rights of every human without distinction of race, religion, political belief, economic or social condition.'[10]

Health is first mentioned in Article 55 of the UN Charter as being one of the international issues with which the organization should concern itself.[11] The first appearance of health in a human rights specific document is in Article 25 of the Universal Declaration of Human Rights (UDHR), which provides a broad definition of the right to health in stating,

'Everyone has the right to a standard of living adequate for the health and well-being of himself and of his family, including food, clothing, housing and medical care and necessary social services, and the right to security in the event of unemployment, sickness, disability, widowhood, old age or other lack of livelihood in circumstances beyond his control.'[12]

---

[10] WORLD HEALTH ORGANIZATION, *Constitution of the World Health Organization*, <http://www.searo.who.int/LinkFiles/About_SEARO_const.pdf>. The Constitution was adopted by the International Health Conference held in New York from 19 June to 22 July 1946, signed on 22 July 1946 by the representatives of 61 States (Official Record World Health Organization, 2, 100), and entered into force on 7 April 1948.

[11] UNITED NATIONS, *Charter of the United Nations*, <http://www.un.org/aboutun/charter/>.

[12] UNITED NATIONS, *Universal Declaration of Human Rights* (Geneva, 1948), <www.unhchr.ch/udhr/lang/eng.htm>.

The UDHR serves as the foundation for modern human rights and is often referenced within the preambular text of other human rights treaties, however it is still difficult to determine on this basis alone the precise meaning of the right enshrined in the article.[13] The legally binding twin of Article 25 of the UDHR is Article 12 of the International Covenant on Economic, Social and Cultural Rights (ICESCR). Article 12 has come to be known as the right to the highest attainable standard of physical and mental health or more commonly, the right to health.[14] Article 12 of ICESCR states:

'...1. The states parties to the present Covenant recognize the right of everyone to the enjoyment of the highest attainable standard of physical and mental health.
2. The steps to be taken by the states parties to the present Covenant to achieve the full realization of this right shall include those necessary for:
(a) The provision for the reduction of the stillbirth-rate and of infant mortality and for the healthy development of the child;
(b) The improvement of all aspects of environmental and industrial hygiene;
(c) The prevention, treatment and control of epidemic, endemic, occupational and other diseases;
(d) The creation of conditions which would assure to all medical service and medical attention in the event of sickness...'[15]

In addition to the right to health as outlined in Article 12 of the ICESCR, there are many other health related rights included in both the ICESCR and the ICCPR. Health-related rights under the ICESCR include the right to non-discrimination (Article 2), work (Article 7), food (Article11), housing (Article 11), and education (Article 13).[16]

The United Nations Human Rights Committee (HRC) monitors the implementation of the International Covenant on Civil and Political Rights (ICCPR). Although the ICCPR does not include an article on the right to health *per se*, it does include provisions on other health related rights including the right to non-discrimination (Article 2), life (Article 6), the prohibition of torture (Article 7), freedom of movement (Article 12), privacy (Article 17), access to information

---

[13] Like many other economic, social and cultural rights Article 25 lacks definitive objective measures by which States performance can be measured. While the challenges regarding the measurement of economic, social and cultural rights are beyond the purview of this analysis it is worth noting this point as it relates to the definition of terms and the meaning of the right enshrined in the article. Other authors have aptly addressed this issue. See for example B.C.A. TOEBES, *The Right to Health Under International Law* (Antwerp, 1999) and P. Hunt, Reclaiming Social Rights (Aldershot, 1996).

[14] OFFICE OF THE UNITED NATIONS HIGH COMMISSIONER FOR HUMAN RIGHTS, *International Covenant on Economic, Social and Cultural Rights*, <http://www.ohchr.org/english/law/cescr.htm>.

[15] UNITED NATIONS, *International Covenant on Economic, Social and Cultural Rights* (Geneva, 1967), <http://www.unhchr.ch/html/menu3/b/a_cescr.htm>.

[16] *International Covenant on Economic, Social and Cultural Rights, supra* n. 14.

(Article 19), assembly (Article 21), freedom of association (Article 22) and equality (Article 26).[17,18]

Several other international human rights treaties also include provisions specifically on the right to health including Article 5(e)iv of the International Convention on the Elimination of all forms of Racial Discrimination (CERD), Article 12 of the Convention on the Elimination of all forms of Discrimination against Women (CEDAW) and Article 24 of the Convention on the Rights of the Child (CRC).[19]

Despite the fact that the right to health has been codified in multiple international human rights treaties and the fact that every nation State has ratified at least one human rights treaty including text on the right to health methods for measurement of the right have remained obscure.[20]

Defining a right to health is necessary not only at the level of international treaty documents but also on the more practical level. The work of Special Rapporteurs and soft law texts, such as General Comments issued by the treaty monitoring bodies, provide guidance as to the normative interpretation of treaty provisions as well as clarifying State obligations, identifying violations and guidelines for enforcement.[21] Unfortunately the broad utility of such work has been limited due to the siloed structural composition of these mechanisms. It is in fact because of this silo effect that there is a need for a comprehensive approach that while respecting the existing mechanisms can make use of the entirety of the human rights corpus allowing for the whole to equal more than the sum of its parts. The following section of this paper will present the synergistic approach, including a discussion of the hard and soft law sources that form the foundations for this approach.

---

[17]   OFFICE OF THE UNITED NATIONS HIGH COMMISSIONER FOR HUMAN RIGHTS, *International Covenant on Civil and Political Rights*, <http://www.ohchr.org/english/law/ccpr.htm>.

[18]   The authors recognize the interdependent nature of rights including those other health related rights which exist within other human rights documents such as the Covenants. The importance of these rights and the ways in which they related to the right to health cannot be overstated. However for the purposes of brevity this paper will limit itself to a focused discussion of the right to health.

[19]   OFFICE OF THE UNITED NATIONS HIGH COMMISSIONER FOR HUMAN RIGHTS, *International Convention on the Elimination of all forms of Racial Discrimination*, <http://www.ohchr.org/english/law/cerd.htm>; OFFICE OF THE UNITED NATIONS HIGH COMMISSIONER FOR HUMAN RIGHTS, *Convention on the Elimination of all forms of Discrimination Against Women*, <http://www.ohchr.org/english/law/cedaw.htm>; OFFICE OF THE UNITED NATIONS HIGH COMMISSIONER FOR HUMAN RIGHTS, *Convention on the Rights of the Child*, <http://www.ohchr.org/english/law/crc.htm>.

[20]   WORLD HEALTH ORGANIZATION, *25 Question and Answers on Health and Human Rights*, <http://www.who.int/hhr/NEW37871OMSOK.pdf>.

[21]   J.P. RUGER, 'Towards a theory of a right to health: Capability and incompletely theorized agreements', 18 *Yale Journal of Law & the Humanities* (2006) 273-326 at 312.

4. A NEW THEORETICAL MODEL: THE SYNERGISTIC APPROACH

Human rights have aptly been described as being similar to a *matrishka*, a Russian nesting doll, where document after document produces ever-specific understandings of particular rights.[22] The synergistic approach aims to utilize these understandings to provide a comprehensive understanding of particular human rights. Beginning with the outer-most *matrishka* we gain some understandings of the general principles of human rights. As the seminal human rights instrument, the UDHR includes all of the various types of human rights, civil, cultural, economic, political and social, which despite their interdependence were divided on the basis of political and ideological differences.[23] Unfortunately as Chapman notes, 'the principle of the indivisibility of rights has been honored more in the breach than in the observance' resulting in the need for models to address the unfortunate cases in which rights are not completely fulfilled as intended under the law.[24]

The synergistic approach draws upon the suggestion of the Office of the United Nations High Commissioner for Human Rights that all of the international human rights the treaties are mutually re-enforcing and that, 'rather than being separate free-standing treaties, the treaties complement each other.'[25] Given the interrelated and interdependent nature of human rights, it seems logical to utilize articles and frameworks that are more clearly articulated under human rights treaties to interpret articles on the same topic from a related human rights treaty since all human rights treaties share familial roots in the UN Charter and the UDHR.[26]

While the authors see many potential uses of the synergistic approach across various human rights treaties and the rights enshrined therein this paper focuses on one specific application of this model. The author hopes that others may share the vision that this approach could be utilized across specific vulnerable populations (women, refugees, children) and treaty provisions (right to education et al). In this instance the right to health under the International Convention on the Elimination of all forms of Racial Discrimination (CERD) Article 5(e)iv is examined within the

---

[22] P. WEISS and H.A. FREEDMAN, 'Protecting human rights through international law and national law', in B. S. LEVY and V. W. SIDEL (eds.), *Social Injustice and Public Health* (Oxford, 2006).

[23] *Universal Declaration of Human Rights, supra* n. 12; *International Covenant on Economic, Social and Cultural Rights, supra* n. 14; *International Covenant on Civil and Political Rights, supra* n. 17.

[24] A. CHAPMAN, 'A violations approach for monitoring the International Covenant on Economic, Social and Cultural Rights', 18 *Human Rights Quarterly* (1996) 23-66.

[25] OFFICE OF THE UNITED NATIONS HIGH COMMISSIONER FOR HUMAN RIGHTS, *The United Nations Human Rights Treaty System*, <http://www.ohchr.org/english/bodies/docs/OHCHR-FactSheet30.pdf>.

[26] The existence of the committee of chairpersons of the human rights treaty bodies and their collective works supports the notion that human rights are meant to be understood and interpreted consistently across the various human rights treaties.

contexts of race and health under international law in order to further hone in on a specific issue. Figure C illustrates the synergistic approach.

Figure C. The Synergistic Approach for the Interpretation of CERD Article 5

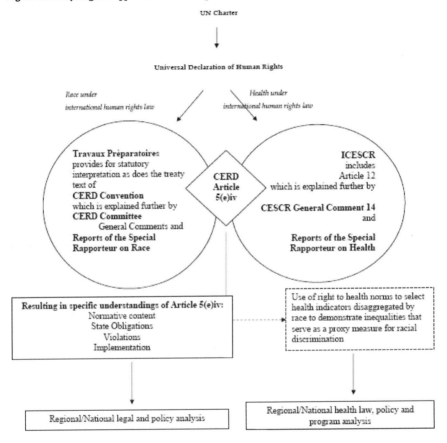

This figure pays due recognition to the UN Charter and the UDHR as the basis for international human rights law, however does not call upon these sources for the specific interpretation of Article 5(e)iv. Rather, the synergistic approach suggests the utilization of even more specific sources of law (both hard and soft). Here application of the synergistic approach means utilization of traditional texts such as the CERD treaty itself as well as familial texts on the right to health, such as General Comment 14 and reports of the Special Rapporteur on Health in order to further clarify the meaning and obligations entailed under CERD Article 5(e)iv. In the following section the relevant elements of race and health under international law are examined in greater detail.

4.1. THE INTERNATIONAL CONVENTION ON THE ELIMINATION OF ALL FORMS OF RACIAL DISCRIMINATION

Brought before the United Nations (UN) General Assembly (GA) for signature under Resolution 2106 (XX) on 21 December 1965, the International Convention on the Elimination of all forms of Racial Discrimination (CERD) is one of the earliest of the core international human rights treaties preceding even the two major human rights covenants on civil and political rights and economic, social, and cultural rights.[27] CERD entered force on 4 January 1969 after the receipt of 27 ratifications and/or accessions in accordance with Article 19 of the treaty. [28] Currently, there are 170 states parties to the treaty with 6 additional signatory states.[29] Given that there are currently 192 member states of the United Nations, nearly ninety percent of the world's nations have ratified this treaty, making it among the most widely adopted of the international human rights texts.[30]

The first binding human rights treaty to follow the UDHR, the CERD includes a substantive article on health. In particular the language of CERD Article 5(e)iv includes,' ...the right to public health, medical care, social security and social services' and naturally parallels that of Article 25 of the UDHR.[31] Yet, in Natan Lerner's detailed commentary on the Convention on the Elimination of all forms of Racial Discrimination, Article 5(e)iv on health is mentioned only once, as a direct quotation of the text of the article along with references to the UDHR and ICESCR as being other sources of information about the meaning of the right to health.[32] The historical documents surrounding the drafting of the Declaration on the Elimination of all forms of Racial Discrimination and the CERD give no other indication as to the intended meaning of CERD Article 5(e)iv. Therefore, in order to ensure consistency across the human rights sphere it seems reasonable to conclude that the text of Article 25 of UDHR and Article 12 of ICESCR as well as the subsequent normative documents coming from the relevant charter monitoring and treaty bodies must be utilized for determining the meaning and interpretation of the right to health under CERD Article 5(e)iv. Thus, the Synergistic Approach suggests examination of the

---

[27]   OFFICE OF THE UNITED NATIONS HIGH COMMISSIONER FOR HUMAN RIGHTS, *International Law*, <http://www.ohchr.org/english/law/>.

[28]   *International Convention on the Elimination of all forms of Racial Discrimination, supra* n. 19.

[29]   OFFICE OF THE HIGH COMMISSIONER FOR HUMAN RIGHTS, *International Convention on the Elimination of all forms of Racial Discrimination, Ratifications and Reservations*, <http://www.ohchr.org/english/countries/ratification/2.htm>.

[30]   UNITED NATIONS, *List of Member States*, <http://www.un.org/Overview/unmember.html>.

[31]   *International Convention on the Elimination of all forms of Racial Discrimination, supra* n. 19; *Universal Declaration of Human Rights, supra* n. 12.

[32]   N. LERNER, *The U.N. Convention on the Elimination of all Forms of Racial Discrimination* (Alphen aan den Rijn, 1980) 59.

soft law texts and work of the Special Rapporteur on the right to health to ensure harmony in the interpretation of CERD Article 5(e)iv.

4.2. SPECIAL RAPPORTEUR ON THE RIGHT TO THE HIGHEST ATTAINABLE STANDARD OF PHYSICAL AND MENTAL HEALTH

In 2002, the United Nations Commission on Human Rights appointed a 'Special Rapporteur on the right of everyone to enjoy the highest attainable standard of physical and mental health' (hereafter referred to as the Special Rapporteur on the right to health). The mandate of the Special Rapporteur on the right to health refers specifically to Article 25 of the UDHR and Article 12 of the ICESCR and includes identifying mechanisms with which to measure the fulfillment of the right to health as outlined in these documents. [33-34] The Special Rapporteur on the right to health is also asked to pay special attention to General Comment 14 of the Committee on Economic, Social and Cultural Rights which is also salient source for the Synergistic Approach.[35]

With a view towards this shared mandate, the Synergistic Approach draws upon the existing work of the Special Rapporteur on the right to health in order to shed light on the obligations under Article 5(e)iv of CERD that have yet to be clarified explicitly. More specifically, the work of the Special Rapporteur on the right to health focuses on two main themes, the right to health, discrimination and stigma, and the right to health and poverty.[36] The theme of the right to health and discrimination is directly relevant to the current investigation while the second theme of the right to health and poverty is at the very least indirectly relevant. Specifically, he has focused chapters within his reports on the topics of discrimination in the enjoyment of the right to health and right to health indicators each of which will be utilized later in this text.[37] Additionally, he has greatly

---

[33] OFFICE OF THE UNITED NATIONS HIGH COMMISSIONER FOR HUMAN RIGHTS, *Special Rapporteur of the Commission on Human Rights on the right of everyone to the enjoyment of the highest attainable standard of physical and mental health*, <http://www.ohchr.org/english/issues/health/right/index.htm>.

[34] In resolution 2005/24 the Commission on Human Rights renewed the mandate of the Special Rapporteur on the Right to Health for a period of three additional years. See OFFICE OF THE UNITED NATIONS HIGH COMMISSIONER FOR HUMAN RIGHTS, *Human Rights Resolution 2005/24*, <http://ap.ohchr.org/documents/E/CHR/resolutions/E-CN_4-RES-2005-24.doc>.

[35] *Human Rights Resolution 2005/24, supra* n. 34.

[36] UNITED NATIONS, *Economic and Social Council, 'The right of everyone to the enjoyment of the highest attainable standard of physical and mental health'*, UN Document E/CN.4/2003/58, 2003.

[37] UNITED NATIONS, *supra* n. 36; UNITED NATIONS, *General Assembly, 'Interim report of the Special Rapporteur of the Commission on Human Rights on the right of everyone to enjoy the highest attainable standard of physical and mental health (Mr. Paul Hunt)'*, UN Document A/58/427, 2003

contributed a report on indicators prepared for the Inter-committee meeting of the human rights treaty bodies.[38]

4.3. GENERAL COMMENT 14

While the treaty text of ICESCR, Article 12 establishes a legal right to health, the substantive nature of the right remains nebulous and somewhat controversial in light of the vague treaty language.[39] In 2000, the Committee on Economic, Social and Cultural Rights (CESCR) published a significant soft law text in the form of a General Comment which provides an interpretive explanation of Article 12 of the ICESCR. General Comment 14 reaffirms health as a fundamental human right.[40] The General Comment asserts the interdependent nature of all rights and particularly mentions the rights of non-discrimination and equality as being instrumental in the fulfilment of the right to health.[41] The General Comment goes on to elaborate the normative content of the right to health, obligations of states parties, violations and implementation at the national level. Elements of each of these four subject areas are relevant to this analysis most often as it relates to the principle of non-discrimination as highlighted below.

The General Comment provides a useful framework of the essential elements of the right to health including what has come to be known as 'Triple-A-Q' namely:

- Availability: a sufficient quantity of functioning public health and health care facilities, goods, services and programs;[42]
- Accessibility: facilities, goods, services and programs are distributed in an equitable and *non-discriminatory* way. Health facilities, goods, services and programs must be accessible especially to *vulnerable populations* with in a State. Additionally, health facilities, goods, services and programs must be physically accessible and they must be affordable for all including to *vulnerable or socially disadvantaged groups;*[43]

---

and UNITED NATIONS, *Economic and Social Council, 'Report of the Special Rapporteur on the right of everyone to the enjoyment of the highest attainable standard of physical and mental health (Mr. Paul Hunt)',* UN Document E/CN.4/2006/48, 2006.

[38] UNITED NATIONS, *International Human Rights instruments, 'Report on Indicators for Monitoring compliance with International Human Rights Instruments – Summary',* UN Document HRI/MC/2006/7, Geneva, 2006.

[39] RUGER, *supra* n. 21, 273.

[40] UNITED NATIONS, *Economic and Social Council, 'The right to the highest attainable standard of health',* UN Document E/C.12/2000/4, Geneva, 2000, § 2.

[41] UNITED NATIONS, *supra* n. 40, § 3.

[42] UNITED NATIONS, *supra* n. 40, § 4.

[43] UNITED NATIONS, *supra* n. 40, § 4.

- Acceptability: systems of medical ethics must be complied with and that health facilities, goods, services and programs are provided in a *culturally appropriate* manner;[44] and
- Quality: medical personnel and scientifically approved and unexpired drugs and hospital equipment should compose health facilities, goods, services, and programmes.[45]

The General Comment recalls Articles 2.2 and 3 of ICESCR which prohibit discrimination in access to health care and the underlying determinants of health. States are also ascribed with a special obligation to provide health insurance to those without other sufficient means and to prevent any discrimination in the provision of health care services especially in regards to the core obligations of the right to health. The General Comment also makes reference to General Comment No. 3, paragraph 12, which states that even in times of resource constraints, the vulnerable members of society must be protected.

The core obligations of any given right are considered to be non-derogable and therefore states have some obligations of immediate effect.[46] In regards to the right to health one immediate obligation outlined in the General Comment is that of non-discrimination.[47] Other core obligations of the right to health include the right of access to health facilities, goods and services on a non-discriminatory basis, especially for vulnerable or marginalized groups and the equitable distribution of health facilities good and services.[48]

Violations of the right to health can result as a direct violation of the right by the State or by non-state actors who are inefficiently regulated by states. The denial of access to health facilities, goods and services to particular individuals or groups as a result of *de jure* or *de facto* discrimination is specifically mentioned as a violation of the obligation to respect. Failure to develop or implement a national health plan, insufficient expenditure and misallocation of public funding for vulnerable groups and failure to reduce the inequitable distribution of health facilities, goods and services are specifically mentioned as violations of the obligation to fulfill.[49]

General Comment 14 calls upon states to develop and adopt a national health strategy with a view towards the fulfillment of the right to health. Specifically, this national health plan should respect the principle of non-discrimination and actively

---

44   UNITED NATIONS, *supra* n. 40, § 4.
45   UNITED NATIONS, *supra* n. 40, § 12.
46   UNITED NATIONS, *Committee on Economic, Social and Cultural Rights, 'General Comment No. 3: the Nature of States Parties' Obligations',* UN Document E/1991/23, Geneva, 1990, § 10; UNITED NATIONS, *supra* n. 40, § 47.
47   UNITED NATIONS, *supra* n. 40, § 30.
48   UNITED NATIONS, *supra* n. 40, § 43.
49   UNITED NATIONS, *supra* n. 40, § 48-52.

solicit the participation of individuals. Health indicators developed as a part of the national health plan should be disaggregated to account for differences across the populations particularly among the vulnerable.[50]

5. APPLYING THE SYNERGISTIC APPROACH

Now that the theoretical foundations of the Synergistic Approach have been clarified, the next part of this paper will strive to apply the model by examining international and national level data related to health and race as suggested in the model. The following section describes the methods employed for the selection of health indicators used for assessing the right to health and presents some illustrative data related to racial health disparities.

In order to measure health status and make comparisons across sub-populations within or between states one needs an agreed upon norm or standard of health.[51] The World Health Organization (WHO) collects data on nearly 200 indicators that it labels as 'core health indicators' for the purposes of its annual World Health Report.[52] Additional indicators for specific populations (i.e. health workers) or health topics (i.e. HIV/AIDS) may also be gathered.[53]

The question as to how to discriminate between a mere health indicator and an indicator that may be used for the measurement of the right to health has been near the top of the agenda for many within the health and human rights community.[54] In one of his earliest reports to the UN General Assembly, the Special Rapporteur on the right to health attempts to address this issue by suggesting a possible framework for measuring the fulfillment of the right to health. This framework defines a right to health indicator as a health indicator that is explicitly derived from specific right to health norms and proposes that the monitoring of the indicator will be used to hold duty bearers to account.[55] The Special Rapporteur suggests three categories of right to health indicators: structural, process, and outcome, a model that has been reinforced by the chairpersons of the human rights treaty bodies.[56],[57] Building on the approaches taken by UNICEF, the Human Development Index (HDI), and Evans et

---

50 UNITED NATIONS, *supra* n. 40, § 53-55.

51 RUGER, *supra* n. 21, 279.

52 WORLD HEALTH ORGANIZATION, *Core Health Indicators*, <http://www3.who.int/whosis/core/core_select.cfm>.

53 WORLD HEALTH ORGANIZATION, *The World Health Report 2006-working together for health*, <http://www.who.int/whr/2006/en/index.html> and *The World Health Report, supra* n. 2.

54 See for example UNITED NATIONS, *supra* n. 36; UNITED NATIONS, *supra* n. 37, A/58/427 and UNITED NATIONS, *supra* n. 37, E/CN.4/2006/48.

55 UNITED NATIONS, *supra* n. 37, A/58/427.

56 UNITED NATIONS, *supra* n. 37, A/58/427.

57 UNITED NATIONS, *supra* n. 38.

al the authors here proposes a methodology for selecting indicators to measure the realization of the right to health.[58]

For the purposes of this research, the authors have chosen right to heath norms and obligations as articulated in Article 12 of the ICESCR and the CESCR General Comment 14 as a starting point.[59,60] The AAAQ framework proposed in CESCR General Comment 14 provides a nice scaffold upon which the elements of the right to health can be categorized but gives little detail as to the selection of health indicators. Instead, these authors draw upon other aspects of CESCR General Comment 14 including the minimum core obligations.[61] Next, a limited number of health indicators that complement these norms and obligations and which fall across the indicators typology described by the Special Rapporteur on the right to health were selected. Indicators were not pre-emptively chosen in order to overemphasize racial health inequalities, rather correlation to right to health norms serve as the primary selection criteria.

As recommended by the Special Rapporteur on the right to health the authors attempt to avoid preoccupation with health indicator selection and analysis.[62,63] The indicators selected for this research are demonstrative, and not meant as a prescriptive answer to the right to health indicators debate currently under way.[64] So as not to become too fixated on indicators, the authors have chosen to utilize a limited selection of health indicators that range across the life spectrum. Recognizing these indicators to be imperfect in their measurement of the right to health and racial discrimination the selected indicators do measure some elements of disease and health status, access and quality indicators, and the social determinants of health.[65] Public health epidemiologists regularly work with incomplete datasets to

---

[58] See for example: P. DASGUPTA, 'Commentary: National Performance Gaps', *The Convention on the Rights of the Child* (UNICEF, 1996), <http://www.unicef.org/pon96/conpg.htm>; UNITED NATIONS DEVELOPMENT PROGRAMME, *Human Development Report 2005. International cooperation at a crossroads: Aid, trade and security in an unequal world* (New York, 2005); D.P. EVANS, M.E. PRICE, T.L. GULRAJANI and A.H. HINMAN, 'Making the grade: A first attempt at a health and human rights report card', 9 *Health and Human Rights* (2006) 280-295.

[59] UNITED NATIONS, *supra* n. 36.

[60] UNITED NATIONS, *supra* n. 40, 4-5.

[61] UNITED NATIONS, *supra* n. 40, 8-9.

[62] D. SHELTON, 'Compliance with international human rights soft law', 29 *Studies in Transnational Legal Policy* (1997) 119-144 at 139.

[63] UNITED NATIONS, *supra* n. 37, E/CN.4/2006/48, 8-9.

[64] EVANS, *supra* note. 58.

[65] The concept of the underlying or social determinants of health is a relatively new one. This concept has been discussed within several fora within the international human rights community including within CESCR General Comment 14 as well as most notably, the World Health Organization's Commission on the Social Determinants of Health (CSDH). See Chapter Three for a broader discussion of the social determinants of health and the work for the CSDH. For the purposes of this study the social determinants of health are defined as in General Comment 14 as, '...access to safe and potable water and adequate sanitation, an adequate supply of safe food, nutrition and housing,

determine patterns of disease, therefore precise measures of the right to health and racial discrimination are not necessarily requisite in order to determine broad issues of importance.

Tables 1-2 below present some right to health norms and obligations as articulated in Article 12 of the ICESCR and the CESCR General Comment 14 as well as the selected health indicators suggested for use by this study. Many of the selected indicators are also consistent with the indicators suggested in the report on indicators prepared for the 5th inter-committee meeting of human rights treaty bodies.[66]

Table 1. Right to health norms and selected health indicators[67]

Right to health norm	Health indicator
- Reduction of infant mortality	- Infant mortality rate
- Sexual and reproductive health services	- Access to sexual report health information - Access to contraceptives
- Access to pre-natal care	- Access to prenatal care
- Prevention of exposure to environmental conditions that impact human health	- Asthma rates
- Discourages the use of tobacco and other harmful substances	- Current cigarette smoking rates
- Prevention of HIV	- HIV-infection deaths and AIDS incidence
- Equal and timely access to preventive and curative health services	- No pap smear and/or no mammogram within the past three years
- Appropriate treatment of prevalent diseases	- Heart disease rates - Cancer rates
- Appropriate mental health treatment and care	- Mental health prevalence rates

---

healthy occupational and environmental conditions, and access to health-related education and information, including on sexual and reproductive health.' UNITED NATIONS, *supra* n. 40, 2.

[66] UNITED NATIONS, *supra* n. 38, table 4.

[67] UNITED NATIONS, *supra* n. 40, 3-4.

Table 2. Right to health obligations and selected health indicators[68]

Right to health obligation	Health indicator
- Ensure that privitization of the health sector does not constitute a threat to AAAQ; Provision of a public, private or mixed health insurance system which is affordable for all	- Coverage by type of health insurance - Health insurance coverage by race/ethnicity
- Take measures to protect all vulnerable or marginalized groups	- Life expectancy rates
- Right of access to health facilities, goods and services...especially for vulnerable and marginalized groups	- No usual source of health care - No health care visits within the past 12 months

Next, one specific health indicator suggested here, that of infant mortality will be examined in further detail. Infant mortality is a frequently used indicator in the field of public health and often seen as strongly indicative of the health of a society. In addition, infant mortality is directly cited as a measure of the right to health within Article 12 of the ICESCR.[69] For these reasons this indicator will be used to illustrate the methods of analysis suggested by the authors. The data presented in this study come from a variety of sources including the World Health Report compiled by the WHO, the World Development Indicators compiled by the World Bank and self-reported national data.[70] The use of self-reported data ensures that states are unlikely to refute the reported data although this would not preclude states from refuting their implications. Additionally, the fact that these data are already regularly compiled means that no additional effort on the part of the State is required.

World Development Indicator data were exported to Excel for data cleaning, then SAS for analysis. The natural log of Gross Domestic Product (GDP) per capita was calculated, creating a new, transformed variable. Infant mortality was plotted against the natural log of GDP per capita, using standard SAS procedures. For the entire dataset, a quadratic least squares regression line was fit to the data, whereas the subset of high income countries was fit using a linear least squares regression

---

[68]   UNITED NATIONS, *supra* n. 40, 6-9.
[69]   *International Covenant on Economic, Social and Cultural Rights, supra* n. 14.
[70]   National health data include publicly reported data compiled by government sources. These data may be analyzed by government sources as in the case of NATIONAL CENTER FOR HEALTH STATISTICS, *Health, United States,* 2006, <http://www.cdc.gov/nchs/data/hus/hus06.pdf> and U.S. CENSUS BUREAU, *Income, Poverty and health insurance coverage in the United States: 2005,* <http://www.census.gov/prod/2006pubs/p60-231.pdf> or by non-governmental organizations as in the case of THE HENRY J. KAISER FAMILY FOUNDATION, *Key facts: race, ethnicity and medical care,* <http://www.kff.org/minorityhealth/upload/6069-02.pdf>.

line. A 95% prediction interval based on individual observations was overlaid on each of these plots, using standard SAS procedures.

Figure D displays data for all 181 states included in the initial analysis of infant mortality by GDP. The x axis of the figure shows the log scale of GDP per capita while the y axis shows infant mortality rates. The infant mortality rate calculates the rate of death of infants within the first year of life per 1,000 live births. Since, as indicated earlier, health outcomes are often resource dependent one would expect that states with a higher GDP (moving left to right on the x axis) would have lower rates of infant mortality than states with a lower GDP.

Figure D. Infant mortality versus log of GDP/capita with quadratic best fit line and 95% prediction interval for 181 states

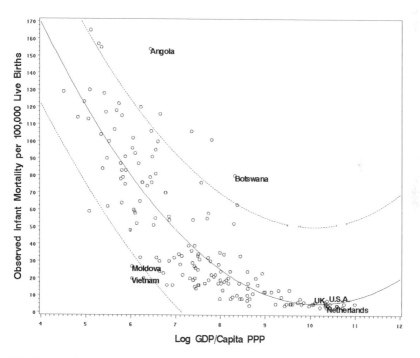

This figure effectively demonstrates the global health inequalities discussed earlier in the paper. However one can also observe that there are outliers. Some states with relatively lower GDP, such as Vietnam and Moldova have lower than expected infant mortality rates. Similarly Botswana, a middle income country has a higher than expected infant mortality rate given its GDP. As expected developed states such as the US, the UK and The Netherlands maintain low infant mortality rates relative to their high GDP.

Figure E takes a closer look at a subset of 39 high income countries. Upon examination one can see that even among developed countries there are differences in infant mortality rates that may not necessarily be attributed to higher GDP. For example while both the UK and The Netherlands have a lower GDP than the US both states maintain lower infant mortality rates.

Figure E. Infant mortality versus log of GDP/capita with linear best fit line and 95% prediction interval for 39 high income states

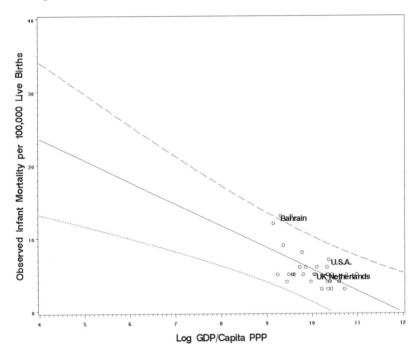

However useful these data may be for demonstrating global health disparities they do little to document the domestic racial inequalities that would fall under the purview of CERD. The data displayed in Figures D and E represent national averages which may mask racial inequalities. In order to address this issue national level data disaggregated by race must be examined. In this instance the authors have elected to examine the infant mortality rate of the US disaggregated by race. Figure F displays US infant mortality rates broken down by racial categories.

Figure F. United States Infant Mortality Rate by Race, 2004[71]

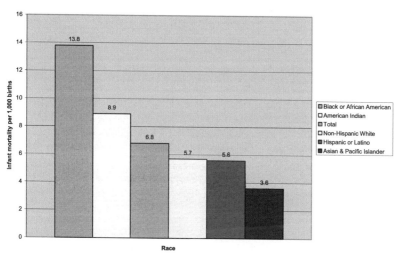

In 1998, the United States ranked 28th in the world in infant mortality far lower than one would expect given its GDP and health care spending.[72] This ranking has been attributed in large part to disparities which continue to exist among various racial and ethnic groups in the country, particularly African Americans.[73] Upon examination of the infant mortality data disaggregated by race one notices that while the total (or average) infant mortality for the country is 6.8 per 1,000 births there is a wide range of rates across the races. The infant mortality of African Americans (13.8 per 1,000) is more than double that of Non-Hispanic Whites (5.7 per 1,000). The significantly higher infant mortality rates of minority populations such as African Americans and American Indians are masked by lower rates among the larger Non-Hispanic White population. As evidenced by these data disaggregation of data by race is necessary in order to more clearly display the health inequalities that may exist between racial sub-populations. Such disaggregation is an important element in identifying areas in which discrimination in the availability of and access to quality health care services may be taking place.[74]

---

71   THE ANNIE E. CASEY FOUNDATION, *Infant Mortality, by Race: Rate per 1,000: 2004*, <http://www.kidscount.org/sld/compare_results.jsp?i=71>.

72   NATIONAL CENTER FOR HEALTH STATISTICS, *Infant Health*, <http://www.cdc.gov/nchs/fastats/infant_health.htm>.

73   NATIONAL CENTER FOR HEALTH STATISTICS, *Table 34. Infant, neonatal, and postneonatal mortality rates by race and sex: United States, 1940, 1950, 1960, 1970, and 1975-201*, <http://www.cdc.gov/nchs/fastats/pdf/nvsr50_15tb34.pdf>.

74   UNITED NATIONS, *supra* n. 37, E/CN.4/2006/48, 12.

The identification of inequalities between racial groups in health outcomes is an important exercise in and of itself. Historically the causes of such differences have been blamed on biological differences between the races. Even while the ultimate conclusion of the scientific community is that race per se does not exist, racism, racial discrimination and their consequent negative effects do. The authors of this paper believe that examination of health indicators such as those suggested here may assist in the analysis of the ways in which racial discrimination continue to exist and exert influence in a variety of social spheres impacting the fulfillment of human rights.

6. BARRIERS AND CHALLENGES TO THE APPROACH

Measuring the fulfillment of human rights generally is no simple task and gauging the fulfillment of economic, social and cultural rights with all of their complexities has proven to be a challenge to many researchers. No one approach to quantifying fulfillment of the right to health has been proven perfect and this approach is no exception to that rule. Here, the authors attempt to link theory to practice by presenting a human rights based theoretical model followed by public health data analysis.

The theoretical model, the synergistic approach, is a novel one that employs both hard and soft law in its analysis. The use of non-binding soft law via this approach may be disconcerting to some strict constructionists. The approach also attempts to bridge the artificial divides within the human rights regime that have arisen as a result of structural stratification. Correspondingly, the challenges that the synergistic approach poses to the existing structural configuration may stimulate a territorial response. Neither of these reactions is the desired intent of the authors. Rather we aim to creatively address the identified needs in order to strengthen the ability of the human rights corpus and mechanisms in practically measuring State fulfillment of obligations.

Challenges related to the application of the model have, for the most part, to do with data. Even data reported at the international level are most often collected nationally. While the measures themselves (i.e. infant mortality) are standardized disaggregated data are not often available at the international level making simultaneous comparisons across countries and racial categories nearly impossible. Variances exist in the way in which data are collected, compiled, and reported at the national level. The unfamiliarity of the researchers with national level data sources outside of the US has limited our ability to perform analyses of these data thus far. Further, access to national level primary data may be limited and secondary data may not be reported in the desired format making cross-country comparisons similar to comparing apples and oranges. Racial categorizations vary across states further complicating international comparisons. Finally, due to time constraints the authors of this paper were only able to begin analysis of some health indicators measuring the right to health. Examination of national level health laws policies and programs are an equally important component of the synergistic approach and should not be overlooked. With additional time and effort the authors believe that such comparisons could and should be undertaken.

7. CONCLUSION AND IMPLICATIONS

The theoretical model and methods employed in this paper wed the normative human rights research methods frequently undertaken in the discipline of law with methods more frequently employed by the social sciences. The synergistic approach utilizes empirical epidemiological research in an attempt to explain, in part the social phenomena of racial discrimination. In this case the synergistic approach is applied to Article 5(e)iv of CERD in order to glean greater understanding of the right to health as it relates to racial discrimination.

The vague treaty language of the CERD convention coupled with the persistent inattention of the CERD Committee and Special Rapporteur on race to specific provisions of the treaty has resulted in a missed opportunity for the application of CERD Article 5(e)iv. The use of complementary texts (such as General Comment 14 and the reports of the Special Rapporteur on health) on the right to health can offer several important lessons. First, the principle of non-discrimination is one which runs throughout the human rights corpus, and which merits attention when examining the right to health as confirmed by the adoption of the theme of non-discrimination in the work of the Special Rapporteur on the Right to Health. General Comment 14 includes statements on the normative content of the right to health, state obligations under the right, what constitutes a violation of the right, and expectations for implementation at the national level. Non-discrimination in the enjoyment of the right to health is an obligation of immediate effect and is not subject to progressive realization. Furthermore, the obligation of states parties to respect and protect the right to health on the whole and to fulfill this core minimum, comprise the most fundamental understanding of the right to health. Along with the work of the Special Rapporteur on health this normative document plays an instrumental role in the application of the Synergistic Approach to the interpretation of Article 5(e)iv of CERD. Therefore, the methods utilized for the selection of indicators here are rooted in the normative content of the right to health as defined in the international human rights treaty documents and supporting soft law texts.

The work presented here places high value on the use of indicators and a discreet methodology for the measurement of human rights. States' signature and/or ratification of relevant human rights treaties forms a precondition for inclusion in the analysis thereby taking into account (in part) structural measures of the right in question. In the formative application of the model attempted here the authors selected standardized health indicators on the basis of their correlation to the normative human rights texts on the right to health such as General Comment 14. This approach results in a discreet list of 15 outcome indicators for measurement of the right to health as it relates to racial discrimination.[75] These indicators are valid, reliable and represent widely accepted standards for the measurement of health. The data used in this analysis comes from State collected data reported at either the national or international level.

Next one variable, that of infant mortality, was selected for more detailed analysis. The selection of infant mortality as an indicator should not lessen the importance of the other suggested indicators. The authors selected one indicator in the interest of brevity and in order to simply demonstrate the approach. This indicator was chosen because of the widespread availability of data and the common use of infant mortality in the health realm as a measure of societal progress. Further analysis utilizing the other suggested indicators is warranted.

The analysis of international infant mortality data clearly demonstrated the global health inequalities that exist across countries. While GDP clearly plays an important role in determining infant mortality outcomes, some State outliers suggest that policy choices may mediate the effects of GDP (either positively or negatively). Since national level data are reported in the aggregate, the authors next elected to examine national level data disaggregated by race. As expected analysis of racially disaggregated data from the US displayed wide variances in infant mortality rates across racial categories. These data seem to indicate that some degree of racial discrimination is in existence in regards to the availability and accessibility of quality health programs and services for racial minority populations.

In order to fully explain these inequalities future analyses should include the examination of the additional indicators suggested in Tables 1-2 at both the international and national levels. The analysis of national level data from additional states should be disaggregated by State specific racial categories. The examination of data over time (i.e. from the time of ratification of CERD up to the present) may also shed light as to whether or not the reduction of racial health disparities is taking place in a progressive manner. Researchers will also need to address the balance between indicators which are universally relevant, such as infant mortality to those which may only be useful in certain settings. For example, access to potable water may be an important indicator in developing settings. However, in developed settings with near universal access to potable water use of this indicator may present an inaccurate measure of State performance with regard to the right in general. The

---

[75] As opposed to the near 50 indicators suggested for the measurement of the right to health. See UNITED NATIONS, *supra* n. 38, table 4.

fact that some measures may need to be customized or change over time adds another layer of difficulty to the undertaking of measurement.

Despite the challenges related with the analysis of such data the authors believe that the analysis of such indicators are both necessary and useful.[76] Further, these authors agree with the Special Rapporteur on the right to health that indicators are one method that can be used in monitoring states progress in achieving health objectives, making requisite policy adjustments and in holding states to account for their responsibilities in regards to the right to health.[77] Since public health data are already routinely compiled the onus is on researchers in the field of human rights to make appropriate use of those data towards these ends.

It is worthwhile noting that while the data presented in this paper are limited in scope and illustrative of the application of the model they are, nevertheless, real. The authors here have taken their discussion of indicators beyond theoretical methodological models and proposed indicators. We have gotten our hands dirty by presenting actual data on specific countries from international and national data sources. It cannot be overemphasized that the only genuine way in which we can determine the utility of proposed theoretical models is in their application. This means facing the ugly truth about the difficulties that researchers and ultimately states will face when preparing data on indicators measuring fulfilment of human rights. However, such primitive attempts are necessary in order to develop a system of human rights measurement that is both scientifically sound and efficacious.

In addition to the use of health data the synergistic approach also suggests the need for in-depth legal and health policy analyses. As asserted in General Comment 14 the availability and accessibility to health care programs and services contribute to the overall fulfilment of the right to health and the synergistic approach would require that non-discrimination is present in any and all health systems both global and domestic. An analysis of health policies and programs as well as legal statues related to health and racial discrimination would be helpful in placing health inequalities data in context. Such an analysis would also identify areas of policy need and legal gaps. Unfortunately due to limitations of time and space this component of the synergistic approach must be left to the future.

This initial presentation of the synergistic approach has sought to link theory and its application in interdisciplinary ways by drawing together social science and legal research methods. In this paper the focus has been on racial discrimination in the enjoyment of the right to health. The authors sincerely hope that readers will find this model interesting and useful especially in regards to the measurement of the fulfilment of human rights in additional contexts or for other vulnerable populations. The primary motivation in developing this model has been the desire to

---

[76] UNITED NATIONS, *supra* n. 37, E/CN.4/2006/48, 8-9.
[77] UNITED NATIONS, *supra* n. 37, E/CN.4/2006/48, 9.

create an informative and practical tool for states, the treaty bodies that monitor them, as well as members of the public with an interest in human rights. The authors are grateful for the opportunity to present this work and welcome feedback on the approach.

METHODS IN HEALTH AND HUMAN RIGHTS RESEARCH: TOWARDS A SPIRAL OF CO-LEARNING

MARIA STUTTAFORD*

1. INTRODUCTION

We need to make room in the academy for serious scholarly work on the multiple dynamics of health and human rights, on the health effects of war and political-economic disruption, and on the pathogenic effects of social inequalities, including racism, gender inequality, and the growing gap between rich and poor. . . . We require a new level of cooperation between disciplines ranging from social anthropology to molecular epidemiology. We need a new sociology of knowledge that can pick apart a wide body of commentary, and scholarship: complex international law; the claims and disclaimers of officialdom; postmodern relativist readings of suffering; clinical and epidemiologic studies of the long-term effects of, say, torture and racism. But remember, none of the victims of these events or processes are asking us to conduct research. . . . because such research would be linked to service, we need operational research by which we can gauge the efficacy of interventions quite different from those measured in the past.[1]

In his book *Pathologies of Power*, Paul Farmer challenges the academy to develop research that: takes account of the complexity of health and human rights, is multi-disciplinary, is applied, and takes account of the sensitivities of conducting research with people who are victims of their rights not being protected, respected and fulfilled. The aim of this paper is to reflect on research designs and research methods adopted when conducting research in the field of health and human rights. The focus is on qualitative research methods and how the application of such methods can be improved in order to ensure quality research. The paper begins with

---

* Acknowledgements to Leslie London, Marion Heap, Jacky Thomas, Nomafrench Mbombo and Zelda Holtman for the stimulating discussion held at the research team start-up workshop of the *Learning By Doing* project on 13th September 2007 in Cape Town. Without them the spiral would never have been committed to paper.

1 P. FARMER, *Pathologies of power: Health, human rights and the new war on the poor* (Berkley, 2003) 241.

---

a short introduction to health and human rights. A brief review of literature on methods in health and human rights research is presented and three research projects are outlined. These research projects are the basis for the reflections in the paper. All three projects were/are multi-disciplinary and use/used mixed methods. The first two, completed projects, used solely qualitative methods and the third project, launched in January 2008 uses qualitative and quantitative methods. The project started in January 2008 aims to overcome the weaknesses in the study design of the previous two projects by aiming to develop a spiral of emancipatory research.[2]

2. HEALTH AND HUMAN RIGHTS

The evolution of the right to the health is covered in key texts on the subject and will not be dealt with here, other than to set out a working definition for use in this paper.[3,4] Article 25.1 of the 1948 Universal Declaration of Human Rights (UDHR) states that: 'Everyone has the right to a standard of living adequate for the health and well-being of himself and of his family, including food, clothing, housing and medical care and necessary social services.' Some 20 years later, in 1966, Article 12.1 of the United Nations International Covenant on Economic, Social and Cultural Rights (ICESCR) refined this right to: 'recognise the right of everyone to the enjoyment of the highest attainable standard of physical and mental health.' Over 30 years later, in 2000, United Nations General Comment 14 further clarified the right to health. Crucially, it sets out minimum core obligations of states for respecting, protecting and fulfilling the right to health, as well as emphasising the underlying determinants of health and not only access to health care services.[5] General Comment 14 clarifies the positive right to the highest attainable standard of health in that it places obligations on states parties, providing a structure of accountability. The added value of a human rights approach to public health, is the clarification of the obligation of states to respect, protect and fulfil not only the access to health services, but also to the underlying determinants of health.[6]

The publication of General Comment 14 took place at a time when those working in the field of health and human rights were moving away from describing what the right to health is, or should be, to focusing on how to implement and

---

2   R. BHASKAR, *Scientific Realism and Human Emancipation* (London, 1986).

3   S. GRUSKIN, M.A. GRODIN, G.J. ANNAS and S.P. MARKS, *Perspectives on health and human rights* (New York, 2005).

4   S. GRUSKIN and D. TARANTOLA, 'Health and human rights', in R. DETELS, et al., *The Oxford Textbook of Public Health (4ʰ edition)* (Oxford, 2004) 311-335.

5   UNITED NATIONS (UN), *Committee on Economic, Social and Cultural Rights (UNCESCR), General Comment 14 (Twenty-second session), The right to the highest attainable standard of health*, UN Document E/C.12/2000/4 (Geneva, 2000).

6   S.P. MARKS, 'The evolving field of health and human rights: issues and methods', 30 *Journal of Law, Medicine & Ethics* (2002) 739-754.

invoke the right to health. The human rights perspective used in this paper goes beyond a purely legal notion of human rights, to also include the role of political and social action in implementing and invoking rights to health.[7,8] Taking into account the holistic conceptualisation of health and the indivisibility of rights set out in General Comment 14 and the growing recognition of the need to move away from purely legal actions to invoke the right to health, this paper, focuses on methods that support multi-disciplinary research. Such research is important to achieve the shift away from simply naming what health and human rights are, to achieving the implementation of such rights.

All three research projects discussed in this paper are under-pinned by an interest in overcoming inequalities in health and the role of collective action in this. Government and non-government programmes focusing on equity and programmes focusing on health as a human right have overcoming marginalization and discrimination as a common goal.[9] Research into the extent to which a human rights approach can be a tool for promoting health equity has found that when rights to health are combined with community engagement, they are a tool for equity.[10] This paper focuses on research in which civil society organisations (CSOs) are the primary unit of analysis and the individuals comprising the CSOs and interacting with CSOs are the secondary unity of analysis. Of particular interest is the way in which CSOs adopt a health and human rights approach for advocacy and action in terms of overcoming discrimination and marginalization with regard to health. For the purposes of this paper, a CSO is understood to be any organisation that is outside of the state and private market sector. Such a broad application of CSO is equally inclusive of, for example, non government organisations with a formal constitution and board directors and of, for example, a member led community based organisation that is informally constituted. All the CSOs in the studies discussed here were 'positively' constituted in that they were characterised by working for equity and human rights and sought to operate in an accountable way in consultation with constituents and members.

3. REVIEW OF METHODS USED IN HEALTH AND HUMAN RIGHTS RESEARCH

The literature reviewed here is intended to be illustrative of the methods and methodology currently in use in research on health and human rights. A systematic

---

[7]   T. CAMPBELL, 'Human rights: a culture of controversy', 26 *Journal of Law and Society* (1999) 6-26.

[8]   FARMER, *supra* n. 1.

[9]   P. BRAVEMAN and S. GRUSKIN, 'Poverty, equity, human rights and health', 81 *Bulletin of the World Health Organisation* (2003) 539-545.

[10]   L. LONDON, 'Can human rights serve as a tool for equity?', *Equinet Policy Paper* 14 (2003), <http://www.equinetafrica.org/bibl/docs/POL14rights.pdf>.

review of the literature has not been undertaken for the purposes of this paper and papers reviewed have been restricted to those in the English language. Three bibliographic databases were searched: Web of Science, International Bibliography of the Social Sciences and PubMed. Of the papers identified, few actually critically discussed or reflected on the methods and methodology. The dearth of literature on research methods in health and human rights is evident by the outputs of these searches. Furthermore, current key texts on health and human rights do not cover research methods.[11,12]

The review of literature is structured to reflect the ways in which a human rights approach can support achieving health equity: to develop policy and programmes; to analyse and critique government performance; to provide evidence in redress for those who suffer violations of their rights and; to support advocacy and civil society mobilization.[13]

3.1. METHODS USED IN RESEARCH INTO DEVELOPING POLICY AND PROGRAMMES

Research aimed at developing policy and programmes is dominated by fixed research designs evaluating new policies. Structured questionnaires have been used to explore population attitudes to changes in government policy, such as the introduction of routine, or 'opt-out' HIV testing; to explore how a population's perceptions of their human rights status may influence the establishment and implementation of rights based health policies and; to exploring the attitudes of patients and health professionals to specific guidelines and rights, such as the rights of hospitalized psychiatric patients.[14,15,16] Randomised controlled trials using a mix of qualitative and quantitative methods have been used for evaluating programmes of welfare rights education delivered through primary health care centres.[17]

---

[11]   J.M. MANN, S. GRUSKIN, M.A. GRODIN and G.J. ANNAS, *Health and Human Rights: A Reader* (London, 1999).

[12]   GRUSKIN, *supra* n. 3.

[13]   LONDON, *supra* n. 10.

[14]   S.D. WEISER, M. HEISLER, K. LEITER, F. PERCY-DE KORTE and S. TLOU, 'Routine HIV Testing in Botswana: A Population-Based Study on Attitudes, Practices, and Human Rights Concerns', 3 *PLoS Medicine* (2006), e261.DOI:10.1337/journal.pmed.0030261.

[15]   M. WILDNER, R. FISCHER and A. BRUNNER, 'Development of a Questionnaire for Quantitative Assessment in the Field of Health and Human Rights', 55 *Social Science & Medicine* (2002) 1725-1744.

[16]   D. ROE, D.J.N. WEISHUT, M. JAGLOM and J. RABINOWITZ, 'Patients' and Staff Members' Attitudes About the Rights of Hospitalized Psychiatric Patients', 53 *Psychiatric Services* (2002) 87-91.

[17]   S. MOFFAT, M. WHITE, J. MACKINTOSH and D. HOWEL, 'Using Quantitative and Qualitative Data in Health Services Research – What Happens When Mixed Methods Conflict?', 6 *BioMed Central Health Services Research* (2006), DOI:10.1186/1472-6962-6-28.

Less research adopts a flexible research design. Focus group interviews have been used with health professionals to explore their attitudes towards rationing of health services following changes in government policy.[18] Iterative consultations based on dialogue with professional groups have also been used to explore professional guidelines, such as Dual Loyalty.[19] An area of ongoing development are investigations into human rights impact assessments, using both qualitative and quantitative methods. One approach to developing human rights impact assessment is to develop specific tools for use during the formulation and implementation of public health policies.[20] A second approach is to adapt existing impact assessment tools, such as health impact assessments (HIAs), to include human rights.[21]

3.2. METHODS USED IN RESEARCH INTO ANALYSING AND CRITIQUE GOVERNMENT PERFORMANCE

Research in the field of health and human rights monitors government implementation of relevant conventions through methods of document review and analysis.[22] Reviews of case laws also indicate the extent to which States parties fulfil obligations to, for example, essential medicines.[23] Monitoring, analysing and critiquing government performance also takes place through the application of right to health indicators.[24,25] Both process and outcome indicators are important for

---

[18] B. CARLSEN and O.F. NORHEIM, ' 'Saying No is No Easy Matter' A Qualitative Study of Competing Concerns in Rationing Decisions in General Practice, 5 *BioMed Central Health Services Research* (2005), DOI:10.1186/1472-6963-5-70.

[19] L. LONDON, 'Dual Loyalties and the Ethical and Human Rights Obligations of Occupational Health Professionals', 47 *American Journal of Industrial Medicine* (2005) 322–332.

[20] L. GOSTIN and J. MANN, 'Toward the Development of a Human Rights Impact Assessment for the Formulation and Evaluation of Public Health Policies', in J.M. Mann, et al., *Health and Human Rights: A Reader* (London, 1999) 54-72.

[21] P. HUNT and G. MACNAUGHTON, *Impact Assessments, Poverty and Human Rights: A Case Study Using The Right to the Highest Attainable Standard of Health* (UNESCO, 2006).

[22] H. NYS, L. STULTIËNS, P. BORRY, T. GOFFIN and K. DIERICKX, 'Patient Rights in EU Member States After the Ratification of the Convention on Human Rights and Biomedicine', 83 *Health Policy* (2007) 223-235.

[23] H.V. HOGERZEIL, M. SAMSON, J.V. CASANOVAS and L. RAHMANI-OCORA, 'Is Access to Essential Medicines as Part of the Fulfilment of the Right to Health Enforceable Through the Courts?' 368 *The Lancet* (2006) 305-311.

[24] S. VENKATAPURAM, 'Survey of Monitoring and Measurement Tools of Health and Human Rights Programs. Background Paper: Doctors of the World-USA', Staff Seminar, 14 November 2002. <http://people.pwf.cam.ac.uk/sv266/DOW%20Monitoring%20and %20Measuring%20HR%20&%20H.pdf>.

[25] DEPARTMENT OF ETHICS, TRADE, HUMAN RIGHTS AND HEALTH LAW, *Consultation on Indicators for the Right to Health*, Château de Penthes, Geneva, 1-2 April 2004.

monitoring the progressive realisation of rights to health.[26] However, these are problematic to develop and implement in terms of their reliability and validity as well as bias, variance truncation and aggregation problems.[27,28,29] In addition, such indicators often focus on detecting violation of rights, rather than the achievement of positive rights.[30]

In many instances, existing data, including indicators and health impact assessments, are used to assess government performance on providing access to health care services and supporting the underlying determinants of health.[31,32] While the use of such secondary data assists in rationalising data collection, by not making explicit links to rights to health, it is possible that vital information is missed in terms of the progress towards achieving the highest attainable standard of health. In addition, many of these measures focus on outcomes. However, there is increasing recognition that in order to see greater implementation of rights, it is important to focus also on process. These problems are alleviated to some extent by the use of benchmarks, rather than indicators. Benchmarks focus more on the context in which rights are being implemented, the progressive realisation of the right to health and linking progress to structures that are accountable.[33,34]

3.3. METHODS USED IN RESEARCH PROVIDING EVIDENCE IN REDRESS FOR THOSE WHO SUFFER VIOLATIONS OF THEIR RIGHTS

In response to the complex data collection contexts and processes, evidence for reporting and redressing violations of rights follows mainly a flexible research design. The presentation of violations of rights to health through a case study

---

[26]   P. HUNT, *Report of the Special Rapporteur on the right of everyone to the enjoyment of the highest attainable standard of physical and mental health*, UN Commission on Human Rights E/CN.4/2006/48 (2006).

[27]   R.L. BARSH, 'Measuring Human Rights: Problems of Methodology and Purpose', 15 *Human Rights Quarterly* (1993) 87-121.

[28]   T. LANDMAN, 'Issues in the Global Comparative Analysis of Human Rights Violations', ESRC Research Methods Festival, St Catherine's College, Oxford, 2 July 2004.

[29]   K. RAWORTH, 'Measuring Human Rights', in S. GRUSKIN, et al., *Perspectives on Health and Human Rights* (New York, 2005) 393-411.

[30]   BARSH, *supra* n. 27.

[31]   A. HASSIM, M. HEYWOOD and J. BERGER (eds.), *Health and Democracy: A Guide to Human Rights, Health Law and Policy in Post-Apartheid South Africa* (Cape Town, 2007).

[32]   E. O'KEEFE and A. SCOTT-SAMUEL, 'Human Rights and Wrongs: Could Health Impact Assessment Help?', 30 *Journal of Law, Medicine & Ethics* (2002) 734-738.

[33]   H.J. STEINER and P. ALSTON, *International Human Rights in Context: Law Politics Morals (2nd ed.)* (Oxford, 2002).

[34]   H. WATCHIRS, 'Review of Methodologies Measuring Human Rights Implementation', 30 *Journal of Law, Medicine & Ethics* (2002) 716-733.

approach, commonly using qualitative methods of interviews and observations is a long standing method in health and human rights research.[35] A similar method is to collect verbal and photographic testimonies of violations, such as through the Truth and Reconciliation Commission hearings (TRC) in South Africa.[36] Providing evidence of human rights violations does also take place using quantitative methods such as structured questionnaires.[37]

3.4. METHODS USED IN RESEARCH INTO SUPPORTING ADVOCACY AND CIVIL SOCIETY MOBILIZATION

There is a particular gap in the literature focusing on methods used for research with programmes exploring health and human rights approach and links to advocacy and civil society mobilisation. Given that it is increasingly recognised that legal process alone will not improve health equity and achieve implementation of the right to health, this is of particular concern. There is much work being conducted in terms of 'human rights approaches to development' and often rapid ethnographic assessment and participatory methods are used in this work, which do engage with civil society. However such methods have received little critical attention, especially in their application to the field of human rights.[38,39] It is a positive step that research on the role of civil society in invoking the right to health, is starting to emerge. Strengthening collective agency of communities has been found to be an important element of human rights approaches achieving the goal of promoting health equity.[40] Such research has used qualitative methods of document review and in-depth interviews.

The above review provides an insight into the range of methods used in research on health and human rights. New methods and adaptation of existing methods, such as HIAs, are being undertaken for research on developing polices and programmes aimed at the right to health. Indicators, and increasingly benchmarks, are being developed for monitoring the performance of duty bearers and flexible research

---

[35] H.J. GEIGER and R.M. COOK-DEEGAN, 'The Role of Physicians in Conflicts and Humanitarian Crises. Case Studies from the Field Missions of Physicians for Human Rights, 1988 to 1993', 270 *The Journal of the American Medical Association* (1993) 616-620.

[36] L. BALDWIN-RAGAVEN, J. DE GRUCHY and L. LONDON, *An Ambulance of the Wrong Colour: Health Professionals, Human Rights and Ethics in South Africa* (Cape Town, 1999).

[37] L.L. AMOWITZ, G. KIM, C. REIS, J.L. ASHER and V. IACOPINO, 'Human Rights Abuses and Concerns About Women's Health and Human Rights in Southern Iraq', 291 *The Journal of the American Medical Association* (2004) 1471-1479.

[38] J. PETTIT and J. WHEELER (eds.), 'Development Rights?', 36 *Institute of Development Studies Bulletin* (2005).

[39] S. HICKEY and G. MOHAN (eds.), *Participation: From Tyranny to Transformation?* (London, 2004).

[40] L. LONDON, "Issues of Equity are Also Issues of Rights': Lessons from Experiences in Southern Africa', 7 *BioMed Central Public Health* (2007), DOI:10.1186/1471-2458-7-14.

designs continue to be used to evidence violations of the right to health. There is a particular paucity of research into advocacy and civil society mobilisation around the right to health. Furthermore, few papers reflect on the use of the methods and consider how methods and research design can be improved to meet the challenges of focusing on the implementation of the right to health through multi-disciplinary, applied research aimed at improving equity in health. The following section outlines three research projects which will be used to undertake such critical reflection and suggest ways for improving design and methods in future applied research. The third research project discussed in this paper seeks to contribute to filling the gap in research exploring civil society mobilization and advocacy.

4 REFLECTIONS ON RESEARCH DESIGN AND METHODS USED TO EXPLORE HEALTH AND HUMAN RIGHTS

This paper is based on the critical reflections of the author who has been and is involved in three research projects in the field of health and human rights (Table 1). These projects are used here for the basis of the following discussions. The section begins by briefly outlining the projects and the methods used before going on to reflect on the strengths and weaknesses of the methods.

Table 1. Summary of research projects reflected on in the paper

	Completed research		Research to commence January 2008
Title	Exploring Collective Rights to Public Health for Homeless People	Towards Establishing a Learning Network to Advance Health Equity Through Human Rights Strategies	Learning by Doing and Doing by Learning: A Civil Society Network to Realise the Right to Health
Year	2004-05	2005-06	2008-10
Funding	Economic and Social Research Council (ESRC), United Kingdom, RES-000-22-0618-A	Centre for Civil Society Research (CCS), University of KwaZulu-Natal, South Africa	South African-Netherlands Research Programme on Alternatives in Development (SANPAD)
Research Team	Maria Stuttaford, Gillian Lewando-Hundt, Panos Vostanis, Lynnette Kelly	Leslie London, Jacky Thomas, Maria Stuttaford, Marion Heap, Laurel Baldwin-Ragaven	Leslie London, Marion Heap, Maria Stuttaford, Lucy Gilson, Nomafrech Mbombo, Jacky Thomas, Zelda Holtman, Wendy Neft, Esther Nakao, Fons Coomans
Disciplines	Geography, anthropology, clinical psychiatry	Public health, adult education, geography, anthropology	Public health, anthropology, geography, nursing, adult education, psychology, law, gender studies
Methods	Interviews, participant observation, participatory diagramming and visualisation	Interviews, focus groups	Surveys, structured interviews, in-depth interviews, focus groups, written and photographic diaries and participatory diagramming and visualization
Experienced Strengths	Flexible design enabled researchers to respond to complex research context Elicited voices of homeless people and service providers on beliefs and understanding of rights to health Provided data for inductive analysis towards a framework of collective rights	Elicited voices of CSO members and duty bearers on how they do/do not explicitly use a health and human rights framework Provided data for deductive analysis testing theoretical framework and inductive analysis on meaning of rights to health	-
Experienced Weaknesses	The topic of health and human rights was a complex one for respondents to grapple with in the moment of the interview Flexible design failed to capture depth of knowledge and experience of participants Analysis was weakened by insufficient theorisation of health and human rights	While respondents well versed in human rights discourse, the implementation of such approaches remains a goal rather than a reality The data did not capture the depth of potential knowledge and potential application of health and human rights approach	-

4.1. EXPLORING COLLECTIVE RIGHTS TO PUBLIC HEALTH FOR HOMELESS PEOPLE

The first project was undertaken in a city in England during 2004-05 and was funded by the UK Economic and Social Research Council (ESRC) (RES-000-22-0618-A). The aims of the research were to develop a conceptual framework on collective rights to health and to explore the extent to which homeless families access their rights to health care services. The research sought to identify aspects of partnerships that might foster the adoption of a collective rights framework where there is a shared responsibility for health across the health and social care sectors and across agencies. It was intended that this would be done by engaging in a process of dialogue between researchers, homeless families and partner agencies.

Methods of data collection included interviews with residents of two hostels for homeless people. Interviews were also carried out with a number of individuals who provided health or health related services to residents of the hostels. Other methods included observations by the researcher during time spent at the hostels, interacting informally with residents, and attending coffee mornings, lunches, and other gatherings. The final method was three workshops using participatory diagramming and visualisation techniques conducted with the parents of homeless families and service providers. Analysis was thematic and Nvivo qualitative analysis software was used. Inter-rater reliability was used to improve reliability, as did the use of multiple methods.

The general aim of the project was to elicit vulnerable people's understandings of the right to health and the use of human rights frameworks. Not only understanding the events (for example of human rights violations), but also the people, places and processes influencing the realization of rights to health. The focus was on social, rather than legal, aspects of human rights. It was found that invoking rights to health for homeless families in this study were the product of individual and collective, or partnership, action. The research attempted to capture the various levels and organisations that contribute to fulfilling rights to health in order to develop a framework of sites for health rights that can be used in the ongoing development of human rights based approaches to health. This framework focuses on where the right to health is invoked, or thwarted, as well as how and by whom.

4.2. TOWARDS ESTABLISHING A LEARNING NETWORK TO ADVANCE HEALTH EQUITY THROUGH HUMAN RIGHTS STRATEGIES

The second project was undertaken during 2005-2006 and was funded by the Centre for Civil Society Research in South Africa.[41] It aimed to test a model developed for the Network on Equity in Health in Southern Africa (EQUINET) with three civil society organisations (CSOs) in rural and urban areas in Western Cape, South Africa.[42] The study examined the role of both the rights holders and duty bearers. In particular it explored how human rights are understood and utilised within the CSOs, and the relative importance of individualised versus collective conceptions of human rights and how these understandings of rights contribute to processes such as advocacy and mobilisation. It also explored how human rights are understood and used in approaches to service delivery. It was intended that the data collected would be used as the basis for initiating a learning network with CSOs.

Methods of data collection included interviews and focus groups. These were conducted with members of the CSOs and staff of the CSOs, as well as government officials and political leaders whose mandate was addressed by the CSO. Thematic content analysis was used to review and reflect on the data. This was first done manually and more in-depth analysis is currently (February 2008) being undertaken, supported by Nvivo qualitative analysis software.

It was found that CSOs have a general sense of the types of rights which exist but lack clear understanding of what a human rights approach implies, and therefore, what a human rights approach could add to their work. However, organisations did acknowledge that collective agency is a key mechanism through which vulnerable people can take action to redress the challenges they face when involving the right to health. It was also found that human rights approaches and practices can act to unite vulnerable groups and that it is important to build alliances across sectors in the context of scarce resources. At the same time, CSOs need to work to guard against their own agency divesting the state of its responsibilities in a market economy. This is particularly important because organisations understand increasingly that rights are integrated across a range of indivisible social, cultural, civil and political entitlements.

---

[41]   J. THOMAS and L. LONDON, *Towards Establishing a Learning Network to Advance Health Equity Through Human Rights Strategies*, Final Project Report to the Centre for Civil Society (Cape Town, 2006).

[42]   LONDON, *supra* n. 10.

4.3. LEARNING BY DOING AND DOING BY LEARNING: A CIVIL SOCIETY NETWORK TO REALISE THE RIGHT TO HEALTH

This project builds on the substantive findings of the project *Towards Establishing a Learning Network to Advance Health Equity through Human Rights Strategies* and the methodological experiences of this project and the project *Exploring Collective Rights to Public Health for Homeless People*. The project commenced work in January 2008 and will be completed in December 2010, although it is hoped to continue the civil society network beyond this. Funding is from the South African-Netherlands Research Programme on Alternatives in Development (SANPAD).

The project aims to answer the following research questions: can a human rights approach help to mobilize the agency needed, individually and collectively, to overcome factors driving health inequalities, and help realize the right to health? If so, what kinds of strategies are most effective, and what roles do health care providers play in either facilitating or acting as obstacle to such agency? The project will address these questions by exploring: the understanding and practice of human rights by civil society groups; the understanding and practice of human rights by health care providers; and the interaction between CSOs and health care providers in a learning network. Through a process of participatory action research, lessons will be drawn on how best the right to health can be operationalised, and to lay the basis for a learning network of CSOs using a rights-based approach to advance health. The design is discussed in more in Section 5. It is essentially a flexible design following an iterative process of knowledge sharing between co-researchers and participants through a spiral of data collection, analysis and dissemination. Methods of data collection are also described in more detail below and will include questionnaires, structured interviews, in-depth interviews, focus groups, written and photographic diaries and participatory diagramming and visualization. Data will be managed in Statistical Package for the Social Sciences (SPSS) and the qualitative analysis software, Nvivo.

4.4. STRENGTHS AND WEAKNESSES OF METHODS USED IN THE COMPLETED RESEARCH PROJECTS

The general strengths and weaknesses of the named methods are covered in key texts on methods in the social sciences.[43] The focus here is on the strengths and weaknesses of the methods in these particular projects exploring social aspects of health and human rights.

---

[43]   A. BRYMAN, *Quality and Quantity in Social Research* (London, 1988); D. SILVERMAN, *Doing Qualitative Research: A Practical Handbook* (London, 2000); C. ROBSON, *Real World Research (2nd ed.)* (Oxford, 2002).

In the first project, while it was intended that a dialogue be established between all participants, in reality this did not emerge in a sustained way. An explanation of this, could lie in the fact that the research was being conducted with a highly mobile population, but also in the fact that the researchers failed to move discussions beyond normative concepts of the right to health to really engage people in debates on implementation. The flexible design did allow for the research to respond to a complex and fluid research context, however, it failed to capture the depth of people's experiences of the right to health. Furthermore, analysis was weakened by insufficient theorisation of health as a human right.

In the second project, the theorisation of the right to health was stronger and, as before, the flexible design enabled researchers to respond to the complexity of the processes and contexts of the CSOs. However, as with the first project, the data did not capture the depth of knowledge and potential application of a health and human rights approach by CSOs.

The main problem encountered when asking people about health and human rights during in-depth interviews and focus groups, is that people have been unclear as to what is meant by the right to health. In the main, people have heard about health being a human right. However, they are unclear how it might be applied, both for the individual, but also in terms of collectives, such as CSOs. In order not to bias responses, researchers in the projects did not set out with a definition of health or of human rights but rather waited to see what themes or concepts emerged during the interview or focus group. This often led to discussions that were overly simplistic and did not reach the depth of knowledge or experience of the participants. Applied research should recognise the skills and expertise of research participants and the research design and methods should be appropriate for eliciting these. However, at the same time, there may be gaps in knowledge and learning may need to take place before action research can be applied. According to the work of Friere, it is sometimes necessary for people to have their consciousness raised, before action can be undertaken.[44] In other words, it may be necessary for there to be some learning and consciousness raising, before CSOs can take action using a health and human rights approach. Such learning should not be imposed from outside but rather be inclusive of all participants. The next section draws on critical and emancipatory theory to propose a research design and methods which attempt to support co-learning and promote inclusivity.

---

[44]   P. FREIRE, *Pedagogy of the Oppressed (revised ed.)* (London, 1996).

5. A LEARNING NETWORK TO FACILITATE A SPIRAL OF CO-LEARNING

Building on the experiences to date of using qualitative methods for research in the field of health and human rights, a methodology has been developed for the Learning Network research launched in January 2008. The following section sets out the theoretical rationale for the approach drawing on the concepts of structure, agency and critical social science. The research design follows a participatory action research approach. The vehicle for facilitating participation is a network of researchers, members of CSOs and health professionals in which all members are seen as co-researchers and co-learners. Through an iterative process of workshops, data collection, analysis and dissemination, experiential learning will be promoted. [45] Furthermore, the importance of developing the participatory learning network in terms of adult learning will be taken into account.[46]

Participatory action research can be used as 'a vehicle for undertaking applied research, co-constructing a shared knowledge base'.[47] Arnstein's 'eight rungs on a ladder of citizen participation' are now widely known.[48] As one moves from manipulation to therapy, informing, consultation, placation, partnership, delegated power and citizen control, the distinguishing shift is in the power between the 'haves' and 'have-nots'. The alignment of power within the research process is a distinguishing characteristic between participatory and conventional research and participatory research is 'a process of sequential reflection and action, carried out with and by local people rather than on them'.[49] Participatory approaches recognise the 'greater involvement of 'local' people's perspectives, knowledge, priorities and skills'.[50] This involves identifying what people do know, not only what they do not know. Therefore the data collected will focus on the research goals, as well as the goals of the CSOs. Where CSO members are willing and have the time, they will be invited to participate as peer researchers in data collection, analysis and dissemination.

---

[45]   D. KOLB, *Experiential Learning* (New Jersey, 1984).

[46]   M. KNOWLES, *The Adult Learner: A Neglected Species* (Houston, 1990); M. STUTTAFORD and C. COE, 'The 'Learning' Component of Participatory Learning and Action (PLA) in Health Research: Reflections from a Local Sure Start Evaluation', 17 *Qualitative Health Research* (2007) 1351-1360.

[47]   T.R. HILL, N. MOTTEUX, E.L. NEL and G. PAPLOIZOU, 'Integrating Rural Community and Expert Knowledge Through Applied Participatory Rural Appraisal in the Kat River Valley, South Africa', 83 *South African Geographical Journal* (2001) 1-7 at 1.

[48]   S.R. ARNSTEIN, 'A Ladder of Citizen Participation', 35 *Journal of the American Institute of Planners* (1969) 216-224.

[49]   A. CORNWALL and R. JEWKES, 'What is Participatory Research?' 41 *Social Science and Medicine* (1995) 1667-1676 at 1667.

[50]   B. COOKE AND U. KOTHARI (eds.), *Participation: The New Tyranny?* (London, 2001) 11.

The project does not engage in 'pure' participatory research in that members of the CSOs and health professionals have not participated in the design of the research and the funding application. However, they will participate in the workshops, as peer researchers where they would like to and where feasible, and in dissemination. All participants — academics, CSO members and health professionals — are therefore seen as co-learners and co-researchers. As co-researchers and co-learners, participants seek to take part in a research process in which no one knowledge is valorised over another.[51] The academics learn from the CSOs and health professionals about their experiences of health and human rights, and CSOs and health professionals learn from each other and from academics about the implementation of a health and human rights approach.

By adopting a participatory action research design, researchers seek to create a more equal balance of power in the research relationship than in conventional research. Critical theory seeks to redress conventional balances of power within the researcher-researched relationship. A critical social science is one that has 'an emancipatory interest in knowledge' and is critical of the social practices it studies as well as of other theories.[52]

Critical realists further argue that we need to engage with structures (the rules and resources) and agency (the interventions of individuals) in order to stimulate change. Structures and agency cannot be separated from one another but are rather a duality with a social system.[53]

'Critical realists do not deny the reality of events and discourses; on the contrary, they insist upon them. But they hold that we will only be able to understand — and so change — the social world if we identify the structures at work that generate those events or discourses'.[54] In the Learning Network project, we seek to engage with the rules, resources and intervention of CSOs and individuals, in order to stimulate learning between all participants and transform people's experience within health and social systems. For example, by learning how health providers exclude patients and working with patients groups and health providers to widen access.

It is the victims of violations of rights that have a direct interest in understanding the structures and agency that promote, respect and fulfil the right to health. 'The oppressed, contrary to their oppressors, have a direct material interest in understanding the structural causes of their oppression'.[55] An emancipatory social science needs to have a specific and directive critical content, identifying what is

---

[51] G. MOHAN, 'Beyond Participation: Strategies for Deeper Empowerment', in B. COOKE and U. KOTHARI (eds.), *Participation: The New Tyranny?* (London, 2001) 151-168.

[52] M. ALVESSON and K. SKÖLDBERG, *Reflexive Methodology: New Vistas for Qualitative Research* (London, 2000) 110; A. SAYER, *Realism and Social Science* (London, 2000).

[53] A. GIDDENS, *The Constitution of Society: Outline of the Theory of Structuration* (Cambridge, 1984).

[54] BHASKAR, *supra* n. 2.

[55] BHASKAR, *supra* n. 2.

wrong and what specifically needs to be done to make improvements.[56] The CSOs in the learning network are all working to overcome the historical inequalities in South Africa, by focusing on the right to health. Emancipatory research explores: the lives and experiences of groups that have traditionally been marginalized; how and why inequities are reflected in asymmetrical power relations; how the results of social enquiry into inequities are linked to political and social action; and uses emancipatory theory to develop the research approach[57]. 'The relationship between social knowledge or theory and social . . . practice will take the form of an emancipatory spiral in which deeper understanding make possible new forms of practice, leading to enhanced understanding and so on'[58]. This is similar to the Aristotlian notion of *phronesis* or 'practical wisdom' in which 'social decision making is an ongoing, iterative process which incorporates new information as it becomes available'.[59] Within the Bhaskar's 'emancipatory spiral' and Aristotle's 'practical wisdom' it is necessary to consider the role of power, especially in the context of research.[60] It has already been explained how power is acknowledged in the research by following a participatory action research design. This is translated in a practical way, through the adoption of a spiral of inclusive research activities during data collection, analysis and dissemination.

In the *Learning By Doing* project, an attempt is made to create an iterative, emancipatory spiral (Figure 1). This is done through a process of: identifying gaps in knowledge by the CSOs and researchers stating their research goals during the workshops; data collection; data analysis and; addressing knowledge gaps and feeding back research findings at the next workshop. Establishing a dialogue at the outset is vital for the spiral to be launched. Dialogue between co-researchers will set the goals for each phase of the spiral. A research network of 'reseachers' and 'researched' can support agency by these co-researchers to establish a 'dialogical process'.[61] In order for the dialogue to take place, participants need to engage in critical thinking in which researchers and researched act as 'co-investigators'.[62] As co-investigators, they explore their themes of reality through narratives and images (collected during interviews and visual data collection methods) rooted in everyday

---

[56] SAYER, *supra* n. 52.

[57] ROBSON, *supra* n. 43.

[58] BHASKAR, *supra* n. 2.

[59] J.P. RUGER, 'Toward a Theory of a Right to Health: Capability and Incompletely Theorized Agreements', 18 *Yale Journal of Law & the Humanities* (2006) 273-326.

[60] B. FLYVBJERG, *Making Social Science Matter: Why Social Inquiry Fails and How it can Succeed Again* (Cambridge, 2001).

[61] P. DE VRIES, 'A Research Journey: on Actors, Concepts and the Text', in N. LONG and A. LONG (eds.), *Battlefields of Knowledge: The Interlocking of theory and Practice in Social Research and Development* (London, 1992) 47-84, at 47.

[62] FREIRE, *supra* n. 44.

experiences and in so doing the validity of knowledge is increased.[63] The CSOs forming the learning network, all participated in the pilot study and a relationship has been established with them. The dialogue started at the launch workshop in January in which the academics stated the goals of the funded research and the CSOs stated what their goals were. The dialogue continues throughout the spiral, with CSOs learning from each other and from the academics and the academics learning from the CSOs and from each other at each of the workshops and during each phase of the research. This co-research and co-learning is the active element of the shift in power compared to traditional research.

Figure 1. The iterative learning process envisaged for supporting emancipatory research

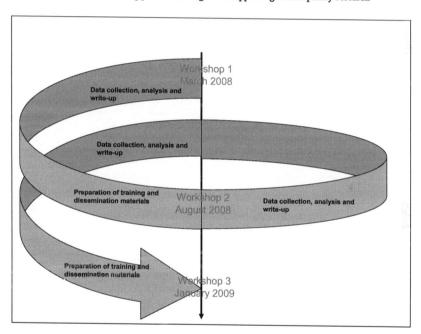

Texts on participatory research rightly attribute much of the theoretical underpinnings of the approach to the writings of Paolo Freire and his work described in *Pedagogy of the Oppressed*, first published in 1971, on the consciousness raising, or learning, needed before 'the oppressed' can take action. The term *conscientização* 'refers to the learning to perceive social, political and economic contradictions and to take action against the oppressive elements of reality'.[64]

---

[63]   P. REASON, 'Learning and Change Through Action Research', in J. HENNY (eds.), *Creative Management* (London, 2001) 182-193.

[64]   FREIRE, *supra* n. 44.

Learning is thus central to action in participatory research. However, a key concern about participatory approaches is that they focus on individuals becoming more self-aware of their knowledge but are then not clear on how this individual conscious raising is transformed into political learning and capability.[65] The intention of the learning network is that the network becomes a vehicle for building learning and capacity for activating collective rights to health. Co-researchers and co-learners will, in the research workshops, identify common goals for further learning. The data collection, analysis and dissemination will focus on these specific topics. In particular a tool-kit on health and human rights will be developed for use by CSOs and may link the findings of the research to social action. Through the research, learning between CSOs will be captured and disseminated and researchers own knowledge transferred. Introductory information about rights to health have been provided to participants following the launch workshop.[66] These materials will be adapted in response to participant feedback during subsequent training workshops and research. The material has provided a common starting point for more in-depth discussion and dialogue.

The pilot phase with CSOs, the launch workshop, follow-up meetings and provision of pamphlets, recognises the need for consciousness raising before action. At each workshop, participants will reflect on progress and learning since the last workshop. Reflection is an important part of the experiential learning process.[67] Learning is defined in terms of experiential learning because of its emphasis on reflection and action and learning by doing. Experiential learning draws on the work of Friere and is defined as 'the process whereby knowledge is created through the transformation of experience'.[68] The model of experiential learning follows four phases: a concrete experience (e.g. advocating for access to medicine for people with epilepsy); reflection on the experience (e.g. during the workshop identifying what worked well and less well); formation of new ideas based on the reflection (e.g. how to use a human rights approach to advocate for essential medicine) and; putting the new idea into practice (e.g. using a human rights approach to contact health professionals to request to make medicine available). The experiential learning cycle then begins again. The spiral in the learning network seeks to establish a similar iterative process of learning. Moreover, in establishing a network of adult learners, it is necessary to build into the network those factors that influence adult learning: adults need to know why they need to learn something before undertaking to learn

---

[65] G. WILLIAMS, 'Towards a Repoliticization of Participatory Development: Political Capabilities and Spaces of Empowerment', in S. HICKEY and G. MOHAN (eds.), *Participation: From Tyranny to Transformation?* (London, 2004) 92-107.
[66] UNIVERSITY OF CAPE TOWN AND OXFAM, 'Six Pamphlets on the Right to Health', The University of Cape Town (Cape Town, 2007).
[67] KOLB, *supra* n. 45.
[68] KOLB, *supra* n. 45.

it; people become adults psychologically when they accept responsibility for their decisions; adults have a diversity and depth of experience which means that a group of people undertaking a learning activity need to be recognised as being heterogeneous and; adults are often motivated to learn by internal pressures such as increased self-esteem and quality of life.[69] Finally, the workshops will be facilitated in such a way that recognises that place influences knowledge and power and that there are spaces that promote and/or inhibit participation[70]. Workshops will be held at a time and place appropriate and accessible to CSOs, as will the other data collection activities.

Based on critical and emancipatory theory, the *Learning By Doing* research network seeks to engage in operational research that addresses health inequalities through a spiral of co-learning. This is done by being sensitive to: power relations within the research; the need to practically address structures and agency within an emancipatory research approach; where and how the workshops are established; the motivation of CSO members for wanting to learn; and the processes which stimulate learning. By being reflective and in open dialogue about these aspects of the research process, the research will not only contribute to the objectives of CSOs in terms of overcoming inequity in health, but also address the goals of the research to explore the use of health and human rights frameworks by CSOs and health service providers.

6. MIXED METHODS OF RESEARCH IN THE LEARNING BY DOING NETWORK

The participatory action research design incorporates mixed methods. Quantitative methods generally seek to quantify phenomena and test hypotheses whereas qualitative methods seek to elicit the voices of people and to interpret social phenomena from the point of views of the meanings employed by the people being studied. Qualitative methods usually use natural settings for data collection and lead to the generation of theory.[71] The main advantage of using mixed methods is to improve validity through triangulation of data sources and methods.[72] Multiple methods can also assist in answering different but complementary questions in a study. In recent years, mixed methods have gained popularity, but there remain

---

[69]   KNOWLES, *supra* n. 46.

[70]   M. KESBY, 'Retheorizing Empowerment-Through-Participation as a Performance in Space: Beyond Tyranny to Transformation', 30 *Signs: Journal of Women in Culture and Society* (2005) 2037-2065; J. GAVENTA, 'Towards Participatory Governance: Assessing the Transformative Possibilities', in S. HICKEY and G. MOHAN (eds.), *Participation: From Tyranny to Transformation?* (London, 2004) 24-41.

[71]   A. BRYMAN and R.G. BURGESS, *Qualitative Research (vol. 2)* (London, 1999).

[72]   N.K. DENZIN and Y.S. LINCOLN (eds.), *Handbook of Qualitative Research* (London, 2000).

several difficulties in combining methods, especially across disciplines and criteria for evaluating the quality of mixed methods research needs to draw on criterion from both quantitative and qualitative traditions.[73,74] Several methods are outlined in this section and they are discussed in relation to the *Learning by Doing* research. Further details of the methods themselves can be found in the references provided.

The first method of data collection to be employed in the research is a survey generating mainly quantitative data with a limited number of open ended questions. The survey will be completed by every member of the learning network (CSO members and heath care providers). When new members join, they will be requested to complete the same survey. The questions will be related to individual demographics as well as factual data about organizational structure.

Semi-structured interviewing takes place when set questions are asked but not in any particular order.[75] This may be particularly useful in the research on health and human rights to ask all respondents similar questions on their understanding and beliefs about particular core phenomena, which have been identified in the learning network. It may provide the opportunity for the researchers to ask the same questions at different intervals in the research to see how knowledge in the network is evolving through the cycles of experiential learning.

While semi-structured interviews focus on the individual, focus group interviews are particularly useful for eliciting views on a specific collective topic, such as rights to health.[76] They are also particularly useful in a participatory action research design as they can lead to shared learning and consciousness raising for all participants, including the researchers.

In-depth interviews are particularly useful for engaging with people with regard to meanings of phenomena. In the research on health and human rights, in-depth interviews as narrative may improve the focus and rigour of data, compared to the first two studies. This is, firstly, because the research is particularly interested in individuals and collectives and personal narratives link the individuals and wider social context.[77] Second, it is possible to identify three different types of narrative, each of which will assist in achieving a greater focus on the depth of knowledge and experience of participants than in the previous research.[78] First, contingent narratives will explore beliefs and knowledge about factors influencing health. Second, moral narratives will explore value judgements, justifications, explanations

---

[73]   MOFFAT, WHITE, MACKINTOSH and HOWEL, *supra* n. 17.

[74]   S. BECKER, A. BRYMAN and J. SEMPIK, '*Defining 'Quality' in Social Policy Research: Views, Perceptions and a Framework for Discussion'*, Social Policy Association (Lavenham, 2006).

[75]   ROBSON, *supra* n. 57.

[76]   F.A. KRUEGER, *Focus Groups: a Practical Guide for Applied Research (2nd ed.)* (London, 1994).

[77]   S. LAWLER, 'Narrative in Social Research', in T. MAY (ed.), *Qualitative Research in Action* (London, 2002) 242-258.

[78]   M. BURY, 'Illness Narratives: Fact or Fiction?' 23 *Sociology of Health and Illness* (2001) 263-285.

for adopting a health and human rights approach. Third, core narratives will take account of the cultural and social context in which the CSOs work to overcome health inequalities. When developing the topic guides for the interviews, the different types of narrative will be given attention to ensure participants are prompted with the opportunity to voice all forms of narrative and therefore voice a wider and deeper account of their experiences of health and human rights approaches.

While focusing the in-depth interviews on eliciting particular types of narratives will assist in grappling with the complex discourse of health and human rights, it still requires participants to respond to the interviewer at a particular point in time with little opportunity of reflection. By using diaries, the participant is provided with the time to reflect on answers to open-ended question. If completed over several months, it is also a longitudinal record of phenomena as they unfold, rather than relying wholly on recall.[79,80] Furthermore, the use of diaries may support consciousness raising in participatory action research through the application of reflective practice. This may assist in overcoming the shortcomings in the previous studies of insufficient depth of data in terms of how health and human rights approaches are applied. The diaries of respondents can also be compared and contrasted to the researcher's diary to provide a further point of co-learning. The researcher diary will be largely based on participant observation and reflections on the research process. In participant observation the researcher immerses him/herself in the context and watches and listens rather than asks, allowing time for reflection.[81]

Interview transcripts and diaries rely on the spoken and written word. Photographs, video and participatory diagramming and visualisation challenge the written word and encourage interaction between all research participants. In addition, photographs and video captures a particular moment or event as well as providing context for phenomena being researched.[82] They may in particular capture the places for invoking rights (e.g. clinics, meeting rooms, pharmacies) and events (e.g. public demonstrations, meetings, signing of agreements).

Building on the above discussion of critical realism, a realist and ethnographic approach to analysis will be undertaken.[83,84] In keeping with the spiral of the research design, analysis will be iterative and on-going throughout the research.

---

[79]   ROBSON, *supra* n. 57.

[80]   A. BOWLING, *Research Methods in Health: Investigating Health and Health Services* (Buckingham, 1997).

[81]   ROBSON, *supra* n. 57.

[82]   C. HEATH and J. HINDMARSH, 'Analysing Interaction: Video, Ethnography and Situated Conduct', in T. MAY (ed.), *Qualitative Research in Action* (London, 2002) 99-121.

[83]   M.B. MILES and A.M. HUBERMAN, *Qualitative Data Analysis: A Sourcebook of New Methods* (Newbury Park, 1984).

[84]   M. HAMMERSLEY and P. ATKINSON, *Ethnography: Principles in Practice (2nd ed.)* (London, 1995).

Initial 'broad-brush' concepts will be generated from the initial reading of the date. Through multiple readings these concepts will be grouped into general categories and typologies and models developed. Meanings of concepts will be clarified and relationships explored as the analysis moves towards the generation of theories. Researchers will independently analyse a variety of data sources and compare categories and typologies to improve the quality of analysis through inter-rater reliability.

It has already been mentioned how the triangulation of data sources and methods will improve the validity of the study. The traditional criteria of quality research will be applied to the survey element of the study. External validity (establishing the domain to which a study's findings can be generalised), construct validity (establishing correct operational measures for the concepts being studied) and reliability (establishing that the operations of a study can be repeated, with the same results) will be monitored and reported on with regard to the survey. For the qualitative methods being used, the quality criteria of credibility (the extent to which the informants view the findings and conclusions of a study to be acceptable), transferability (the ability to transfer the methods and findings of a study in one context to another context), dependability (the researcher aims to take into account factors within the research design that may effect the findings of the research) and; confirmability (the extent to which the findings are evidenced and coherent) will be applied.[85] Such tests of rigour have been found to be particular relevant to participatory action research.[86]

The mixed methods increase validity. They also support the multi-disciplinary nature of the research by support different epistemologies. Of particular importance in this research design, the mixed methods support the flexibility needed in the design to respond to the learning objectives of the CSOs in the network following each workshop, while still answering the research questions.

7. CONCLUSIONS

The right to the highest attainable standard of health is a positive right placing obligations on states to protect, respect and fulfil rights to health services as well as the underlying determinants of health. A human rights approach, in conjunction with community engagement, can provide the structure and agency for promoting equity in health. The field of health and human rights research is relatively new and there has been insufficient attention paid to date on the methods used for studies in this field. A review of the literature shows that a range of quantitative and

---

[85]   Y. LINCOLN and E.G. GUBA, *Naturalistic Enquiry* (Beverly Hills, 1985).

[86]   M.J. MELROSE, 'Maximising the Rigor of Action Research: Why Would You Want To? How Could You?', 13 *Field Methods* (2001) 160-180.

qualitative methods are being used. In this paper, the focus has been on research exploring how CSOs use human rights approaches for advocacy and mobilisation in terms of overcoming health inequalities. Previous experience has shown the shortcomings of using purely qualitative research methods and in addition, failing to acknowledge the need for the consciousness of research participants to be raised. This is not done in a paternalistic way, but rather in a way that places equal value on the knowledge of all participants in the research process. A participatory research design using mixed methods has been proposed as a way to achieve quality, multi-disciplinary research concerned with the implementation of the right to health. Such an approach acknowledges power within research relationships. Furthermore, taking a critical and emancipatory approach provides a framework in which co-researchers and co-learners can act to transform structures and agency and at the same time meet the learning goals and research objectives of all participating in the research process. Drawing on theories of critical, emancipatory and participatory research it has been proposed that a spiral of co-learning may achieve the operational research called for by Paul Farmer.

TELLING TRUTH?
THE METHODOLOGICAL CHALLENGES
OF TRUTH COMMISSIONS

PAUL GREADY

1. INTRODUCTION

Research methods are a relatively recent concern of both human rights organizations and academics studying human rights. Many years ago, starting work with Amnesty International and then with other agencies, I was struck by the prevailing assumption that people would know how to do research and should just get on with it. Things have moved on, but not perhaps enough. For an enterprise requiring the manufacturing of legitimacy, it is surprising that research methods have received such little attention. How should we read reports that do not identify their author(s), contain little or no discussion of the methodology actually employed, and/or completely pass over power relations in this most power saturated research domain? In this contribution, I will focus on truth commissions, and particularly the Truth and Reconciliation Commission (TRC) in South Africa.[1] Truth commissions are suggestive because they raise a range of dilemmas common to all human rights reporting, as well as two additional teasers: 1) They are the largest scale human rights research projects ever undertaken and, therefore, pose challenges of scale and scope; 2) Such commissions are quintessentially hybrid institutions (human rights-based but also profoundly political; using qualitative and quantitative methodologies; with one foot in the academy and another in practice; spanning various disciplines) and so raise questions about coherence that are increasingly also facing mainstream human rights research.

What, for starters, is an official truth commission? It is possible to distil the core characteristics of these bodies down to 1) a focus on the past; 2) their origins at the point of transition away from war or authoritarian rule; 3) the investigation of patterns of abuses and specific violations committed over a period of time, rather than a single event; 4) a focus on violations of human rights, and sometimes of

---

[1]   The analysis provided here draws on work done for a forthcoming book, *Aftermaths: Truth, Justice and Reconciliation in Post-Apartheid South Africa*.

humanitarian norms as well; 5) a temporary, short-term life span, usually culminating in the production of a report with recommendations; 6) official status, as commissions are sanctioned, authorized, or empowered by the state (and sometimes by armed opposition groups, in the context of a peace accord); and 7) a victim-centred approach.[2]

We can already begin to see that the scope of truth telling is both contained and ambitious. The Promotion of National Unity and Reconciliation Act (No 34 of 1995) outlined the truth-objectives of the TRC in the following terms in Section 3 (1) (a):

> [to establish] as complete a picture as possible of the causes, nature and extent of the gross violations of human rights which were committed during the period from 1 March 1960 to the cut-off date, including the antecedents, circumstances, factors and context of such violations, as well as the motives and perspectives of the victims and of the persons responsible for the commission of the violations, by instituting investigations and holding hearings.

The mandate required a focus on individual victims and perpetrators as well as broader patterns, and on facts informed by understanding and interpretation (motives, perspectives, antecedents, causes and context).

In what follows, I address three issues of importance to truth commissions and human rights practitioner research more generally. Two are dealt with quite briefly – the relationship between concepts and methods on the one hand and qualitative and quantitative methods on the other – while the notion of hybridity is lingered over because, on a canvas that is inclusive of its two precursors, it raises methodological challenges but also suggests possible solutions. An entry-point to hybridity is provided by a discussion of truth as genre, with truth commission reports characterised as state inquiries, human rights reports and official histories.

2. CONCEPTS AND METHODS

My research on the TRC started out as an inquiry into the keywords of transition (truth, justice, reconciliation) as the main body of the TRC's work came to a close in 1998. The TRC was the first truth commission to make a significant contribution to understandings of these terms, but its conceptual insights were post-hoc rationalizations for a politically informed mandate and working methods often devised on the hoof.[3] To provide just one conceptual example, the Commission's

---

[2]   P. HAYNER, *Unspeakable Truths: Facing the Challenge of Truth Commissions* (New York, 2002) 14-23; J. QUINN AND M. FREEMAN, 'Lessons Learned: Practical Lessons Gleaned from Inside the Truth Commissions of Guatemala and South Africa', 25 *Human Rights Quarterly* (2003) 1117-1149 at 1119.

[3]   There are any number of comments to the effect that the TRC methodology was to a significant degree made up as it went along - for example, the changing definitions of what constituted a gross

four-fold categorization of truth – factual or forensic truth (objective, corroborated evidence with regard to individuals, patterns and causes), personal and narrative truth (subjective, experiential story telling to restore dignity), social or 'dialogue' truth (affirmative processes of inclusive participation, transparency and public debate), and healing and restorative truth (emphasizing the context of human relationships and acknowledgement)[4] – was not coherently reflected in its work and report. The conceptual schema arose out of the hearings and research rather than informing them. Put simply, this is bad social science. The lesson is: consider your objectives, define your keywords, then design your methods and institutional scaffolding accordingly. That said, this four-fold categorization does provide a useful starting point for discussions about what is meant by truth in transitional contexts.

A more recent development in transitional justice discourse is also problematic methodologically. There is now a growing tendency to adopt holistic understandings of the problems faced and solutions required. Firstly, it is common practice now to define transitional justice extremely broadly, to include some or all of the following: prosecutions, reparations, commemorative practices, truth-seeking, institutional reform, vetting and dismissals, educational reform, reconciliation initiatives, and more. Such definitions usefully move beyond legal responses to include wider political and social processes, and can serve to integrate official, top-down mechanisms and unofficial, bottom up, community or grassroots initiatives. Secondly, keywords are also viewed through the holistic prism.[5] Thirdly, in a shift from substitution to complementarity, interventions are seen in both/and more, rather than either/or, terms. Whilst in the past it was often assumed that truth commissions would take place where trials could not now it is argued that the two can, and should, coexist.[6] One influential framing of holism is the 'ecology model' of social reconstruction, which emerged from the Human Rights Center at the University of California Berkeley.[7] This approach suggests interventions at multiple

---

violation of human rights or who was a victim (L. BUUR, '"In the Name of the Victims": the Politics of Compensation in the Work of the South African Truth and Reconciliation Commission', in P. GREADY (ed.), *Political Transition: Politics and Cultures* (London, 2003) 148-164, at 151-153; L. BUUR, 'The South African Truth and Reconciliation Commission: A Technique of Nation-State Formation', in T. HANSEN and F. STEPPUTAT (eds.), *States of Imagination: Ethnographic Explorations of the Postcolonial State* (Durham, 2001) 149-181, at 166-167). Lessons-learning processes mean there is less reason now for truth commissions to falter in this way, or at least to quite this extent.

4 TRUTH AND RECONCILIATION COMMISSION, *Truth and Reconciliation Commission of South Africa Report, Vol. 1* (Cape Town, 1998) 110-114.

5 For a critique of the excessive claims made in truth's name, see D. MENDELOFF, 'Truth-Seeking, Truth-Telling, and Postconflict Peacebuilding: Curb the Enthusiasm?' 6 *International Studies Review* (2004) 355-380.

6 N. ROHT-ARRIAZA and J. MARIEZCURRENA (eds.), *Transitional Justice in the Twenty First Century: Beyond Truth Versus Justice* (Cambridge, 2006).

7 E. STOVER and H. WEINSTEIN (ed.), *My Neighbor, My Enemy: Justice and Community in the Aftermath of Mass Atrocity* (Cambridge, 2004); L. FLETCHER and H. WEINSTEIN, 'Violence and

levels of society – state, community, individual – and spanning fields as diverse as the rule of law and justice, security, education for democracy, economic development, and reconciliation. Here we begin to see the advantages and some of the pitfalls of holism.

That trade offs are not always inherent and more than one intervention can be required in circumstances where none standing alone would succeed, are useful ways of reshuffling the transitional justice pack. Yet, transitional justice is the art of imperfect solutions and difficult choices in the context of competition for finite resources and delicate political dynamics. While we now know more about what should be done, we know relatively little about how these objectives might be achieved. How should interventions be prioritized so that they are sequenced rather than permanently traded off against one another? Bosire, for example, in a piece with the suggestive title 'Overpromised, Underdelivered: Transitional Justice in Sub-Saharan Africa', argues that strengthening state institutions should be seen as a precondition or entry-point for successful transitional justice measures in this part of the world.[8] Without functioning institutions little will be achieved. In transitional justice circles this domain is normally consigned to the wish-list of potential outcomes (via truth commission recommendations, for example), rather than being seen as a necessary enabling environment.

To this reservation I would add another: Should transitional justice be taking on more when it is far from clear that it can successfully achieve its original, far more modest, remits (truth, justice)? Holism is characteristic of the expansionary phase of transitional justice in that while it is not unreflective, its criticisms are of the 'more work' variety. In other words they anticipate transitional justice doing more not less. As such, holism is both a reaction to past shortcomings, and runs the risk of reproducing them on a broader canvas. Keyword conceptualization, for example, remains weak. While it is important to interrogate linkages between keywords, many analyses slide into a mire where truth entails pretty much everything, and justice does too. Any methodology would struggle to deliver on this ambition. It is a sleight of hand to overcome what were previously seen as tensions – truth versus justice, peace versus justice – by defining the terms indistinguishably.

A coherent conceptualisation of truth needs to be found somewhere between no conceptualisation at all and a holistic understanding of the term that renders it virtually meaningless. The TRC's four-fold categorisation is one place to start. Clearly, it is also necessary to decide what work truth is being required to do, its desired outcomes, to a greater degree of specificity and to link these desired outcomes cogently to research methods and institutional designs. The latter two will

---

Social Repair: Rethinking the Contribution of Justice to Reconciliation', 24 *Human Rights Quarterly* (2002) 573-639.

[8]   L. K. BOSIRE, 'Overpromised, Underdelivered: Transitional Justice in Sub-Saharan Africa', 5 *Sur – International Journal on Human Rights* (2006) 71-107.

vary, for example, depending on which of the following, in isolation or combination, is prioritised: *truth as acknowledgement, truth as apology, truth as justice, naming names, patterns vs. individuals, exchanging amnesty for truth, truth and reconciliation.* In conclusion, methods should be determined by truth objectives and not vice-versa.

3. QUALITATIVE AND QUANTITATIVE METHODS

Non-governmental human rights research and reporting are archetypally about the individual and qualitative in nature. This can be framed in a variety of ways – Richard Rorty has argued that the emergence of the human rights culture owes 'everything to hearing sad and sentimental stories', for example,[9] while Stephen Hopgood's depiction of Amnesty International as internally divided, with 'keepers of the flame' pitted against 'reformers', is predicated in part on their preference for research and campaigning based on individuals/countries on the one hand and thematic issues on the other.[10] Yet for truth commissions, the privileging of individual stories can clash with an emphasis on investigating patterns of abuse (*patterns vs. individuals*). It is the highlighting of patterns, providing an authoritative account of the abuses of a particular era or regime (also called the 'global' truth), that is widely seen as a key role of truth commissions, and one that sets commissions apart from trials. What level of analysis should prevail?

An article by Chapman and Ball raises very clearly some of the dilemmas introduced by a focus on patterns. They state: 'it is our view that truth commissions are far better suited to pursue what we have termed "macro-truth", the assessment of contexts, causes, and patterns of human rights violations, than "micro-truth" dealing with the specifics of particular events, cases, and people'.[11] The authors are critical of the TRC for focusing too much on the latter and too little on the former. They, and others, applaud the Guatemalan Commission for Historical Clarification (CEH) for its greater success at establishing macro-truths. A number of claims are made by Chapman and Ball to support this argument: it is the big picture that is often most incomplete and victims also want systemic truths; commissions are not particularly good at investigating individual cases; micro-truths should mainly be left to the courts; commissions should prioritize the objective over the subjective dimensions of truth, outcomes (reports) over process (hearings); and responsibility should be attributed at the macro-level too, focusing on institutions, parties, structures,

---

[9]   R. RORTY, 'Human Rights, Rationality, and Sentimentality', in S. SHUTE and S. HURLEY (eds.), *On Human Rights: The Oxford Amnesty Lectures 1993* (New York, 1993) 112-134, at 118-119.

[10]   S. HOPGOOD, *Keepers of the Flame: Understanding Amnesty International* (Ithaca, 2006).

[11]   A. CHAPMAN and P. BALL, 'The Truth of Truth Commissions: Comparative Lessons from Haiti, South Africa, and Guatemala', 23 *Human Rights Quarterly* (2001) 1-43 at 41.

ideologies and patterns of abuse, and only secondarily on individuals and particular cases.[12]

It is the case, as the TRC illustrated, that truth commissions are ill-equipped to investigate potentially thousands of individual victim/survivor or perpetrator cases. The TRC's investigation unit, for example, predominantly provided corroboration rather than new information for victims/survivors. Pigou states that probably over 90% of people who appeared before the TRC did not receive meaningful new information about their cases.[13] This was not simply a resource question though: greater priority was given, ultimately, to making perpetrator findings and to the amnesty process.

The focus on patterns of abuse clearly matters, but it is also important to be honest about what a privileging of patterns means. To leave individual cases to the courts means that for the overwhelming majority nothing further will happen. To conclude, after outlining the framework detailed above, that findings should be 'victim-centered, telling the story from their point of view and validating their experiences' is somewhat disingenuous.[14] Many victims/survivors want information about or acknowledgement of their particular experiences; their truths are particular truths. Others yearn to get beyond 'bad apple' exculpations to situate their experiences within broader policies of abuse. Both levels of analysis, in short, are vital. The methodological challenge is how to integrate, whilst giving appropriate attention to, individual experiences *and* broader patterns. If reports may well in the main have to resort to illustrative or representative examples – 'window cases' in the TRC's jargon – to highlight patterns or important events, ways can also be found to name names, and summarize and acknowledge each and every individual victim/survivor story.[15]

---

[12]   CHAPMAN and BALL, *supra* n. 11, 41-43.
[13]   P. PIGOU, 'False Promises and Wasted Opportunities? Inside South Africa's Truth and Reconciliation Commission', in D. POSEL and G. SIMPSON (eds.), *Commissioning the Past: Understanding South Africa's Truth and Reconciliation Commission* (Johannesburg, 2002) 37-65, at 37.
[14]   CHAPMAN and BALL, *supra* n. 11, 43.
[15]   TRUTH AND RECONCILIATION COMMISSION, *Truth and Reconciliation Commission of South Africa Report. Vol. 7* (Cape Town, 2002). Naming names, of both perpetrators and victims, can be an important truth commission activity (P. HAYNER, *supra* n. 2, 107-132). Truth commissions have adopted different, and often highly contested policies, on naming perpetrators, with some choosing to name (El Salvador, South Africa, Sierra Leone) but the majority not. The issue raises questions of profound methodological importance about what kind of procedures and methodologies truth commissions should employ. Naming, in short, entails a balancing of, if not necessarily an equivalence between, victim/survivor and perpetrator rights. Before leaving the issue of naming one final, often overlooked point is crucial. That is the importance of naming both perpetrators *and* victims/survivors (as a form of acknowledgement) in human rights work, where information and security concerns allow. While neither form of naming is done widely or consistently, as Bronkhorst notes, the potential implications of rectifying this situation are significant:. Names can remake the world for individuals. If human rights organisations produce extensive or exhaustive

A particular quantitative research methodology is increasingly influential in the work of truth commissions. Much less work is being done on how imaginatively to use qualitative methods in large-scale human rights projects or how to integrate a range of methodologies. The quantitative agenda has been driven by the American Association for the Advancement of Science (AAAS), which has helped to design information management and database systems for a number of commissions, including those in El Salvador, Haiti, South Africa, Guatemala, Peru, Sierra Leone and Timor Leste.[16] This 'who did what to whom' methodology has its strengths, particularly when multiple data sources can be cross-referenced to overcome the limitation of unrepresentative, convenience samples. It can identify, sometimes hitherto unknown, patterns of violence and challenge prevailing myths about past violence.

But this methodology is complex and resource intensive, essentially descriptive, and thin on context and as an interpretive and explanatory tool. For example, it may produce but not explain paradoxical findings. An over-reliance on such methods also constitutes report 'fetishization' writ large[17] – more on this anon. In much of the writing about such methodologies the 'human' is sadly absent from discussions of human rights. In South Africa, there were criticisms from those orchestrating the information management system that the TRC, including its research staff, did not use the database effectively and to the full, while commission staff criticized the accessibility and utility of the methodology and database. Interestingly, and perhaps in recognition of its shortcomings, the TRC report in its recommendations called for more quantitative analysis of the data it had amassed.[18]

While qualitative methods can provide a more effective entry point to interpretation and understanding, Fiona Ross highlights a weakness in the TRC's deployment of qualitative data.[19] Ross details how the TRC circumscribed and

---

lists of victims for each situation, they stress the principle that each individual victim is a life as valuable as that of any other person. In naming the names of perpetrators, they render individuals accountable for crimes committed, instead of sketching only the more elusive patterns of violations. D. BRONKHORST, 'Naming Names: Identity and Identification in Human Rights Work', 16 *Netherlands Quarterly of Human Rights* (1998) 457-474 at 472.

[16] P. BALL, H. SPIRER and L. SPIRER (eds.), *Making the Case: Investigating Large Scale Human Rights Violations Using Information Systems and Data Analysis* (Washington DC, 2000); A. CHAPMAN and P. BALL, *supra* n. 11; T. LANDMAN, *Studying Human Rights* (London, 2006) 107-125; TRUTH AND RECONCILIATION COMMISSION, *supra* n. 4, 140-145, 158-164, 322-325.

[17] S. COHEN, *Denial and Acknowledgement: The Impact of Information About Human Rights Violations* (Jerusalem, 1995).

[18] TRUTH AND RECONCILIATION COMMISSION, *Truth and Reconciliation Commission of South Africa Report*, Vol. 5 (Cape Town, 1998) 312.

[19] F. ROSS, *Bearing Witness: Women and the Truth and Reconciliation Commission in South Africa* (London, 2003a), and F. ROSS, 'The Construction of Voice and Identity in the South African Truth and Reconciliation Commission', in P. GREADY (ed.), *Political Transition: Politics and Cultures* (London, 2003b) 165-180.

misrepresented the lives and concerns of women. She argues, for example, that the emergence of 'women' as a category in the Commission's work carried with it assumptions about the nature and severity of particular harms, notably privileging sexual violence while silencing other kinds of experience:

> diverse identities, activities and experiences were obscured through the emphasis on sexual difference and harm. The result is an overemphasis on the similarity of bodily experience at the expense of an understanding of the subjectivities produced through apartheid and resistance to it.[20]

The experience of Yvonne Khutwane, a veteran political activist for the ANC, exemplifies these patterns, demonstrating 'the elicitation, condensation and crystallisation of testimonies in circulation'.[21] Khutwane was the first woman to include a description of sexual violation in her public testimony. During her testimony at the victim hearings in Worcester in the Western Cape during June 1996 she spoke about her experience of abuse, including solitary confinement, torture, sexual molestation, and the petrol bombing of her house and alienation from her political community due to rumours that she was an informer. Sexual violation in the form narrated at the hearing was not part of Khutwane's written statement (in which a threat of rape was mentioned not actual sexual molestation). Despite her reticence at the hearing, the new revelations were both solicited and returned to by the persistent interventions of HRV Committee member and psychologist, Pumla Gobodo-Madikizela.[22] In the end, one third of the time was taken up by questions and answers about an event of sexual violation that Khutwane seemingly had not intended to narrate. In this collaborative testimonial narration, subsequent media coverage, the TRC report (in four separate entries) and academic studies, sexual violence is represented as the primary violation. The narrative Khutwane wanted to tell is thus displaced; certain kinds of violence and her political activism are downplayed as she is reduced to a victim of sexual abuse. This is a failure of methodology, among other things.

More research is required on qualitative *and* quantitative methodologies in human rights research, *and* on ways of integrating the two. Choices need to be informed by foundational questions about what conceptual understandings are being privileged and whose interests are being served. For example, if truth commissions are victim-centred, what is it that victims actually want from truth? We can already begin to see with regard to methodology that hybridity is both the problem and,

---

[20]   ROSS, *supra* n. 19, 2003b, 175.
[21]   ROSS, *supra* n. 19, 2003a, 93.
[22]   Also see P. GOBODO-MADIKIZELA, *A Human Being Died that Night: A Story of Forgiveness* (Cape Town, 2003) 90-94.

necessarily, needs to be part of the solution. What might a coherent hybridity look like?

4. TRUTH AS GENRE

The truth commission report is a new genre of document in human rights and transitional politics, 'a new or incipient genre on the world scene'.[23] The truth established by such official commissions is forged in the coming together of three tributary genres: the state inquiry, the human rights report and the official history. Truth as genre provides a means of acknowledging and interrogating truth commission work across diverse methods, objectives and interests. Many of the strengths and weaknesses of truth commissions can be traced to the fact that they constitute an imperfectly realized hybrid genre. Genre confusion needs to be more rigorously understood before confusion can become coherence.

If we identify, with Bhatia, reporting genres as an example of a 'genre colony', the communicative purpose of which is 'reporting on events', the state inquiry, human rights report and official history can all be placed within such a colony.[24] More interesting is the idea that part of colony formation is colonization and 'a process whereby generic resources are exploited and appropriated to create hybrid' forms.[25] Thus, notwithstanding hybridity, certain methodologies and discourses come to the fore. The truth commission report is such a hybrid genre – drawing on a legal, human rights-based mandate; the organizational culture and powers of a state inquiry; a cross-cutting set of research methodologies; a diverse skill and personnel base (by disciplinary background, professional experience, ideological persuasion); and subject to often competing expectations (that it will identify human rights perpetrators and map related violations, legitimize the new state/government, write a revisionist national, official history). How did these dynamics play out within the TRC?

The TRC was a state inquiry in the sense that it was established by the state, or more precisely by parliament and its enactment of the Promotion of National Unity and Reconciliation Act (No 34 of 1995), which bestowed upon the Commission its mandate and powers. The State President appointed the commissioners in consultation with the cabinet of a Government of National Unity, which included the National Party and Inkatha Freedom Party (IFP), following an extensive public

---

[23] J. TAYLOR, 'Body Memories: Aide-Memoires and Collective Amnesia in the Wake of the Argentine Terror', in M. RYAN and A. GORDON (eds.), *Body Politics: Disease, Desire, and the Family* (Boulder, Colorado, 1994) 192-203, at 201.

[24] V. BHATIA, Worlds of Written Discourse: A Genre-Based View (London, 2004) 57-59, 81-82.

[25] BHATIA, *supra* n. 24, 58.

nomination and selection process.[26] The TRC also enjoyed considerable powers (for example, to subpoena witnesses, and of search and seizure). In the academic literature, state inquiries are normally understood to perform a range of political functions.[27] The primary function and desired legacy is that of legitimacy, and specifically enhanced state legitimacy. In times of crisis, controversy and change, in which they are themselves usually complicit, states turn to such inquiries to educate the populace, frame public discourse and official policy, and to provide closure and signal a break from the past. Periods of turmoil can be assuaged by the inquiry function of social repair. But alongside these anticipated and desired functions, such inquiries can take on a life of their own and rub against the grain of expectation. The TRC's even-handedness enshrined and tried to operationalize the ANC's ethos of speaking truth to reconciliation, but was also ultimately more critical of the ANC's past conduct than the latter anticipated or was prepared to accept.

The TRC was tasked with writing a human rights report in the sense that gross human rights violations were the lens through which it viewed and represented the past. Its report has been described as 'one of the most important and influential human rights documents of our time'.[28] A new role for human rights forged through an alliance between truth and power is understandably an intoxicating prospect for those in the human rights community. Through truth commissions, such unrivalled research opportunities and their reports, can have, or appear to have, the ear of the state.

Human rights organizations, like state inquiries, are deeply dependent on the manufacturing of legitimacy. Organization-specific factors such as reputation and mandate are important in this regard. But more important for this analysis are the features common to all human rights actors. While one cross-cutting source of legitimacy – objectivity and impartiality – allies their work with that of state inquiries, not least in relation to the methods employed, the other marks a departure: human rights activists seek to legitimize both their own activities and to legitimize or delegitimize state and sometimes non-state practice with reference to international human rights law. This marks a parting of the ways with state inquiries – which although embedded in a legal framework, are more likely to use the law to protect the state – as rather than speaking truth mainly through power it often also demands the more strident function of speaking truth to power. In short, human rights organizations work with a similar methodological legitimacy regime as state

---

[26]   Internationally, truth commissions have often been established by presidential decree (Chile, Argentina) or as part of peace agreements (El Salvador, Guatemala, Sierra Leone).

[27]   G. GILLIGAN and J. PRATT (eds.), *Crime, Truth and Justice: Official Inquiry, Discourse, Knowledge* (Cullompton, Devon, 2004).

[28]   R. DUDAI, '"Can You Describe This?" Human Rights Reports and What They Tell Us About the Human Rights Movement', in R. WILSON and R. BROWN (eds.), *Humanitarianism and Suffering: The Mobilization of Empathy* (Cambridge, forthcoming).

inquiries, but in this case truth-as-objectivity usually serves a different interpretive function.

There is no agreement among commentators as to whether the TRC report is a form of official history. Among those who present and analyze it as an historical text, Bundy states that '[i]t goes without saying that the TRC was charged with writing an official history'.[29] The TRC itself, and its staff, were generally more cautious.[30] The Director of Research at the TRC, Villa-Vicencio, states, 'I think [Bundy] is wrong in suggesting that the Commission was charged with "writing an official history"', preferring the phraseology of a 'historical comment' and 'the first stages of historical narrative'.[31] In part, this difference of opinion arises because, as we have seen, the TRC was mandated to go beyond lists of facts and litanies of abuses to address what are interpretive and historical questions – to establish 'as complete a picture as possible' and to address the antecedents, causes and context of gross violations of human rights – without specifically being asked to write 'a history'.

An official history is a state-sanctioned history. Such histories, like state inquiries, are officially legitimized and also have a legitimizing function, in the TRC's case sanctioning the discourse of speaking truth to reconciliation. Leman-Langlois and Shearing talk of '[a] history that is at once not a history – it repairs rather than establishes a past'.[32] Why, beyond the need for legitimation, is an official history needed during periods of political transition? The writing of such a history is in itself righting a past wrong, 'setting the record straight', by writing a revised official history to replace its distorted and divisive counterpart from, in this case, the apartheid era. An official history can also serve the related function of 'drawing a line under the past', establishing the essential difference between the past and present. Du Toit contrasts historians' concerns with the past with the objective of truth commissions to establish a new moral and political order: 'If truth commissions are backward-looking, they are so precisely as historical founding projects; they deal with the past not for its own sake but in order to clear the way for a new

---

29   C. BUNDY, 'The Beast of the Past: History and the TRC', in W. JAMES and L. VAN DE VIJVER (eds.), *After the TRC: Reflections on Truth and Reconciliation in South Africa* (Cape Town, 2000) 9-20, at 13.

30   See, for example, the TRUTH AND RECONCILIATION COMMISSION, *supra* n. 18, 257.

31   C. VILLA-VICENCIO, 'On the Limitations of Academic History: The Quest for Truth Demands Both More and Less', in W. JAMES & L. VAN DE VIJVER (eds.), *After the TRC: Reflections on Truth and Reconciliation in South Africa* (Cape Town, 2000) 21-31, at 22, 25.

32   S. LEMAN-LANGLOIS and C. SHEARING, 'Repairing the Future: The South African Truth and Reconciliation Commission at Work', in G. GILLIGAN & J. PRATT (eds.), *Crime, Truth and Justice: Official Inquiry, Discourse, Knowledge* (Cullompton, Devon, 2004) 222-242, at 228-231, 239.

beginning'.[33] Addressing civil-political abuses that could be consigned to the past rather than economic-social issues that could not, is a clear example of this function. Also, in South Africa, constructing a more inclusive, consensual narrative history to further national unity was seen as one dimension of speaking truth to reconciliation. This involved writing an official history based on the stories of the previously voiceless and an attempt to include all relevant political parties. Rewriting the past was predicted on new patterns of inclusion, and new kinds of relationship with the benign state. This is part of a broader trend in history-writing, in which the victorious and elite have made way for the marginalized: 'Over the last two generations the writing of history has shifted focus from the history of perpetrators to the history of victims'.[34] Official histories, in short, rewrite the past, draw a line under the past, create a moral community/nation, and provide a foundation for the future.

In what follows three questions are addressed as a means of interrogating the methodological implications of hybridity. Firstly, to what extent did the TRC suggest ways of securing legitimacy *and* enhanced impacts beyond report 'fetishization'? Secondly, how did it negotiate the tensions between speaking truth both with and to power? And, thirdly, to what extent do historical methods provide a solution to the challenges faced by the prevailing methods employed by truth commissions?

5. LEGITIMACY AND IMPACTS BEYOND REPORT 'FETISHIZATION'

Political interests, ideologies and judgments, including the author's own, are always part of the human rights report writing process.[35] In an attempt to distance itself from this reality 'the whole enterprise of reporting has generated its own styles of talking and working',[36] with established methodologies of data collection and processing, corroboration techniques, and report writing styles and formats. Dudai memorably describes the interpretive repertoire of fact-finding with legal analysis as 'advocacy with footnotes'.[37] Objectivity and impartiality are secured, therefore,

---

[33]   A. DU TOIT, 'The Moral Foundations of the South African TRC: Truth as Acknowledgement and Justice as Recognition', in R. ROTBERG and D. THOMPSON (eds.), *Truth v. Justice: The Morality of Truth Commissions* (Princeton, 2000) 122-140, at 125.

[34]   E. BARKAN, *The Guilt of Nations: Restitution and Negotiating Historical Injustice* (Baltimore, 2000) 34.

[35]   T. FARER, 'Looking at Looking at Nicaragua: The Problematique of Impartiality in Human Rights Inquiries', 10 *Human Rights Quarterly* (1998) 141-156.

[36]   COHEN, *supra* n. 17, 9.

[37]   R. DUDAI, 'Advocacy with Footnotes: The Human Rights Report as a Literary Genre', 28 *Human Rights Quarterly* (2006) 783-795; also see DUDAI, *supra* n. 28.

through rigorous methodologies, stylistic and structural features, and reference to legal standards.

The methodological scaffolding of the state inquiry and human rights report, although not formalized, makes use of a virtually identical set of sources and strategies. Information gathering is based on interviews/testimony, on-site visits and written documentation – and data can come from such sources as victims and survivors, witnesses and their families, government or security force officials, and laws, legal judgments and court or medical records. Reliability and corroboration are secured through the use and evaluation of direct testimony, careful questioning and cross-checking (with other sources, identifiable injuries, location descriptions).[38] The TRC used a system of 'corroborative pointers', and the balance of probabilities as its standard of proof.[39] There are also similarities of presentation and rhetorical style in the reports themselves. These include the use of collaborative, impersonal authorship; an emphasis on facts ('speaking for themselves') over interpretation; measured language and a transparent acknowledgement of sources; a lack of reflection on methodology, researcher subject position and research context; a legal discourse that deliberately speaks the language of the state and of power; and standardized report structures. But this truth infrastructure is not unchallenged and does not necessarily translate into impact.

Reporting is the main activity of many human rights organizations, and it is both an end in itself and a means to implementation and compliance. Cohen, however, critiques a 'fetishization' of the report by human rights NGOs as an end in itself, a focus on the report writing process accompanied by a comparative neglect of the report's wider impacts.[40] NGOs give too little attention to dissemination and how their information is communicated to and received by the public beyond the human rights community. Resulting problems, which resonate clearly with the TRC and truth commissions or state inquiries more generally, span an excessive faith in the power of transforming ignorance into knowledge rather than examining how knowledge is acknowledged and acted upon; and poor or non-existent evaluation.

There is a very strong element of report 'fetishization' in the work of truth commissions and accompanying academic analysis. 'The document becomes an end in itself, an absolute value, a magical notion indeed. What is the magical role assigned here to public memory as a guarantee that what we remember will never

---

38   H. THOOLEN and B. VERSTAPPEN, *Human Rights Missions: A Study of the Fact-Finding Practice of Non-Governmental Organizations* (Dordrecht, 1986); D. WEISSBRODT and J. McCARTHY, 'Fact-Finding by NonGovernmental Organizations', in B. RAMCHARAN (ed.), *International Law and Fact-Finding in the Field of Human Rights* (The Hague, 1982) 186-230.

39   TRUTH AND RECONCILIATION COMMISSION, *supra* n. 4, 91-92, 139, 142-143, 164; TRUTH AND RECONCILIATION COMMISSION, *supra* n. 18, 208.

40   COHEN, *supra* n. 17.

again occur?"[41] To provide just one example of report 'fetishization', the Sierra Leone TRC spent 'considerably more time' writing up its report than on the operational phase of its activities. This was in part due to over-ambition. Schabas continues: 'It was decided that the report should be several volumes in length, perhaps so as to match that of the South African Commission. A shorter and more succinct report would have been far more accessible to Sierra Leoneans, and yet could have covered all of the essentials'.[42] Even beyond countries with widespread illiteracy, such practices beg the question: Who reads truth commission reports?

The short answer is that we do not know. The TRC report consists of five weighty volumes, complemented by two equally voluminous stragglers, one to mark the completion of the amnesty process ('the codicil' - 2003) while the final member of the family contained the comprehensive list of victims (2002).[43] A scattergun approach to the publishing, over a five-year period, is hardly ideal in terms of optimizing impacts; neither is the high price charged for the hardback editions. Allocation of the publishing contract to a private publisher inevitably meant that the report is expensive and the full text was only available on the internet for a limited period. It has not been widely read, beyond a small set of transitional justice groupies like me.[44]

Truth commission reports have been best sellers – for example a shorter version of the report of Argentina's National Commission on the Disappeared (CONADEP), *Nunca Más (Never Again)* – when, following a research process behind closed doors, they represent a dramatic act of first disclosure. And truth commissions have disseminated and adapted their often very long reports (12 volumes in Guatemala, 9 in Peru) for different audiences and to be more media-friendly. Moderate pricing, publication of a summary of some kind (for the general public; for children and schools), translation of certain products into relevant languages, press supplements

---

[41]   TAYLOR, *supra* n. 23, 196.

[42]   W. SCHABAS, 'The Sierra Leone Truth and Reconciliation Commission', in N. ROHT-ARRIAZA and J. MARIEZCURRENA (eds.), *Transitional Justice in the Twenty First Century: Beyond Truth Versus Justice* (Cambridge, 2006) 21-42, at 27.

[43]   TRUTH AND RECONCILIATION COMMISSION, *Truth and Reconciliation Commission of South Africa Report,* Vols. *1-5* (Cape Town, 1998); TRUTH AND RECONCILIATION COMMISSION, *Truth and Reconciliation Commission of South Africa Report,* Vol. 6 (Cape Town, 2003); TRUTH AND RECONCILIATION COMMISSION, *supra* n. 15.

[44]   Based on January 2008 figures obtained from the South African publishers of the report, Juta and Company Ltd. Publishers, domestic sales figures were as follows: +2,400 copies of Volumes 1-5 as a set; +37 copies of Volumes 1-7 as a set; +800 copies of Volume 6; and +281 copies of Volume 7. The very small sales figures for Volume 7 are particularly striking given its potential role in acknowledging victims and survivors. As a point of comparison, Random House, the publisher of Antjie Krog's *Country of My Skull,* perhaps the best known book about the TRC, reported that by the end of 2007 17,000 copies of the book had been sold, with the bulk of these sales having been within South Africa. Both sets of sales figures were obtained via personal communications with the publishers.

or serialization, accompanying television broadcasts, internet access, a CD-ROM or video version, a photographic record, free distribution of relevant products to libraries, schools and universities, and copies sent to each named victim's family, are among the strategies that have been used. In South Africa, dissemination of the TRC's report has been inadequate. Successes (press supplements and coverage at the time of the report's publication) are outweighed by the failures (a popular summary and school version of the summary, both in all 11 official languages, have yet to see the light of day). The TRC made recommendations designed to increase access to its reports that are as yet unimplemented by the government.[45] Nevertheless, a broader claim remains valid: truth commissions have explored a range of representational forms and are at the forefront of efforts to combine such diversity with objectivity and legitimacy in human rights work.[46]

At this juncture it is important to cite two important differences between conventional human rights reports and state inquiries. Firstly, while human rights reports generally have a short life-cycle – they make an impact immediately or not at all – state inquiries and truth commission reports, and indeed the archives they generate, as state-sanctioned enterprises have greater potential to enter into a dialogue with history and seep into institutionalized pores of influence. They can feed into memorial practice, educational curricula, cultural production and ongoing academic debate. Secondly, and also moving beyond report 'fetishization', public hearings are rarely used in human rights investigations but are a common feature of state inquiries, and increasingly constitute a key component of truth commission activities. Such hearings were absolutely central to the impacts of the TRC.

The reality is that the testimony of a single victim relayed to the country by the media will ultimately have had more of an impact upon the national consciousness than any number of volumes of the report. The enduring memory of the Commission will be the images of pain, grief and regret conveyed relentlessly, week after week, month after month, to a public that generally remained spellbound by what it was witnessing. For other truth commissions, their final reports may have represented the crowning achievement of their work. We feel that our report takes its place humbly in a wider range of achievements, and should not be the only or final measure of the Commission's success.[47]

---

[45] TRUTH AND RECONCILIATION COMMISSION, *supra* n. 18, 312; TRUTH AND RECONCILIATION COMMISSION, *supra* n. 43, Vol. 6, 732.

[46] Cohen, in the context of his interest in how human rights reports impact on the general public, illustrates that campaigns and appeals supplement reports with a wide variety of other documentation, and that these materials are often characterized by less contextual information but greater subjectivity and personalisation (*supra* n. 17, 110, 140-3). Thus, human rights organizations also often speak through a range of discourses and genres.

[47] J. CHERRY, J. DANIEL and M. FULLARD, 'Researching the "Truth": A View from Inside the Truth and Reconciliation Commission', in D. POSEL and G. SIMPSON (eds.), *Commissioning the Past:*

The TRC was in fact one of the first truth commission to hold public hearings. Security concerns can render such hearings impractical, but one of the TRC's impacts on international transitional justice has been to render them part of mainstream truth commission work. It was the Human Rights Violations hearings in particular, alongside public amnesty and sector hearings (for institutions and social groups), and their coverage in the media, that spread the work and word of the TRC beyond an elite group of government officials and human rights activists. The hearings were the media and public awareness short term 'bit hit', while the report's, hopefully complementary, impacts will only become clear in the much longer term.

This discussion highlights the need to be aware of the uncomfortable fact that both human rights reports and state inquiries, although they may spur debate, shine a spotlight on priorities for advocacy and change, provide a reference point for public mobilization and have unanticipated longer-term impacts, often change very little. Extraordinarily '[t]o date, there has been no thorough review of how many of the hundreds of recommendations by truth commissions have been put in place'; less surprisingly: 'It is clear, however, that the record of implementation of truth commission recommendations has been among the weakest aspects of these commissions to date'.[48]

And yet a prognosis of unread reports and unimplemented recommendations is too bleak. The TRC has left a legacy of both intended and unintended effects. Its most interesting contribution to the legitimacy beyond report 'fetishization' debate is the four-fold truth classification it provides. After this reflective moment, the TRC's report largely proceeds in conventional factual truth mode, but the truth – gloriously! – was already out of the bag; or perhaps one should say liberated from the report. Critiques of the truth categorization have been scathing. Posel writes: 'This is a very wobbly, poorly constructed conceptual grid'.[49] Many of the critiques are valid: it represents a post-hoc rationalization for the TRC's work, both the grounds for prioritization and the nature of inter-relationships are unclear, and it arguably attempts to make sense of a broad and contradictory mandate that makes no sense.

While inadequate as it stands there is an outline here of a framework for truth that combines testimony, text and public debate, and a variety of qualitative and quantitative methodologies. In short, these are truths that begin to take us beyond the 'fetishization' of human rights reports to explore the intersection of processes, products and potential impacts. Human rights organizations are crying out for new tools that will enhance both the impacts and legitimacy of their work. The TRC

Understanding South Africa's Truth and Reconciliation Commission (Johannesburg, 2002) 17-36 at 35.

[48] HAYNER, *supra* n. 2, 168-169.

[49] D. POSEL, 'The TRC Report: What Kind of History? What Kind of Truth?', in D. POSEL and G. SIMPSON (eds.), *Commissioning the Past: Understanding South Africa's Truth and Reconciliation Commission* (Johannesburg, 2002) 147-172, at 155.

provides some points of departure. For example, process (how we work; who we reach) matters as much as product (what we write); and processes can be products (hearings). Crucially, if the TRC's experience is anything to go by, the old fashioned sources of legitimacy (fact finding, legal analysis) can withstand the competition from a range of products that are more in tune with the media age.

6. SPEAKING TRUTH WITH AND TO POWER

Moving on, the second question requires an unpacking of truth commissions' complex balancing act, speaking truth both with and to power, and the magnificent prospect that they may be able to do both. This necessitates an analysis of the fact finding and legal analysis rubrics of human rights reporting and the way in which they sideline individual subjectivity and testimony on the one hand, and broader political context on the other. Through such acts of inclusion and exclusion the parameters of truth and power and the relationship between the two are defined. Political and strategic concerns are also relevant, as any understanding of the TRC's relationship to power cannot overlook its positioning in the post-apartheid political firmament.

Wilson argues that the realist and legalistic language of human rights reports serves to decontextualize and depoliticize events. A universal human rights template strips events of their individual subjective and local meanings. '[L]ife becomes text becomes genre' in a way that may speak truth to power, but it also privileges a liberal, universal, legal agenda over personal and local politics.[50] The clearest illustration of this face of human rights within the TRC came with a shift in its focus and working methods in mid-1997, from its first year's prioritization of victim hearings and narratives to the making of victim and, in particular, perpetrator findings and amnesty hearings. It is true to say that the whole identity and legacy of the TRC turned on this axis which distilled its truth tensions to an essential core: 'its own dual role as a fact-finding, quasi-judicial enterprise obsessed with forensic truth and verifiable information on the one hand, and a psychologically sensitive mechanism for victim storytelling and "healing" on the other'.[51] The change encompassed a variety of interlinked and incomplete transitions: from a victim to a perpetrator focus; from hearings to findings; from public, onstage to backstage and invisible activities; from testimony to text; from qualitative to quantitative methods; from the listening state to the bureaucratic state.

---

[50]   R. WILSON, *The Politics of Truth and Reconciliation in South Africa: Legitimizing the Post-Apartheid State* (Cambridge, 2001) 146.

[51]   G. SIMPSON, '"Tell no Lies, Claim no Easy Victories": A Brief Evaluation of South Africa's Truth and Reconciliation Commission', in D. POSEL and G. SIMPSON (eds.), *Commissioning the Past: Understanding South Africa's Truth and Reconciliation Commission* (Johannesburg, 2002) 220-251, at 237.

In this context, both Buur and Wilson critique the triumph of a particular kind of human rights discourse that colonized the work of the TRC.[52] The legalistic, positivist and statistical methodology of the TRC led to the report's focus on forensic truth without an accompanying integrative conceptual framework or unifying, explanatory historical narrative. Individual narratives were progressively decontextualized and dissected as data, deconstructed and reconstructed into the 'higher' grammar of human rights. The statement form or 'protocol' became 'a highly structured questionnaire',[53] re-structured to privilege facts over narrative; during data processing statements were broken down and categorized as discrete human rights violations (acts) and categories of persons (victims, perpetrators, witnesses); while the report, organized by universal parameters – chronology, spatial coordinates and geography, political actors, human rights abuses[54] – similarly fragmented individual stories, as well as local histories, to different sections and volumes. Buur remarks: 'the memories of victims materialised first as narratives, and then, through a chain of translations, became *signs* of gross human rights violations under apartheid'.[55] What is lost in such analysis is the integrity, framing and subjectivity of individual narratives, instructive ambiguity and instabilities of meaning, everything that does not fit the prevailing 'controlling vocabulary' of human rights abuses, and local, social and political context. The flattening of context is accompanied by the flattening of language, into a 'cold', neutral, institutional prose.[56]

In a frequently cited and complementary critique, Mamdani states that the TRC had 'the power to define the terms of a social debate and, in doing so, define the parameters of truth-seeking'.[57] He accuses the Commission of establishing a narrow, diminished truth, focusing on a tiny, elite minority (individualized perpetrators and victims, state agents and political activists) rather than the majority (beneficiaries and a broader category of victims), who were written out of its history. By drawing

---

[52]   L. BUUR, 'Monumental Historical Memory: Managing Truth in the Everyday Work of the South African Truth and Reconciliation Commission', in D. POSEL and G. SIMPSON (eds.), *Commissioning the Past: Understanding South Africa's Truth and Reconciliation Commission* (Johannesburg, 2002) 66-93; BUUR, *supra* n. 3; WILSON, *supra* n. 50, 33-61.

[53]   WILSON, *supra* n. 50, 44.

[54]   A. DU TOIT, 'Perpetrator Findings as Artificial Even-handedness? The TRC's Contested Judgements of Moral and Political Accountability for Gross Human Rights Violations'. Paper presented at the Truth and Reconciliation Commission: Commissioning the Past conference, a joint project of the History Workshop of the University of the Witwatersrand and the Centre for the Study of Violence and Reconciliation, Johannesburg, 11-14 June 1999, 20-22.

[55]   BUUR, *supra* n. 52, 2002, 80.

[56]   CHERRY, DANIEL and FULLARD, *supra* n. 47, 22.

[57]   M. MAMDANI, 'A Diminished Truth', 3 *Siyaya!* (1998) 38-40 at 38; also see M. MAMDANI, 'The Truth According to the TRC', in I. AMADIUME and A. AN-NA'IM (eds.), *The Politics of Memory: Truth, Healing and Social Justice* (London, 2000) 176-183; and M. MAMDANI, 'Reconciliation without Justice', 46 *Southern African Review of Books* (1996) 3-5.

on the analogy of Latin America, and using the prism of brutal dictatorship and gross human-rights abuses, the TRC obscured what was distinctive about apartheid – violence directed at communities and population groups more than individuals, systemic socio-economic as well as political abuse, 'the colonial nature of the South African context: the link between conquest and dispossession, between racialised power and racialised privilege, between perpetrator and beneficiary'.[58] While Mamdani is incorrect to categorize the TRC's constituency as an elite (political activists often kept away), he is correct that majority beneficiaries and victims were excluded. Such decontextualized human rights truths remake conflicts and histories in a single image. This is a feature of human rights reports as a genre, which normally take no position on broader political questions (apartheid *per se*, or the Israeli occupation of Palestine) and thereby 'distort a total system of domination by looking only at the particularly brutal manifestations of it'.[59]

Further narrowings of perspective fostered by this particular conception of human rights were the focus on political violence and motivation as opposed to criminal acts, and the tendency to see much racist violence as outside its mandate, as not linked to political organizations and conflicts but rather a matter of private belief. Victims and perpetrators often found such distinctions puzzling and irrelevant to their understandings of conflict. The political-criminal distinction undermined the TRC's capacity to penetrate patterns of violence such as the merging of politics and crime in the 1980s and early 1990s (the 'third force', 'black on black violence', Self Defence Units [SDUs]) and trajectories of continuity and change in violence pre- and post-1994). The TRC's reluctance to conceive of racism as political *per se*, and its conception of the political in largely party or organizational terms, particularly affected rural areas writing a swathe of violent history out of the TRC's narrative. Racism was largely excluded as a relevant motive in the amnesty process, with similar results. Understandings of politics and racism were impoverished, and the relationships between political and criminal violence, between public and private racism, between politics, crime, race, poverty, gender, class and other variables, were not adequately addressed in what became an exercise in thin description.[60]

The weakness of human rights, narrowly construed, as an analytical tool, and some of the ways in which it constructs a one-dimensional truth and past, is clear. To the extent that such human rights discourses dominated the work of the TRC they diminished individual subjectivities and political contexts, and as a result a decontextualized truth was spoken to an analytically impoverished and incomplete

---

[58] MAMDANI, *supra* n. 57, 1998, 40.

[59] DUDAI, *supra* n. 28.

[60] See M. FULLARD, *Dis-Placing Race: The South African Truth and Reconciliation Commission and Interpretations of Violence* (Johannesburg, 2004); SIMPSON, *supra* n. 51; TRUTH AND RECONCILIATION COMMISSION, *supra* n. 4, 84-85; WILSON, *supra* n. 50, 79-93.

notion of (political) power. This truth-power nexus was problematic in South Africa not only because it smothered the individual and the local and warped history, but also because it highlighted apartheid's symptoms (torture, killings...) rather than its structural violence and enduring legacies (racism, inequality, violent crime). It also framed narrow understandings of accountability and responsibility. Human rights can be critiqued for speaking partial truths to similarly selective constructs of power.

Nevertheless, this human rights critique is not without its merits. One strength of the exclusion of political context in human rights narratives is the argument that no amount of contextual thickness can be used to justify gross human rights abuses. While the genre of state inquiry had to balance the regime of speaking truth to reconciliation with the need for truth-as-objectivity, to the extent that it produced a human rights report the TRC refracted a similar imperative for objectivity and reconciliation through a more assertive, if specific and partial, critique of power. Speaking truth with and to power produced some unexpected results, arising from the chosen methodology and the TRC's political self-positioning. While on occasion the TRC sacrificed truth to reconciliation (all parties could have been criticized more), it also told unpopular truths to all parties, asserting its own truth-as-objectivity legitimacy over the legitimization of the ANC and parties across the political spectrum, and a specific discourse of nation-building (legal equality) over the more partisan valorization of the ANC or the protection of parties deemed necessary for democratic consolidation. This is a considerable achievement by any fair estimation.

But could alternative methodologies achieve more? Well, firstly, there are research methodologies that provide a thicker description of violence.[61] Secondly, human rights reports are more diverse, complex and contested documents than many critics suggest and therefore need to be read with greater subtlety.[62] Dudai's argument that human rights reports include first person testimony to say the otherwise unsayable within human rights discourse – 'rain and cold enter the otherwise bare forensic tone' – and to complement the rational (required to secure legitimacy) with the emotional (necessary to generate empathy for victims), acknowledges both the authoritarian interpretive impulse within human rights and that it is never fully realized.[63] On these terms, the TRC reports went beyond purely

---

[61]   See for example the action research approach used by Penal Reform International (PRI) in its monitoring of the *gacaca* courts in Rwanda. This longitudinal research goes beyond a narrow monitoring remit to mine the perceptions and behaviours of a range of actors in order to understand the *gacaca* process and the broader context in which it is unfolding <www.penalreform.org>. And yet PRI's difficult relationship with the current Rwandan government begs the question of the implications of such thick description for effectiveness. With at least some governments it is likely that human rights reports will have more purchase if facts precede analysis, rather than the reverse.

[62]   See T. GODWIN PHELPS, Shattered Voices: Language, Violence and the Work of Truth Commissions (Philadelphia, 2004).

[63]   DUDAI, *supra* n. 37, 789-791; DUDAI, *supra* n. 28.

forensic truths. Thirdly, an alternative reality could be uncovered by operationalizing the human rights mantra that civil-political and social-economic rights are indivisible and interdependent as an interpretive framework.[64] By focusing on certain key events or pieces of legislation (pass laws, migrant labour, forced removals), and linking specific symptoms to structural contexts, a broader picture could have been both acknowledged and contained. At the same time the critique of power would be deeper and the net of responsibility thrown wider. That the TRC did not go down this path is a choice it must own; it is not, any longer, an inevitable characteristic of human rights. In short, the truth-power interface within the TRC constituted as much an act of colonization within human rights (elevating certain kinds of research methodologies, certain understandings of rights) as it did an act of colonization by human rights.

This section and its predecessor, discussing the TRC report largely within the generic possibilities of human rights, have sought to explore the potential for legitimacy and impacts beyond report "fetishization" and to unpack the linkages forged between truth and power. There are at least two legitimate responses to the picture that has emerged. One is to castigate the TRC for its contradictions and inconsistencies, the other is to applaud it for achieving something in human rights terms in a context in which human rights was one objective to be balanced against others. What is its legacy for human rights? The TRC made a contribution to long-standing human rights debates: To rely on the power of critique and/or constructive engagement with the state? To produce objective knowledge to inform and educate and/or manipulate emotions to engage and mobilize? In both cases the TRC was at the cutting edge of human rights work in suggesting hybrid responses.

7. HISTORY AS SAVIOUR?

We have already outlined some of the methodological challenges faced by the TRC and truth commissions more generally, in particular the dominance of a particular quantitative research approach. Could historical methods provide a solution? To see truth commissions as a form of history raises questions about methodology, meta-narrative and context; each will be considered in turn.

In the South African setting, the difficulties of writing an official history have been explored most fully by Posel. She identifies three mandate-related tensions linked to different kinds of historical knowledge and writing: objectivity versus acknowledging contending voices and experiences; a comprehensive record versus a representative and politically strategic account (balancing memory and forgetting, forms of reconciliation and truth); and focusing on apartheid as mere backdrop to a descriptive account of gross violations of human rights versus a fuller engagement

---

[64] See SCHABAS, *supra* n. 42, 24-25, on the broader remit of the Sierra Leone TRC.

with apartheid as source and explanation.[65] The methodological challenges facing the TRC resonate in many ways with the historian's craft. As Posel notes, the dilemmas raised by her three tensions were in some respects not unlike the routine challenges confronting practising historians: how to reconcile conflicting versions of the past; how to paint a national picture that takes sufficient account of regional or local specifics; how to adjudicate between different types of historical evidence (particularly the tensions between oral and written modes of recording the past). But they confronted the TRC in a particular form: how to construct knowledge about the past in a form that satisfied a range of competing criteria of adequacy and validity arising from the different facets of its mandate?[66]

Truth commissions and history share significant overlapping methodological practices and objectives (multiple sources, strategies for corroboration, a focus on both individuals and patterns). Where methodological differences emerged in South Africa – such as the TRC's shift over time to the use of quantitative methods and making findings – these linked particular understandings of truth and reconciliation to particular objectives in the mandate. Arguably, the TRC's research process came to represent not just the marginalization of testimony, but also the marginalization of history, if history is understood as contested, contextual (for individuals and events), interpretive and explanatory, exploring patterns of social relations and institutional dynamics. The sidelining of a historical regime of truth occurred due to a variety of interlinked processes, including 1) an overwhelmed research capacity – the TRC employed very few researchers (12-14) in comparison to data analysts and investigators (about 60); 2) the legalization of the TRC process (making findings, amnesty functions etc.); 3) an increasingly reactive research agenda; 4) limited engagement with secondary sources and archival material; 5) and a report editing process that sacrificed detailed case studies, local histories, analysis, context, causality and explanation.[67] These processes together amounted to a shift from historical analysis to the investigative repertoires of the state inquiry and human rights report, and from academic history to the nation-building and legitimizing functions of official history.

---

[65]   POSEL, *supra* n. 49, 150-153.

[66]   POSEL, *supra* n. 49, 153.

[67]   CHERRY, DANIEL and FULLARD, *supra* n. 47. FULLARD (*supra* n. 60, 23) provides some background to the writing of the 'historical context' chapter in the TRC report (TRUTH AND RECONCILIATION COMMISSION, *supra* n. 4, chapter 2). A lengthy, detailed history chapter written by academic historians was deemed to be 'too academic' and ultimately unsuitable; it was replaced at the last minute by a shorter chapter written by a TRC researcher. For further, rather exasperated, reflections on the writing and editing process, from an academic involved in the drafting of the TRC report's chapter on the business sector (TRUTH AND RECONCILIATION COMMISSION, *supra* n. 43, Vol. 4, chapter 2), see N. NATTRASS, 'The Truth and Reconciliation Commission on Business and Apartheid: A Critical Evaluation', 98 *African Affairs* (1999) 373-391 at 374, 386.

The second historical imperative is that truth commission reports undertake the conventional historians' task of providing a containing meta-narrative, or interpretive framework, for the past. Posel problematizes the TRC's failure to link individual cases to more general causative patterns in a coherent analytical synthesis, and an absence of serious engagement with apartheid in preference for a moral narrative about wrongdoing across the political spectrum, rooted in the over-riding evil of the apartheid system. Wilson argues that in the service of national building and reconciliation, more easily modified and unifying notions of morality and values were often preferred to political confrontation and challenging analysis: '[m]orality ventured where analysis feared to tread'.[68]

This moral parable is all that binds together a report characterized by description, fragmentation, repetition and multiple messages. Endless examples could illustrate this point. Suffice to note the failure to integrate testimonies and statistical analysis; the need to relate things treated separately (time periods, regional profiles, categories of abuse, parts of individual stories); and the treatment of sector hearings and related structural issues in a separate volume.[69] Consideration of 'causes, motives and perspectives of perpetrators' takes place in a very insightful separate chapter in the 1998 report,[70] and is then treated somewhat superficially in the long consideration of the truths emerging from the amnesty process in the 2003 report.[71] To this unfortunate list should be added the decision to begin, and therefore frame, the whole report with a chairperson's foreword (genre: sermon – a sermon that both encourages further debate and closure on the past, and that seeks to balance moral differentiation, legal equivalence and national unity). Much that follows the foreword in the first volume of the report is a tedious and highly repetitive manual of methods and bureaucratic arrangements, where a strong statement of core findings would surely have been preferable. The absence of an index is similarly 'symptomatic of the lack of an intellectual map'.[72] All these qualities detracted from the TRC's capacity for historical analysis and explanation.

In interviews with former Commissioners, and commission staff,[73] it is clear that there was no agreement about the meta-narrative of the TRC report, even amongst those closely associated with its production: 'In 1998, I don't think anyone writing had a major sense of the uber-points we were trying to make'.[74] The meta-narrative

---

[68] WILSON, *supra* n. 50, 93.
[69] TRUTH AND RECONCILIATION COMMISSION, *supra* n. 43, Vol. 4.
[70] TRUTH AND RECONCILIATION COMMISSION, *supra* n. 18, Vol. 5, chapter 7.
[71] TRUTH AND RECONCILIATION COMMISSION, *supra* n. 43, Vol. 6, 181-501; D. FOSTER, P. HAUPT & M. DE BEER, *The Theatre of Violence: Narratives of Protagonists in the South African Conflict* (Oxford, 2005) 13-24.
[72] POSEL, interview 14/8/2002.
[73] For example: FULLARD, interview 21/4/2005; ORR, interview 19/4/2005; SOOKA, interview 20/4/2005.
[74] FULLARD, *supra* n. 73.

of the codicil report,[75] a document drafted less inclusively by a smaller group of writers, largely to incorporate material gleaned from the amnesty hearings, is much clearer: accountability and reparation. The codicil is characterized by a strong legal justification for its meta-themes, a focus on 'unfinished business', and certain elements of self-critique (a clearer meta-narrative; modest re-writings of earlier findings and recommendations). As weaknesses of the TRC were acknowledged, new material emerged within the commission and old material was better analyzed, and the outlines of a government response, or lack thereof, became clearer, this process of reflection was perhaps inevitable; but it is nonetheless intriguing, and both the internal political processes and textual re-writing deserve further study. However, while the battle for legitimacy was re-engaged, the historical interpretive framework remained weak largely because the codicil draws on human rights and the law rather than historical analysis for its justifications.

Some argue that the weakness of the report's meta-narrative may also be a strength, inviting rather than curtailing further debate.[76] One strategy for combining both multi-vocality and some kind of meta-narrative is provided by Phelps's reading of truth commissions and their reports.[77] Bakhtin's carnival serves as a template, allowing storytelling within the polyphonic TRC hearings to be conceived as liberating victims and survivors by disrupting existing social structures, equalizing social relationships and temporarily inverting the established official order. The inclusion of such stories in the master narratives of truth commission reports 'allows for the *carnivalization* of history, an entirely new kind of history telling and nation making'.[78] With reference to such reports, and exemplified in the Argentine report, *Nunca Más*, Phelps[79] invites a reading that recognizes a plurality of voices not completely subordinated to the governing master narrative, a blend of chaos pitted against order, of victim/survivor and authorial/commission voices: 'and the two together manifest a unique sharing of power reflecting the promise of democracy'.[80] Beyond providing evidence, testimonies become explanatory, exemplary and disruptive partners in a conversation, thereby preventing an appropriative master narrative from becoming too authoritarian or totalizing, or too focused on perpetrators at the expense of the victims and survivors. If the TRC victim hearings represented a rare example of the carnivalesque in contemporary political life, the TRC report was an exercise in order and control, an effort to 'contain the

---

[75]   TRUTH AND RECONCILIATION COMMISSION , *supra* n. 43, Vol. 6.
[76]   DU TOIT in WILSON, *supra* n. 50, 54; POSEL, *supra* n. 49, 168-169; D. POSEL and G. SIMPSON, 'The Power of Truth: South Africa's Truth and Reconciliation Commission in Context', in D. POSEL and G. SIMPSON (eds.), *Commissioning the Past: Understanding South Africa's Truth and Reconciliation Commission* (Johannesburg, 2002) 1-13, at 12-13.
[77]   GODWIN PHELPS, *supra* n. 62.
[78]   GODWIN PHELPS, *supra* n. 62, 69, see 67-69, 104, 113.
[79]   GODWIN PHELPS, *supra* n. 62, 74-128.
[80]   GODWIN PHELPS, *supra* n. 62, 81.

uncontainable',[81] in which residues of the carnival perhaps remain. The report's three typefaces provide an initial mapping of its voices: regular for the master narrative, italics for the first-person victim and perpetrator stories, and bold for the TRC's findings. The master narrative, according to Phelps, is one of forgiveness and reconciliation.

A third area where history and historians ask important questions of the truth commission enterprise – context – revisits the discussion of human rights and its tendency to decontextualize. Human rights abuses, in truth, are a narrow and idiosyncratic prism through which to attempt a rewriting of history. Posel writes that the 'inability to grapple with the complexities of social causation is compounded by the TRC's having to tie its account of apartheid to the story of gross human rights violations. Having to focus a narration of the past around the clash between "victims" and "perpetrators" provides very blunt tools for the craft of history-writing'.[82] Bundy reiterates the point that the narrow focus on gross human rights violations served to diminish the full iniquity of the apartheid past.[83] The decontextualization critique applies at various levels, encompassing individual testimony, community histories and macro- or meta-narratives.

Historians and social scientists have begun to critique the community analyses and impacts of the TRC in relation to often complex local dynamics of power and violence.[84] Local histories of this kind lack the clear lines and unified, crisp agendas of official histories. Before signing off on this subject, a cautionary comment is required with reference to historical and other academic analyses. History as context, while rectifying the decontextualization of legal discourse and human rights reporting, can simply provide another, broader narrative and set of external agendas with similarly expansive truth claims into which testimony and community are appropriated as sources of evidence and facts. The interpretive context is still imposed from above, filtering voices from below. If truth commissions and social historians are to fulfill their claims to give voice to the ordinary and the voiceless, to democratize history, they need to incorporate insights into power relations in narrative construction, understandings of oral testimony and memory beyond

---

[81] GODWIN PHELPS, *supra* n. 62, 115.
[82] POSEL, *supra* n. 49, 166.
[83] BUNDY, *supra* n. 29, 16-19.
[84] See, for example, P. BONNER and N. NIEFTAGODIEN, 'The Truth and Reconciliation Commission and the Pursuit of "Social Truth": The Case of Kathorus', in D. POSEL and G. SIMPSON (eds.), *Commissioning the Past: Understanding South Africa's Truth and Reconciliation Commission* (Johannesburg, 2002) 173-203; H. VAN DER MERWE, 'National Narrative versus Local Truths: The Truth and Reconciliation Commission's Engagement with Duduza', in D. POSEL and G. SIMPSON (eds.), *Commissioning the Past: Understanding South Africa's Truth and Reconciliation Commission* (Johannesburg, 2002) 204-219; VAN DER MERWE in TRUTH AND RECONCILIATION COMMISSION, *supra* n. 18, 423-429; WILSON, *supra* n. 50.

evidence, and interpretive worlds as well as voices from below.[85] The TRC's record as history has rightly been subject to rigorous critique across the concerns addressed here – methodology, meta-narrative, context – but both truth commissions and the academy have lessons to learn from transition, notably from the rise of public history. Nevertheless, history clearly does provide some insights, and tools, for the necessary hybridity of truth commission and human rights research.

8. CONCLUSION

Official truth commissions work within the generic confines of the state inquiry, the human rights report and the official history. A basket of generic methodologies seeking objectivity were linked, in South Africa, respectively to an impulse towards speaking truth to reconciliation, to power, and to context and meta-narrative. Such priorities map different routes through which the TRC sought legitimacy, a spectrum of functions and objectives, and the Commission's deepest struggles over power. Its report, and work more generally, represents a 'genre colony' that failed to achieve a hybrid coherence. Rather, genre status changed over time and through different sections of the organization and report. An initial focus, at least within sections of the TRC, on narrative and history was overtaken midstream by quantitative methodology and a focus on making findings. This was an act of colonization by human rights, narrowly construed. But it was also an internal coup within human rights, elevating to power a particular set of civil-political rights and research methodologies.

The methodological challenge is how to render the multiple genres, truths and methodologies productive rather than fragmentary and mutually undermining. Less ambition is one option, through perhaps choosing to privilege one genre tributary. Another is to acknowledging the different emphases in different facets of commission work, while seeking to integrate the parts into a coherent whole. Greater conceptual and methodological sophistication would also help, and the TRC's four truths provide the basis on which to begin the discussion. In raising questions about legitimacy and impacts beyond report 'fetishization', the possibility of speaking truth with and to power, and the potential of historical methodologies, the TRC and commentary on the TRC spoke to and through hybridity in a way that

---

[85]   J. DU PISANI and K-S. KIM, 'Establishing the Truth about the Apartheid Past: Historians and the South African Truth and Reconciliation Commission', 8 *African Studies Quarterly* (2004), <http://web.africa.ufl.edu/asq/v8/v8i1a5.htm>; P. LALU and B. HARRIS, 'Journeys from the Horizons of History: Text, Trial and Tales in the Construction of Narratives of Pain', 8 *Current Writing* (1996) 24-38; G. MINKLEY and C. RASSOOL, 'Orality, Memory, and Social History in South Africa', in S. NUTTALL and C. COETZEE (eds.), *Negotiating the Past: The Making of Memory in South Africa* (Cape Town, 1998) 89-99.

makes a valuable contribution to our understandings of possible futures for truth commission methodologies, and for human rights research more generally.

METHODOLOGICAL CHALLENGES IN COUNTRY OF ORIGIN RESEARCH

Marco Formisano*

1. INTRODUCTION

"The provision of protection information is a core protection function". This strong announcement is typically characterized by the new era of global information management and information sharing. Protection-related information has become crucial in many areas of modern asylum law and policy. This is even more evident when it comes to operational functions like the protection of asylum seekers, voluntary return and resettlement of refugees, and, obviously, refugee status determination (RSD).

The use of Country of Origin Information (COI) reports and studies in the adjudication of asylum claims brings this category of refugee research into a peculiar field of analysis. Researching COI, in fact, implies a different mindset and a particular care in the application of research standards. The research methodology is robustly influenced by the quasi-judicial nature of their function in asylum procedures, their overall protection finality and the degree of persuasion of their content. These driving factors shape the way researchers should approach COI investigations.

Hence, COI research requires specific awareness of what the exploration should really centre on, on how to assess sources, how to use them, and how to generally structure the research and the presentation of results. This can be examined under a twofold approach, namely reviewing procedural and substantive research principles.

Country reports intended for RSD procedures are normally produced and collated by dedicated COI units within national administrative structures, as well as from the United Nations High Commissioner for Refugees (UNHCR), and non-governmental organizations (NGOs) with some expertise in forced displacement like

---

* The views expressed in this contribution are exclusively those of the author and are not those of the UNHCR. Special thanks go to Jerome Sabety for our exchange of views and his stimulating ideas on this subject.

the Austrian Centre for Country of Origin and Asylum Research and Documentation (ACCORD) managed by the Austrian Red Cross.[1]

Irrespective of the diversities amongst the compilers, when researching COI the investigators should legitimately put forward some self-interrogations like: What are the fundamental research questions a researcher should come up with? What shall be included in the research scrutiny and what should more appropriately stay out of it? How can we evaluate the best reporting authorities and most respected sources that analyze country situations and human rights violations? What distinctive traits should they bear? Shall we use exclusively publicly available sources or can we exploit anonymous sources? What is the tone admissible in the report? Can we act as human rights defenders or should we employ a more neutral wording? And finally and more generally, how can we draft a research strategy that will respect a set of codified standards for high quality research?

There is extremely little literature on research methodology and standards for searching and producing COI. This paper aims therefore at setting the fundamental principles that lie behind accurate and efficient research tactics and methods, as well as first-rate principles to be observed when researching COI. In particular, the analysis will open focusing on the peculiar nature of COI as a branch of refugee research. In this context the quasi-judicial nature of the use of COI will be addressed, together with the implications this entails for researching and producing COI. Once the peculiarity of COI research is assessed, we will elaborate in detail on the research methodology and doctrine. We will focus on the dichotomy "procedural and substantive" principles, codifying principles for high quality research. The issues of relevance, reliability, accuracy, currency, and neutrality of sources will be treated as well as legal and country-related searching processes and reporting techniques.

The commentary will conclude linking the two sections of the analysis (nature of COI – specific methodology), with the aim of demonstrating that, because of the very nature of COI, traditional rigid schemes for research standards are not applicable and that a set of principles, to be observed and adapted on a case-by-case basis, should rather constitute the more appropriate approach to COI research.

---

[1]   While governmental COI compilations are often not available to the general public, the UNHCR offers free access through its Refworld system, available at <www.refworld.org>, to a vast collection of country, legal and refugee-related information, and ACCORD provides a similar service through its European Country of Origin Network (Ecoi.net), available at <www.ecoi.net>.

2. A DEFINITION OF COUNTRY OF ORIGIN INFORMATION

Before proceeding to any dissertation on the methodological system related to COI research, we should attempt to provide a definition of the object of our analysis. The 1951 Convention relating to the Status of Refugees is indeed silent on the possible meaning of Country of Origin Information. When identifying who is a refugee, it simply affirms that the person should be outside his/her country of nationality (or habitual residence for stateless persons) and should have a fear of persecution which, in addition to corresponding to one of the so-called Convention grounds (Nationality, Race, Religion, belonging to a Particular Social Group or Political Opinion), ought to be also *well-founded*.[2] By this, the drafters of the 1951 Convention implied that besides the subjective element of the fear of being persecuted there should be an objective component of the applicant's apprehension that justifies the legitimacy of the claim. This can be established on the genuine convincement that persecution is likely to happen if the person is returned to his/her country of origin, involving some appreciation of the situation in the country of first flight. Despite being indirectly clear on the fact that the knowledge of conditions in the applicant's country of origin becomes essential in establishing the well-foundedness of the fear, we still have to define what to look for and how.

Some interpreters give a broad description of COI as "[a]ny information that should help to answer questions about the situation in the country of nationality or former habitual residence of a person seeking asylum or another form of international protection".[3] Direct experience proved that many caseworkers, frantic to find any piece of information they may deem essential in order to assess a case, would also marry this definition. Nevertheless this characterization risks being so extensive as to miss its purpose, not telling much about what COI really is other than just 'any' information. We may name this approach the 'open sea approach'.

Others attempt to give a functional definition of COI based on their evidentiary scope in RSD.[4] Here the object of research is the required evidence to be used in

---

[2]   Article 1A of the 1951 Convention also requires that the person, having the fear of persecution, is unable or unwilling to return to the country of origin (or habitual residence for stateless). UN General Assembly, Convention Relating to the Status of Refugees, UN Doc. A/RES/429 (V), New York, 1951.

[3]   See H. STOREY, *Judicial Criteria for Assessing Country of Origin Information (COI): A Checklist*, Paper for 7th Biennial IARLJ World Conference, Mexico City, 6-9 November 2006, quoting Barbara Svec in a presentation to the IARLJ November 2005 Budapest Conference.

[4]   See Austrian CENTRE FOR COUNTRY OF ORIGIN AND ASYLUM RESEARCH DOCUMENTATION (ACCORD), *ACCORD COI Network and Training, Researching Country of Origin Information: A Training Manual*, September 2004, 4 and 20, where their use as evidence in asylum claims is stressed. Along the same line, see also New Zealand Refugee Status Appeals Authority, *Refugee*

administrative decisions or judicial remedies for the determination of refugee status. Again, the object of research is not directly and precisely defined in its substance and we are still unclear on what type of evidence we shall concentrate our investigation on. We may refer to this scheme as the 'functional approach'.

Closer to a more accurate definition is probably the text of the so-called 'EU Qualification Directive'. In order to assess the facts and circumstances of the asylum application, Article 3(3) solicits that "all relevant facts as they relate to the country of origin at the time of taking a decision on the application, including laws and regulations of the country of origin and the manner in which they are applied" should be taken into account.[5] Along the same line is the UK Home Office when it considers COI the "provision of complete, accurate and timely" information.[6] Although still summarily defined, these scant indications bring with them (though probably without direct intention) two important elements: a qualitative assessment (the reference to the 'relevant', 'accurate', 'complete', 'timely', facts and to the way laws are implemented) and a quantitative description (the reference to 'including laws' of the EU qualification directive). We may name this the 'selective approach' (although still in its latent meaning).

This selective approach while limiting the scope and field of research to certain types of support instruments (quantitative characteristic) already contains some indications on the substantive and procedural fundamentals (qualitative aspect) that should make up the research methodology. This interpretation of COI has the advantage of eliminating the "noise" of thousands of available but defective sources in the provision of country information and guarantees a solid basis for sound refugee-status decisions. Its final aim is to guide the researcher to use robust research products that will serve as evidence in the delicate process of asylum determination.

Therefore, a correct definition of COI shall not abstain from referring to qualitative and quantitative constitutive elements. Hence we cannot omit using adjectives to describe the substance of COI, nor can we desist from limiting the number of items that may form information on the country of origin. Thus COI maybe identified as: relevant, reliable, precise, accurate, current, publicly available,

---

Appeal No. 73545/02, 11 October 2002, §53, available at <http://www.refugee.org.nz/Fulltext/73545-02.htm>.

[5] EUROPEAN UNION, Council Directive 2004/83/EC of 29 April 2004 on Minimum Standards for the Qualification and Status of Third Country Nationals or Stateless Persons as Refugees or as Persons Who Otherwise Need International Protection and the Content of the Protection Granted, *Official Journal of the European Union*, L 304/12, 30 September 2004.

[6] B. MORGAN, V. GELSTHORPE, H. CRAWLEY & A. JONES, *Country of origin information: a user and content evaluation*, Home Office Research Study 271, Home Office Research, Development and Statistics Directorate (London, 2003) 1. See also International Centre for Migration Policy Development (ICMPD), *Practical Guide to the effective Gathering and Usage of Country Information*, sponsored by the EC Odysseus Programme and the Swiss Government, Prague, 13-15 February 2002, p. 4.

neutral, and balanced factual and legal country-reporting that is included in reports on the application of international instruments and national legislation, applicable case law, guidelines, recommendations and resolutions, human rights reports, country-news, country-profiles, and experts' analysis. We will be thus focusing on looking for impartial, authoritative and trustworthy examinations of the political situation, the potential human rights abuses, the effective application of the law, the civil and religious freedoms, the ethnic composition, etc. of the relevant country of origin.

3. THE QUASI-JUDICIAL CHARACTER OF COUNTRY OF ORIGIN INFORMATION AND ITS ROLE IN ASYLUM LAW

Having attempted to clarify what COI is we may now try to locate it within the practice of determination of refugee status. In a standard RSD procedure, an individual's testimony should normally be sufficient for reaching a decision. The importance of the applicant's statements during the interview is a concept that might be referred to as the psychological and communicative aspects of a lawsuit, integrating the so-called subjective element of the claim.[7] Nevertheless, the UNHCR Handbook for Procedures and Criteria for Determining Refugee Status (from now on the 'RSD Handbook') establishes that "the applicant's statements cannot [...] be considered in the abstract, and must be viewed in the context of the relevant background situation. Furthermore "a knowledge of conditions in the applicant's country of origin – while not a primary objective – is an important element in assessing the applicant's credibility".[8] This specification involves a shift from the one-sided assertion to a more objective element in the analysis of the claim. State practices are also oriented in this direction, using external reports for adopting a decision on the claim.

The main function of Country of Origin Information in refugee law is therefore closely comparable to the verification of evidence required in judicial proceedings. On the other hand, we are not in the presence of a judiciary process, being the recognition of refugee status rather an administrative practice of a descriptive and non-constitutive nature.[9] The procedure is thus non-adversarial and does not

---

[7]   UN HIGH COMMISSIONER FOR REFUGEES, *Handbook on Procedures and Criteria for Determining Refugee Status under the 1951 Convention and the 1967 Protocol relating to the Status of Refugees*, HCR/IP/4/REV.1, 1992, §42, available at <http://www.unhcr.org/cgi-bin/texis/vtx/refworld/rwmain?docid=3ae6b3314>.

[8]   See *Handbook on Procedures and Criteria for Determining Refugee Status under the 1951 Convention and the 1967 Protocol relating to the Status of Refugees*, supra n. 7.

[9]   Refugee determination is, in fact, the recognition of a pre-existing status (that is the status of being forcibly uprooted for one of the Convention's grounds and the inability or unwillingness of availing

confront the claimant with the decision maker, who is ultimately asked to certify the existence of the conditions for granting refugee status. The parties in this process are not contending to produce valid attestations *pro* or *contra* the fulfilling of the Convention's criteria, but are both requested to cooperate in ascertaining that all the decisive factors for reaching a fair executive determination are respected. Furthermore, beside the humanitarian and solid nature of asylum, the absence of cross-examination is also due to the fact that there is an inner impossibility of crosschecking the legitimacy of the claim calling direct testimonies, verifying premises, and acquiring evidence directly from the country of origin. The only viable evidentiary tool is thus the recourse to COI. We have to bring into play reports whose content is gathered and produced by others, with different approaches, different methodologies and different quality outputs.

During this non-antagonistic adjudication, and besides the other legal requirements to be looked at, the caseworkers who conduct the interviews and draft their legal analysis will base their convincement on the well-foundedness of the fear of persecution on both the testimony (subjective element of the claim) they receive and the legal and factual reporting on the situation in the related country of origin that is ultimately available to them (objective element of the claim).

As argued by Zahle (2003), evidentiary aspects of a refugee claim may be divided into two topical elements: one pertaining to the degree of probability or certainty with which we may assess that, in a particular country, a specific group is persecuted or risks persecution (termed 'risk-group existence') and the other one based on the degree of probability or certainty that a particular asylum seeker effectively belongs to a group-at-risk (termed 'risk-group affiliation'). This dichotomy may be read as the translation of the objective and subjective element of the claim discussed above, imported into a different theoretical construction.[10]

The substantiation of the 'risk-group existence' is thus given by the available COI in both a retrospective (ascertaining that the facts are likely to have happened) and prospective (prophesying the potential occurrence in the future) outline. In this framework, the role of COI is fundamental in corroborating the chronicle reported by the claimant, helping to predict with a certain degree of reliability the consequences for the person in case s/he is returned to the country of origin.

In addition, the COI contributes in helping to assess the credibility of the claim, functioning again as evidence for confirming or contesting the 'risk-group affiliation'. Two elements are worth underlining at this stage. The first one relates to the COI function in credibility assessments and the second one to the object of the assessment. Concerning the former, it is fundamental to stress that COI should

---

oneself of one's country's protection) resulting in granting international protection as well as the set of specific rights attached to it.

[10]   H. ZAHLE, 'Competing Patterns for Evidentiary Assessment', in G. NOLL, *Proof, Evidentiary Assessment and Credibility in Asylum Procedures*, (The Hague, 2005), p. 21.

restrictively be used to 'help' assess credibility, but it cannot alone determine it. The trustworthiness should be built around a communicative approach that takes into account the various elements of the claim: the vulnerability of the person (e.g. women, children, persons with disabilities, etc.), past traumatic experience, the degree of literacy, inner integrity and the consistency of the testimony. The RSD interview is indeed a complex process for acquiring information that includes psychological, cultural, gender and socio-environmental issues. When using distant reporting on facts that have allegedly happened in the country of origin with the aim of evaluating credibility, much attention should be paid to all these factors. The second aspect to note is that it is the credibility of the applicant's statement that should be tested and not the general one of the applicant. COI cannot cross the borders of their fact-reporting scope to defeat the reliability of the whole person.

But COI is also used for other protection purposes than RSD. For example in authorizing cessation of a certain group because of supervening circumstances in their home country, decision makers necessitate solid information on the current situation in the country of origin. On the operational side as well, when organizing repatriation and voluntary return of refugees, COI is essential in verifying and predicting conditions upon return. Furthermore, when seeking durable solutions for refugees through resettlement, resettling countries need accurate COI in order to prioritize cases and process files.

Last but not least and coming back *ab initio* to refugee determination, COI plays a fundamental role in preparing for the RSD interview. After registration, the caseworker should be in a position to know the main elements of the claim and be able to carry out some focused preparatory work, searching and studying the available COI. If this statement appears superfluous, sometimes the added value of having a clear sense of the specific matter in the country of origin prior to the interview is often underestimated. Being able to drive the interview according to the known facts increases the efficiency (time-savings and better focus) and the quality (meeting the right point for corroboration) of the whole interviewing exercise and helps either to be attentive to what the asylum seeker may not even realize or qualify as an important element of his/her testimony, or assist in spotting potential credibility issues when the testimony contradicts known facts (opening in this case more room for enquiry).

Given the overall quasi-judicial nature of COI as evidence, it may merit a word on the burden and standard of proof in RSD, because this regulates the 'who' should produce 'what' and 'how'. Concerning the former point, the relevant facts of the individual case will have to be furnished in the first place by the applicant himself (orally or documentarily), and after that it is up to the examiner to assess the validity of any other supplementary evidence (both generic and case-specific) and to evaluate the legitimacy of individual claims for refugee status (including exclusion and cessation) or other forms of international protection. There is here a substantial difference from the general legal principles of the Law of Evidence. In view of the particular character of the refugee situation and the vulnerability of the uprooted people, in fact, the burden of proof does not lie merely on the person who lodges the case and makes the assertion, but also on the examiner who should bring into the process all the relevant aspects for verifying and substantiating the alleged facts. According to international standards, it exists in RSD what we may define as 'equality of arms' between the applicant and the examiner. The latter shall thus contribute to the truthful establishment of facts (i.e. addressing the right questions), and has an obligation to refer to reliable, accurate, current, etc. COI.[11]

If it should be common practice to share the burden of proof between the applicant and the caseworker, the threshold up to which relevant evidence should be assessed varies according to different jurisdictions. While it is generally accepted that the standard of proof in RSD should never reach the level of the *"beyond reasonable doubt"* as applied in criminal proceedings, common law jurisdictions (e.g. Canada, Australia, New Zealand, the UK and USA) have moved away from the "balance of probability" test and have developed a wide range of more liberal formulae for setting their applicable standards stemming from *"serious possibility"*, *"good grounds"* and *"reasonable degree of likelihood"* to *"substantial grounds for thinking"* and *"reasonable chance"*.[12] Along the same line, civil law jurisdictions have also elaborated a variety of concepts such as *"plausibility"* of persecution, *"sufficient probability"* and *"significant probability"*.[13] The international standard is slightly more generous in situating the threshold for attaining a convenient degree of likelihood within the limit of a *"reasonable degree"*.[14] Moreover, the set threshold of the 'possibility', 'probability' or 'likelihood' of an event happening (persecution if returned) apparently brings on pure quantitative measures rather than qualitative

---

[11]   See UN HIGH COMMISSIONER FOR REFUGEES, *Note on Burden and Standard of Proof in Refugee Claims*, 16 December 1998, 2, available at: <http://www.unhcr.org/cgi-bin/texis/vtx/refworld/rwmain?docid=3ae6b3338>.

[12]   See for example [1971] 1 WLR 987, 994. Cf. Art.2, Draft Convention on Territorial Asylum, proposing a 'definite possibility of persecution' as the criterion for the grant of asylum; B. JACKMAN, 'Well-founded fear of persecution and other standards of decision-making: A north American perspective', in J. BHABHA & G. COLL (eds.), *Asylum Law and Practice in Europe and North America*, (Washington, 1992), p. 44.

[13]   For a full account of the various cases that contributed to establish both Common and Civil Law standards see B. GORLICK, 'Common Burdens and Standards: Legal Elements in Assessing Claims to Refugee Status', 15 (3) *International Journal of Refugee Law*, 2003, 357-376.

[14]   *Handbook on Procedures and Criteria for Determining Refugee Status under the 1951 Convention and the 1967 Protocol relating to the Status of Refugees*, supra n. 7. Furthermore, in case of uncertain cases, UNHCR elaborated the so-called 'Principle of the Benefit of the Doubt', which states that "if the applicant's account appears credible, he should, unless there are good reasons to the contrary, be given the benefit of the doubt" (Handbook, §196). The benefit of the doubt should thus be granted when: a) all evidence has been obtained and checked; b) the examiner is satisfied with the applicant's general credibility; and c) the applicant's statement is coherent, plausible and does not run contrary to generally known facts.

ones. Calculation of probabilities is indeed an algebraic experience. Nevertheless the quality of the examined data that enters the quantitative computation plays a fundamental role in determining the ultimate result. Thus, only qualitatively sound reports should enter the balancing of the available evidence that will constitute the 'reasonable degree' of likelihood that persecution may take place in the country of origin.

Notwithstanding the slim disparity in the various scales for reaching the required probation boundary and the different approaches in weighing up and using COI of governments, we may legitimately affirm that the type and quality of the researched COI that serves this purpose, penetrates transversally the diverse refugee systems and is of extreme sensitivity in the adjudication of the case. In this sense is also Gulyai (2007) who presents the results of a comparative study on different approaches to country information in EU asylum procedures, and stresses the common need for the superior quality of the used information.[15]

Hence, although not in isolation from the other essential elements of the RSD procedure, COI contributes substantially to the adoption of a sound versus an incorrect decision on the life of a person who is applying for protection. In this sense, taking a solid first instance verdict will reduce the human resources and financial costs of an appeal, boosting the consolidation of a secure status, and sparing the claimant the additional psychological distress of an uncertain position. More generally, a well-motivated decision based on qualified substantiation will reinforce the integrity and consistency of the institute of asylum.

The legal use of COI as probation instrument in a humanitarian setup requires a particular reflection and inclination in the way country information is investigated, both procedurally and substantially. Accordingly, the peculiar scope of COI should shape the entire research method, from the basic characteristics of the researcher, to the correct measurability of human rights-related facts to look into, up to the formulation of appropriate research questions, the implementation of thoughtful inquiry and collecting techniques, and the application of definite research principles. Relying on this assumption, we will now try to construct a model of efficient COI research.

---

[15]   G. GULAI, *Country Information in Asylum Procedures, Quality as a Legal Requirement in the EU*, Hungarian Helsinki Committee, 2007, also available at <http://www.helsinki.hu/docs/COI in Asylum Procedures FINAL WEB version.pdf>.

Marco Formisano

4. THE THREE ELEMENTS OF COI RESEARCH: THE OBSERVER, THE FACTS AND THE RESEARCH INSTRUMENTS

The main components of any COI research may be summarized as: the observer, the facts and the instrumentation (the actual way of collecting data). In this three-pillar 'research house' we need to insert a bridge associating the observer and the facts from one side to the instrumentation on the other side. This connecting passage is the formulation of a firm research strategy that is the preliminary step to the actual investigation.

4.1. THE OBSERVER

The principal actor of any research is the observer. In COI studies, the researcher is a secondary observer, someone that in most of the cases is not directly reporting the facts, but who is using someone else's observations. Typically country researchers will be based in COI units within national administrations, usually the ministry of the interior and immigration, the ministry of justice or the ministry of foreign affairs. Most frequently these departments will communicate between them in a functionally organized structure with a responsible office (e.g. the COI unit of the ministry of justice or the ministry of immigration) and a complimentary one (the foreign office) with inquiry functions. Different combinations of the three are also possible. These units will also operate though their networks of foreign offices and embassies in order to obtain direct information from the ground. International organizations and non-governmental organizations may function in a similar way, having a dedicated section for country research and making use of their country offices as antennas in the field. Nevertheless, in most of the cases the observer will be conducting his/her research from the country of asylum or from the headquarters of the international organization, predominantly accessing information through the web.

Thus, unless directly participating in a fact-finding mission, the COI researcher would normally have the only option of relying on the works of primary field experience observers. In some cases his position will also shift to the third or fourth place according to the availability of sources. In any event the country of origin researcher should possess some specific characteristics that will ensure the sound outcome of the research.

First of all the observer should be a distinct person from the decision makers. A disconnected researcher, not involved in the case and not directly responsible for the final decision, will possibly guarantee the required impartiality in both the research approach and the final production of results. The establishment of a distinct COI unit within national administrations, equipped with a good pool of country experts, should be the basic prerequisite of any asylum system. But while this may seem obvious in theory, in practice, given the shortage of human resources, the high turnover of staff, and/or the need to swiftly process the potentially consistent backlog, it may became a common trend to ask the eligibility officers to conduct their own COI research. In this case the right balance between professionalism, know-how and objectivity may be jeopardized.

The necessary distance from the asylum request and from the corresponding responsibility in the adjudication or denial of refugee status is directly linked to the second important feature that should distinguish the COI observer, which should be his/her total disinterest in the particular case. Only dispassionate researchers will be efficient enough to provide a solution that, at least nominally, goes beyond the single case that generated the question. This qualification is different from the structural division between the caseworker and the researcher and it relates more to having clearly separated the idea of the subject to search, the relative topic and the available tools. More than the relation to the facts is the condition or quality of being sufficiently remotely situated mentally from the case in order to have a universal approach.

Lastly, the observer should be an experienced researcher in refugee issues. This is a key element in order to equally facilitate a clear understanding of the research requirements and the smooth construction of a well-organized research strategy. Only informed refugee specialists will in fact be able to centre their attention on significant issues of the claim such as the convention grounds, the concept of internal flight alternative, the exclusion triggers, etc., and produce the right answer to the COI question. Past track records in asylum affairs will enhance the application of the required standards of the specific law of evidence of the asylum regime.

Hence, the COI observer should be a sort of uncontaminated refugee research technician with a solid background in human rights, law, politics, sociology or anthropology, endowed with pertinent knowledge and expertise in refugee research, and whose work should be organized and delivered in a completely independent manner. This should be the right profile of the main performer of COI research.

4.2. THE FACTS

The object of COI research is twofold: first of all, the observer may want to look at the *static* side of country information, learning about maps, names of villages and cities, ethnic groups composition, locally spoken languages, and all sorts of geo-socially related items that will help assess the credibility of the claimant. Secondly, COI research will focus, in a more *dynamic* fashion, on the facts that generated and/or may anyhow legitimately justify the fear of persecution. Thus the observer will be looking at the existence of human rights abuses, the country's security and political situation, the potential use of violence and repression, the possible subsistence of various forms of discrimination that trespass on the legal threshold actually becoming forms of persecution, the conditions of minority groups, etc., especially focusing on the entries related to the five convention grounds (Ethnicity, Race, Religion, Political Opinion and membership of a Particular Social Group). The observer will also be interested in looking at the existing national legislation and its concrete application.

The explored facts should be legally relevant. A fact is legally relevant if it can have an impact on the case's outcome. While we discuss relevancy as a substantive research principle further on, we may here underline the importance of clearly isolating the few legally significant details of the case that necessitate substantiation and formulate an appropriate research strategy for obtaining precise answers.

Furthermore, COI researchers should use commonly agreed indices and indicators for measurable events, bearing in mind that sound measurement is 'not simply a matter of observation but also of conceptualization'.[16] The concrete object of research is more linked to a relative level of generality rather than a quotation of observables. It is not easy for example to observe alleged abuses of the police in every single prison, but reporting bigger aggregates, e.g. the 'conditions in detention' should be sufficient to demonstrate the existence of indicators that serve as indirect measures for protection rights. A common agreed approach should be reached on the use of internationally recognized human rights standards, both in the investigation and the reporting methods.

4.3. THE RESEARCH STRATEGY

The conjunction ring between the observer and the facts is the formulation of a pertinent refugee research strategy. The research should be academically sound and legally relevant. The investigator should be able to elaborate a pure realistic, non-critical, non-interpretive methodology. The main aim of interpretive research is intended to understand, rather than to predict and serving a correct prediction is rather the aim of the COI research. The critical approach seeks to disrupt rather than reproduce the status quo and, yet again, we should be looking at facts as they are, or better, as they are reported to be. The right COI research philosophy should then be close to the positivist method, which aims at uncovering reality through defining constructs and precise qualitative and quantitative measures. This approach assumes that reality is objectively constructed, that measurement is possible, and that a predictive understanding of phenomena is free from human influence.

Having this principle in mind, the observer should develop good skills in formulating research questions linked to the case under analysis. Hence, if for example the ground of persecution is imputed political opinion because the claimant

---

[16]   R. PAWSON, *A Measure for Measures; A Manifesto for Empirical Sociology*, (London, 1989), 40.

allegedly belonged to a religious group that the authorities perceive rather as a political party opposing the government, the research question will not be on the freedom of religion in Country X of course, but rather freedom of expression, the legal side, and the existence, structure and activities of the religious group, in the pure risk-group assessment. In preparing for this exercise, some suggest using the research-tree method, consisting of drawing from the main facts to be explored a central question to which is attached the other possible research questions as branches to the main trunk. This technique may prove effective for beginners, but as long as research experience is cumulative, researchers should be able to work out their patterns automatically.

As soon as the field of study is delineated and research questions have shaped the investigation hypothesis, the ability of the researcher will be tested in translating the questions in efficient research syntax. Especially with the use of electronic sources, the capacity of devising the right word for running an internet search become crucial for avoiding irrelevant results and speeding up the research process. In the current information seeking and information retrieval systems where only direct search is possible, the observer must think of different kinds of information that could be relevant contextually or situational and formulate a separate question for each one of them. Hence, using our previous example, typing the name of the main pastor of the religious group to which the claimant was directly associated during a specific event such as a public gathering cracked down on by the police, will probably give more precise results then the name of the religious group, but the latter should also be a 'target' of the search. Consequently, the researcher must think both comprehensively and selectively.

When all is set to start the fact-finding task, the COI observer will be called to tie together different standards for expedient implementation. The way in which the collection of data is obtained and the guarantees of quality that the gathered data should offer may be indicated as the *procedural* and the *substantive* principles of COI research. The word 'principles' should be preferred to 'standards' in order to allow for less rigid schemes and more flexibility in approaching the research. Fixing several strict boundaries for research will be counterproductive, especially when dealing with different sources and corresponding methodologies. A set of codified principles, as opposed to prescriptive instructions, leaves more room for evaluation and consequently more responsibility to the researcher in conducting his/her inquiries but in the meantime offers guidance and orientation. In the first category of principles we may include a) the impartial and objective approach, b) the predominant use of publicly available information and c) the skills in assessing sources. In the second category we might include the criteria of d) relevance, e) reliability, f) accuracy, and g) currency of the sought information.

Yet, no standard should stand in the abstract, but must be read in combination with the others in a non-exclusive way and must be applied with a certain degree of elasticity and malleability to the case concerned. The over emphasis on one or two elements or a disproportionate balance between them may render the research too rigid, limiting the admissibility of results otherwise accessible. For example we should not exclude some sources because the intensity of reliability is not equivalent to the perceived accuracy or the information supplier is not totally neutral in its descriptions. Since every claim is different and since the probability of finding that related piece of information may vary considerably, one should be able to handle the different criteria in order to attain the right weighing scale between all of them.

As in a stable and resistant molecule, all the particles, here represented as the procedural and substantive principles, should hold one another together through flexible ties in order to create a solid and adaptable organizational structure for COI query.

4.4. PROCEDURAL PRINCIPLES

Procedural principles are intended to provide guidance to the analyst, suggesting the correct way to grip COI research in a manner that may secure valuable results. They represent the behavioural ground rules and the technical skeleton of the research process. They aspire both to ensure a predisposition to the accurate exploration of facts as well as to the skills and practical solutions to be generally used. They differ from the substantive principles in that they pertain more to the operational attitude rather than to the core qualities of the sought evidence.

4.4.1. Impartiality and Objectivity

COI researchers should abstain from taking a position (*a priori* or *ex-post*). Their attitude to the research topic should be unbiased, equitable and fair-minded. A partial approach tailored based on human rights defence or derived from over-reliance on past caseload will limit and distort the outcome as well as negate preconceived intentions. Yet, value-free data cannot be granted, since the researcher inevitably uses his/her preconceptions and his/her progressive findings to guide the research process, but some efforts to scale down and abstract from presumptions and assumptions should be mandatory.

Applying objectivity in COI research suggests also not using just one source or one category of sources. Information should be sought in 'multi-sources modality', looking for various categories (international, national, non-governmental, etc.) and types (mission reports, field interviews and annual reports) of information providers. This is valid both for weighing up conflicting accounts (an Amnesty International note affirming that 'X' happened under the 'Y' form and a US Department of State report asserting that 'X' did not take place or was manifested in the form of 'Z') and for similar information where the variety of sources hunted for is wide and provides additional corroboration. The application of this principle will lessen the risk of marrying the cause of 'one-way sources'.

The risk of researchers' involvement with the subject of research is real and quite high in the field of human rights and potentially even more in refugee-related inquiries. The danger of being befriended by the stories of persecution, human rights abuses and the various exposures of the uprooted people may result in a selective approach of both what to look at and how to report it. Thus, it might be natural to omit government sources in the analysis of a 'commonly-known' dictatorial environment or rebel-produced information in a context of civil war and abuses of civilians. Exiting the 'emphatic tunnel' without taking sides or engaging in pro-partisan militancy is probably one of the most difficult quality standards to respect when conducting research.

4.4.2. Public vs. Anonymous Sources

The observer should utilize documents obtainable from sources that respect certain publication principles and rules rather than doubtful sources (such as partisan websites, Blogs, Wikipedia,[17] etc.) without an organized methodology that do not grant the necessary quality and confidence of COI.

The burning necessities of eligibility officers to obtain the required detailed information, is often in breach of this basic principle. Consequently, in many instances we may find refugee decisions based on confidential information shared between governments or their specialized agencies or stemming from unscrutinized information springs, considerably lowering the transparency and the overall strength of the pronouncement.

Conversely, publicly available documents are subject to some yardsticks such as multiple editing by the authors, reviewers and editors, preliminary in-depth formal and substantial verification prior to publication, and public scrutiny once the document is published that may correct inaccuracies.[18] Furthermore, the fundamental need for maintaining a certain reputation brings enough assurances of upper quality[19] and validates the predominant recourse to this type of informant.

---

[17] For a critique of the Wikipedia system by one of its founders, see A. FREAN, 'Wikipedia a force for good? Nonsense, says a co-founder', *The Times*, 11 April 2007.

[18] J. W. HOBSON, *The Damned Information. Acquiring and Using Public Information to Force Social Change* (Washington, 1971).

[19] M.L. JORDY, E.L. McGRATH & J.B. RUTLEDGE, 'Book Reviews as a Tool for Assessing Publisher Reputation', 60 (2) *College & Research Libraries Journal*, March (1999) 132-142.

4.4.3. Assessing Sources

Facts are reported in various categories (national, international, governmental and non-governmental) and type (academic, news, research institutes and research departments) of sources in a jungle of ever-growing information opportunities. Assessing the sources becomes thus fundamental in reaching the desired significance of the COI. This is even more important in the uncontrolled proliferation of web-based sources. What are then the critical elements for minimizing the risk of locating undesirable information? Which are the signs the observer should be able to interpret in order to reach the desired conviction of quality?

Developing from the UNHCR (2004) attempt at codification, to appraise any particular source it is important to ascertain the following:

"(i) Who produced the information and for what purposes (taking into account such considerations as the mandate, the mission statement, and the values of the information producer);

(ii) To what extent the information producer is *independent* and *impartial*. [Bearing in mind that every organization has an agenda, we may have to evaluate the possible *ideological* and the *financial* biases];

(iii) Whether the information producer has *established knowledge* (e.g. has regional or country branches, has a geographical specialization, has a specific focus, etc.);

(iv) Whether the information produced is couched in a suitable tone (objective rather than subjective viewpoint, no overstatements, etc.) or whether the source is overtly judgmental;

(v) Whether a scientific methodology has been applied and whether the process has been transparent.

Finally, information sources should be regularly re-evaluated as changing in circumstances can affect the accuracy and reliability of information."[20]

This simple test is an excellent tool for evaluating accountability and credibility through uncomplicated verification, and while is not a scientific instrument, the grid may nevertheless prove to be very useful for systematically delimiting the uneven level of the quality of information.

---

[20]   UN HIGH COMMISSIONER FOR REFUGEES, *Country of Origin Information: Towards Enhanced International Cooperation,* Department of International Protection, Protection Information Section, February 2004, 10.

Other evaluating criteria may be added to enhance the threshold of selection such as the presence of overstatements or oversimplification of the subjects treated, the good mix between primary and secondary sources, the solid argumentation behind opinions, the level of information and assumptions the author makes about the reader, the width of distribution and the accessibility of materials.[21]

4.5. SUBSTANTIVE PRINCIPLES

Substantive principles aspire to direct the observer towards those sources that present some essential warranties of content-reliance. They are designed as methodological assessments to test how robust and trustworthy, and ultimately valuable the available evidence really is.

4.5.1. Relevance

Affirming that the subject of research should be relevant to the case seems an obvious statement. Nevertheless, here the criterion refers more to the legal rather than the logical relevance of the COI.[22] To be more precise, the legal relevance is the tendency of a given item of evidence to prove or disprove one of the legal elements of the case (in our case the well-foundedness of the fear). As reported in a study by Huang and Soergel (2006) "a piece of information is evidentially relevant if it either increases or decreases the confirmation or probability of a conclusion through deductive or inductive reasoning, including plausible and probabilistic reasoning".[23]

The application of this principle has few connotations. First of all, irrelevant facts should not be admissible in the adjudication process. Only pertinent and directly related information that helps answer the key questions should be accepted. Hence, if the research produces an answer upon which we cannot draw a conclusion (not even through inference), then it means that we do not need that information. Secondly, relevance is not subject to individual estimation of what is related to the case but is rather governed by the general rule of evidence and the consequent constant review of applicable standards. Lastly, given the practically inexistent chance of finding direct situational relevance (a precise answer to an individual case's COI question, e.g. 'A' was mentioned in a report as being tortured while in custody) we have to refer to circumstantial relevance that can be used to infer the

---

[21]   J. ORMONDROYD, M. ENGLE & T. COSGRAVE, *How to critically analyze information sources*, Cornell University,   2004,   available   at   <http://www.library.cornell.edu/ okuref/research/skill26.htm>.

[22]   P. TILLERS & E. GREEN (Eds.), 'Probability and Inference in the Law of evidence. The Uses and Limits of Bayesianism', 109 *Boston Studies in the Philosophy of Science (Series)* (1988).

[23]   X. HUANG & D. SOERGEL, 'An evidence perspective on topical relevance types and its implications for exploratory and task-based retrieval', 12 (1) *Information Research* (2006), available at <http://informationr.net/ir/12-1/paper281.html>.

answer (e.g. in the city where 'A' lives, the occurrence of torture in custody is reported) and therefore the relevance analysis assumes huge importance.

Applying one of Wigmore's legal relevance standards we may emphasize the requirement that admissible evidence has more than a "bare minimum" of probative value, and that admissible evidence have a "plus value".[24] Thus, as a first step, the COI source should really be able to add something to the substantiation of the case.

4.5.2. Accuracy

How can someone verify the accuracy of the reported information? How can we trust or mistrust an account of events that normally take place in countries far away from ours? The epistemology of testimony can contribute to solve this rather practical issue. Drawing on Fallis (2004) conceptualization we may indicate four central areas to consider when verifying information: the authority of the source, independent corroboration and transparent retrieval, plausibility and support, and presentation.

The authority of a source can be determined by a positive 'past track record' which one may rely on. Nevertheless, this criterion alone may not be satisfactory when accuracy was not verifiable in the past or the researcher just chances upon the information provider for the first time (especially when navigating the internet jungle and when information tracing becomes difficult because of the scarcity of sources). Certainly one may rely on another's experience such as the selection of sources operated by specialized COI providers such as the UNHCR's Refworld or Ecoi.net, or simply on another researcher's advice. In any case, we many want to rapidly determine the possible bias of a source by looking at its mandate, mission statement or overall scope but we may also become familiar with the source by understanding its principal target, why it should publish distorted information, why should it not be sincere and if there is any indication that the author was not in a position to know the facts that it is reporting (e.g. has no presence in that country, is reporting others' reports only, etc.). The built reputation of a source may sometimes prove not to be absolute. Amnesty International for example can also report inaccurate accounts of events. But what is of interest here is the generic trust that the observer can have in a given source rather than a single report or piece of information.

Accuracy can also be verified through a multiplicity of sources reporting the same event. Agreement between different sources will offer a healthy indicator of accurate information. The numerical verification of independent corroboration

---

[24] J. H. WIGMORE, *A Treatise on the Anglo-American System of Evidence in Trials at Common Law, including the Statutes and Judicial Decisions of all Jurisdictions of the United States and Canada* (Boston, 1940).

reduces the risk of misleading information. It is important to link the increase of trustworthiness given by the agreement between different sources with the analysis of their possible agenda and bias. Only multiple independent sources will grant a good degree of confidence. Cross referencing and triangulation may offer a wider statistical foundation to establish the likelihood that the fact indeed happened, but often one may be brought to the misleading conclusion that if the fact is reported in more than one source it must be true. The reported information might not be obtained first-hand or there could be round-tripping (citation of one single source in various reports).[25] We should pay particular care in detecting the original source and avoid citing a round-tripper as an additional substantiation of evidence.

Another principle to apply when validating accuracy is the plausibility of the reported facts based on the supporting materials surrounding it like appropriate descriptions, good referencing, reasons sustaining the assertions, declared methodologies (direct experience, indirect acknowledgement, deduction, allegation, hypothesis advancement, etc.). Already acquired expertise on a caseload, ethnic group, country characteristics, etc., may substantially help in testing the accuracy of the description of facts. Lipton (1998) maintains that 'if it is very unlikely that a piece of information is accurate given everything else that we know about the topic in question, then we should be inclined to think that the information is inaccurate.[26]

Ultimately, the way in which the information is presented is also an indicator of accuracy, especially for web-based sources. The presence of copious advertisements may indicate a lack of objectivity. The purpose of selling products may override the desire to tell the truth.[27] Furthermore, if the information provider presents texts with wrong spelling or grammar mistakes we may also be tempted to think that if it did not take the time to correct errors it may also present a lack of concern for quality and accuracy.[28] Lastly, if the referencing is not indicated in a clear way (incorrect referencing, use of inappropriate quotations standards, no hypertexting when possible, etc.) provoking irretrievability of the original source, we may be persuaded to think that the author is hiding something or is just revisiting reality for his own interpretation of the facts.

Additionally, completeness of research is a distinct but correlated problem in relation to accuracy. We may want to avoid not only inaccurate reporting but also incomplete reporting. Exact quotations, in the sense of faithful coverage of the facts

---

[25] Goldman refers to such information sources as "non-discriminating reflectors". See A. I. GOLDMAN, 'Experts: Which ones should you trust?', 63 (1) *Philosophy and Phenomenological Research* (2001), 85-110.

[26] P. LIPTON, 'The epistemology of testimony', 29 (1) *Studies in the History and Philosophy of Science* (1998).

[27] J.E. ALEXANDER & M.A. TATE, *Web wisdom: How to evaluate and create information quality on the Web*, (Mahwah, New Jersey, 1999) 27.

[28] A. COOKE, *Authoritative guide to evaluating information on the Internet* (New York, 1999) 61.

and avoiding omissions, are essential. The omissions may have a geographical, quantitative or qualitative character. If an authoritative study on Country X reports that 'torture' is applied in detention centres, and we leave out from the quotation the fact that this happens only in certain regions or provinces of Country X then we are providing inaccurate and misleading information. The same goes for if, e.g. we do not mention the fact that torture is practised only against men or women or is restricted to a single detention centre, or is practised only in a few specific cases (e.g. against terrorist suspects).

In conclusion, if we do not have scientific proof of the accuracy of facts reported from a source, we may nevertheless use a systematic classification applying the mentioned features in order to minimize the risk of using inexact information for making a decision in refugee claims. Practice and experience will help fine-tune the researcher's skills in appraising the accuracy of a determined piece of information.

4.5.3. Reliability

Reliability implies both the trustworthiness of the source as a whole and what we may call the 'fact-happening reliability', that is the approximation of the likelihood of the fact to have truly happened. Here the 'fact-happening reliability' is a sort of specification of accuracy in that we may find problems in relying on a source that may even generally be reliable, but whose reported facts are not mentioned in any other account, leaving the observer with the dilemma of what to do with single reporting. It is rather a matter of lack of verification for which the researcher is largely armless. Conversely, we may have an unreliable source (e.g. Wikipedia) that reports a truly happened event.

In general, reliability reinforces judicial confidence in the report. When looking for information on, e.g. a specific violation of human rights, we will search through reputable specialized sources. But how can we define a source as reliable? Similarly to the assessment test discussed as a procedural principle above, the researcher will tend to look at a certain number of indicators like authorship, the reputation of the publisher, historical accuracy, the existing bias, lack of conflicting interests, corroboration, etc. What can be added here, as an additional meter of evaluation is the reflection on what that particular source may offer more or just differently from other sources. The reasons that rationalize the comparative advantage of a particular information supplier may be found in its specialization (e.g. a research institute focusing exclusively on child soldiers), its stated capacities (e.g. having a pool of researchers that are proficient in Arabic and produce information on the Middle East), and its presence on the ground (e.g. having permanent regional offices opened in Africa). All these elements may help structure the general degree of confidence in a source.

On the other hand, 'fact-happening reliability' may pose a few ontological problems. It is practically impossible to authenticate the reliability of a single event, in particular when only one source is describing it. In some cases, in fact, only a small fraction of the Internet will index key information. This may be generated by the fact that the sought information is too detailed and granular to be captured by general primary observers or because most of the reports are free texts from which it is not easy to extract and combine information.[29] Therefore, the researcher may be confronted with a single piece of information and have little luxury for assessing trustworthiness. Nevertheless, we should not exclude the employ of that evidence using all the necessary caution and caveats in the weighing up mechanism for attaining a decision. Once again, we can only establish a principle and not set a rigid rule.

4.5.4. Currency

The importance of using reports that are published within a recent time frame is directly related to the necessity of establishing the actuality of the fear of persecution and confirming the existing likelihood of being harassed upon return. The objective well-foundedness of the fear of persecution should indeed be assessed at the time when the decision is taken. Hence, we may want to search and use country reports that were produced in the last six months up to one year. Country analyses from the majority of authoritative sources (e.g. US Department of State, Human Rights Watch, ECRE, etc.) are usually issued on a regular annual basis. Most of the major events occurring in the countries of origin at irregular intervals are reported in *ad hoc* reports.

However, we should mention a certain tendency by COI users in the way they approach the topic of currency, which brings on the generalized belief that the report must be "truly" current, not trespassing on the few weeks preceding the consideration of the case. This conviction is normally driven by the structure and functioning of the modern information society, where users are bombarded with a quantity of ever-changing news and media accounts that give the impression that every situation is volatile and that what is true today might not be actual tomorrow or at least not in exactly the same way. In this frenzied environment everything seems to become immediately outdated and therefore is not certain anymore. This alteration of the perception of reality should be reframed and limited, especially when dealing with asylum and persecution. The causes of persecution are generally deep-rooted, based on old ethnic or religious conflicts, on cultural uniqueness that have consolidated through the centuries or on political oppositions with long past track records. It is unlikely that ethnic hate or political repression may disappear or

---

[29]   D. F. NOBLE, *Assessing the Reliability of Open Source Information*, (Vienna (US), 2004).

substantially change from day to night, and we may not want to set aside reported stories based on the fact that they are several months old.

Additionally, even less current reports are extremely useful in assessing asylum cases. The assembly of evidence that may be capable of demonstrating that at the time of the flight the asylum-seeker had a legitimate subjective fear of persecution can only add value to the credibility test. The testimony is corroborated by an investigation of the facts reportedly occurring at the time of escape. Once again, COI accomplishes its evidentiary function by reinforcing the analysis of the case and building a solid base for the concluding decision.

4.6 PRESENTING RESEARCH RESULTS

Bearing in mind that the aim of country reports is to accurately record factual information reported by other observers, we should now consider the methodology to use when presenting the results of the query, because this has deep repercussions on the correct usage of the information provided and, ultimately, on the quality of the decision. Providing a confused, unstructured, and fragmented description of facts will not help the decision maker to easily use the evidence and build a genuine determination. If the reader is somehow lost throughout the document because he cannot access the passage s/he looking for in a straightforward manner, if s/he is puzzled with internal inconsistencies or if the organization of the report is not immediately clear and user-friendly, the COI report would not facilitate but rather slow down the adjudication process. Moreover, interpreting, assessing or evaluating the information instead of faithfully recording what others have reported will influence the legal analysis of the caseworker, distorting his/her independent appreciation of the evidence. Lastly, a lack of citation of original sources or the use of a non-transparent referencing system will weaken the legal significance of the evidence, lowering its probative value. But what are the rudiments of a correct reporting methodology?

First of all, the COI report should present a clear logical structure linked to the refugee determination. The report should use standardized templates that may enhance the harmonization of the reporting method, ease the readability of the document and grant a transparent readability of the account. These templates should contain: (i) an introduction where the aim of the research is explained (e.g. if the report is an update of the previous situation, if it is a specific study of an ethnic group, if the report corrects other descriptions, etc.) and the research methodology with its possible caveats (e.g. lack of independent information, scarcity of available sources, difficulties encountered in differentiating the type of used sources, etc.) are declared; (ii) a brief geographical description, including cities, the population and its ethnic composition, the language spoken and the practised religions; (iii) an historical background, focusing on the main events and on particular facts that have characterized the current social composition, including a detailed chronology of events; (iv) a description of the state structure, the constitutional and political system, the organization and scope of political parties, corruption, the composition and way of functioning of the judiciary, detention centres and prison conditions, citizenship and legislation on immigration and asylum; (v) an assessment of the security situation, including the police and the military; (iv) a thorough human rights appraisal including freedom of religion, freedom of expression, freedom of association, minority rights, freedom of movement, civil liberties, treatment of women, children, and homosexuals, racial discrimination, practices of organized crime and human trafficking; (vii) a section on treatment of rejected asylum seekers and of possible cases of *refoulement*. This is a merely indicative outline of a structured report that may help the reader to increase her/his capacities of swiftly making use of the COI report.[30]

Another key element for ensuring the high quality of research and granting an effective tool for superior RSD is neutrality. According to the UNHCR RSD Handbook *"[t]he competent authorities that are called upon to determine refugee status are not required to pass judgment on conditions in the applicant's country of origin"*.[31] The use of non-opinionated language in reporting the facts is fundamental in order to grant objectivity and avoid guiding the legal analysis of the decision maker. The latter is the only person responsible for the interpretation of the case and for reaching a final decision. This is of particular sensitivity in RSD. Eligibility officers often would like to find the evidence that can alone determine a case, while in most of the cases it would just contribute to its clarification where a weighing up exercise is still required as well as a balance with the other elements of the interview (the testimony, the personal experience of the caseload, credibility issues, etc.).

Avoiding judgmental language increases the legal weight of the report. Neutral accounts will testify the impartial aim of purely factual research. To give a concrete example of how little effort is required to satisfy this important principle, we may affirm that in a COI report we should not mention that the *sharia* law discriminates against women but rather that, according to *sharia* law, girls are not allowed to go to school. The 'discriminatory' element is there, but the researcher stays away from driving the caseworker analysis. Moreover, it would be useful to leave some degree of uncertainty when, like in nearly all the cases, there is no direct observation of the facts. The prudent use of the words 'reportedly' or 'allegedly' will lighten the

---

[30] See also the Advisory Panel on Country Information, *Instructions on Producing Country Reports*, during its second meeting of 2 March 2004 designed for the United Kingdom Home Office's Country Information and Policy Unit, available at <http://www.apci.org.uk/PDF/cipu_instructions.pdf>.

[31] See the *Handbook on Procedures and Criteria for Determining Refugee Status under the 1951 Convention and the 1967 Protocol relating to the Status of Refugees, supra* n. 7.

dogmatization of the reported facts, ease the reading and avoid even more influence on the reader.

Another essential requirement for quality reporting is the use of a transparent referencing methodology. All the reported statements should be sourced and the indication of the information supplier should be clearly mentioned in a footnote. This concern is frequently neglected by COI writers creating a problem of attribution. If no reference is made to the paternity of the information, then the reader will legitimately assume that the writer had direct access to the observation of the facts. While in other human rights reports this may not be so relevant, in COI research the ownership of the information may change significantly the legal weight of a document. For example if the UNHCR affirms something without mentioning the source of the information or without mentioning the fact that the source should remain anonymous but that is anyway trusted by the refugee agency, then the decision maker would reasonably attribute a value to that report that benefits from the UNHCR's general credibility and specialization in refugee and displacement issues. The origin of the information counts in the overall weighing up process and therefore proper referencing should receive particular attention and care. Classical academic standards for footnote referencing determining the citation method such as the Oxford Style or the Harvard Style may be used as well as other document annotation and bibliography building systems.[32]

In conclusion, the way the research results are presented is as important as the observance of the procedural and substantive principles when performing the research. The COI report will have a different usability and a different authority in RSD procedures if it is well structured, non-opinionated and transparent.

5. CONCLUSIONS

The delicate use of Country of Origin Information as probation material in the determination of refugee claims requires some specific care in the way the information is collected and presented.

A selective definition of COI, advocating a predominant use of qualitatively robust reports will offer some guarantees of sound decision-making. The application of some distinctive principles to the structure of country of origin research will contribute to a more candid assessment of the well-foundedness of the fear of persecution.

We may resume the research cycle (as shown in Figure 1) as a structured, logically organized, progressive hierarchy of principles to be applied in a comprehensive but accommodating way. This construct should contribute to

---

[32] See also UN HIGH COMMISSIONER FOR REFUGEES, *Style Guide*, Department of International Protection, Protection Information Section, Second Edition, July 2005.

empowering the country researcher with some tools in order to obtain decent research outcomes. Ultimately, the final beneficiary of this research methodology is either the institute of asylum that will reinforce its integrity, and the asylum-seeker, who will be confronted to a fair and efficient refugee status determination.

Figure 1. The Country of Origin Research Cycle

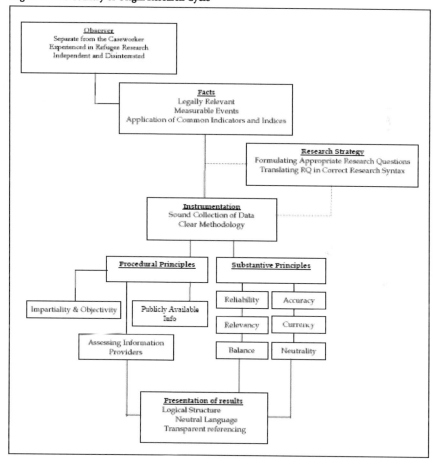

TREATY INTERPRETATION AND THE SOCIAL SCIENCES

Koen De Feyter

1. INTRODUCTION

Lawyers work with text. In international law, interpretation of text allows the attributing of meaning to a treaty provision in the context of a specific dispute. Treaty rules tend to be formulated in the abstract in order to allow general application. At the same time, the abstract general nature of provisions opens the door for disputes on what a rule means in a specific circumstance, perhaps unforeseen at the time of drafting. At this juncture, interpretation is essential.

The law of treaties offers legal professionals rules on interpretation, but law is not the only discipline intent on detecting meaning and there is no obstacle in principle why law should not accommodate input from other disciplines. Semantics is the dominant science of discovering the meaning of expressions used in language or other systems of signs. When law refers to things and situations in the real world, natural sciences are also relevant. The continental shelf is a geographical phenomenon and it makes sense that any legal interpretation of what that concept means takes into account the physical reality.[1]

Here, our main concern is whether the understanding or use of a term in society — as evidenced through the use of social science methodology — can usefully inform the interpretation of human rights treaties.

2. MULTIDISCIPLINARITY IN TREATY INTERPRETATION

The Vienna Convention on the Law of Treaties[2] includes a section on treaty interpretation that is frequently invoked in international litigation. According to the

---

[1]   E.g. on the use of recent scientific developments for the purposes of interpretation in the context of international environmental law, see D. FRENCH, 'Treaty interpretation and the incorporation of extraneous legal rules', 55 *International and Comparative Law Quarterly* (2006) 281-314 at 308.

[2]   Vienna Convention on the Law of Treaties (23 May 1969), entry into force 27 January 1980. Official publication in the UN Treaty Series, vol. 1155, p. 331.

International Court of Justice, the rules in the Convention on the interpretation of treaties constitute customary international law.[3] In many instances, however, the Convention allows the parties to a specific treaty to diverge from the Convention's provisions (on matters such as the entry into force of the treaty, the procedure for amendment, reservations and so on). Similarly, international courts tend to use the section on interpretation as a frame of reference, without offering much clarification on what specific element of the provisions has been paramount to their findings and without considering themselves limited to the methods explicitly spelled out in the Convention.[4] The Convention articles function as an aid to interpretation, rather than as a constraint.[5]

Articles 31 and 32 of the Vienna Convention on the Law of Treaties are relevant to our purposes.[6] The articles were meant to be used in an integrated way — all

---

[3]   E.g. see *Case concerning the Application of the Convention on the Prevention and Punishment of the Crime of Genocide (Bosnia and Herzegovina v. Serbia and Montenegro)*, ICJ 26 February 2007, Judgement, General List No. 91, § 160.

[4]   Compare R. GARDINER, *International Law* (Harlow, 2003) 79.

[5]   For a different argument, see Orakhelashvili, who argues that 'interpretive methods are laid down in the Vienna Convention in a certain order of priority. Tribunals rarely have a free reign in applying them: they have to follow the sequence laid down in the Vienna Convention'. See A. ORAKHELASHVILI, 'Restrictive Interpretation of Human Rights Treaties in the recent jurisprudence of the European Court of Human Rights', 14 *European Journal of International Law* (2003) 529-568 at 537. Orakhelashvili develops the argument to criticize the recent tendency of the European Court to interpret the Convention restrictively in cases dealing with the extraterritorial reach of the treaty. Clearly, there is a hierarchy between Article 31 and Article 32 of the Vienna Convention of the Law of Treaties (See also U. LINDERFALK, 'Is the hierarchical structure of Articles 31 and 32 of the Vienna Convention real or not? Interpreting the rules of interpretation', 54 *Netherlands International Law Review* (2007) 133-154. Within Article 31, there is a huge amount of room for judicial discretion, and, as is argued below, judges also use interpretive methods not explicitly provided for in the Vienna Convention. As Ian Brownlie stated: 'Jurists are in general cautious about formulating a code of 'rules of interpretation' since the 'rules' may become unwieldy instruments instead of the flexible aids which are required'. See I. BROWNLIE, *Principles of Public International Law* (Oxford, 2003) 602.

[6]   Vienna Convention on the Law of Treaties, *supra* n. 2, Articles 31-32:Article 31 *General rule of interpretation*
1. A treaty shall be interpreted in good faith in accordance with the ordinary meaning to be given to the terms of the treaty in their context and in the light of its object and purpose.
2. The context for the purpose of the interpretation of a treaty shall comprise, in addition to the text, including its preamble and annexes:
(a) any agreement relating to the treaty which was made between all the parties in connection with the conclusion of the treaty;
(b) any instrument which was made by one or more parties in connection with the conclusion of the treaty and accepted by the other parties as an instrument related to the treaty.
3. There shall be taken into account, together with the context:
(a) any subsequent agreement between the parties regarding the interpretation of the treaty or the application of its provisions;
(b) any subsequent practice in the application of the treaty which establishes the agreement of the parties regarding its interpretation;

elements referred to are of assistance in determining the proper meaning of a text. Article 31 as a whole establishes a 'general rule' and there is no hierarchy as to preferred method within the article. Article 32 on the other hand, is a 'supplementary' tool that only comes into play in the circumstances as defined in the provision.

The provisions contain a mix of subjective and objective elements. The subjective elements refer to the intentions of the drafters and of the parties to the treaty. States need to consent to being bound by treaty obligations and such obligations should therefore be interpreted in a way that is consistent with the consent given. Hence, clarification of content may result from subsequent agreements made by the parties, subsequent State practice, evidence of the intention of the parties to give a special meaning to a term and from the *travaux préparatoires*. At the same time, the Vienna Convention enables judges to take into account objective elements and thus engage in more independent research that goes beyond investigating the intent of the parties. Courts can hold States to the ordinary meaning of the terms of a treaty. They can interpret a treaty in the light of philosophical foundations set out in the preambular paragraphs. They can determine what the object and purpose of the treaty are, and then construct individual provisions accordingly. Courts usually consider both the objective and the subjective elements,[7] but the weight given may differ on a case-by-case basis, depending on what is deemed to be an equitable outcome.

The court's degree of deference to State sovereignty also plays a role. Clearly, attaching predominant weight to State intent fits within a traditional approach to international law that stresses the sovereign freedom of States to engage (or not) in commitments at the international level. In international human rights law, monitoring bodies tend to stress the importance of the objective elements, even in ways not explicitly envisaged in the Vienna Convention. The Inter-American Court has explicitly stated that 'In the case of human rights treaties (...) objective criteria of interpretation that look to the text themselves are more appropriate than subjective criteria that seek to ascertain only the intent of the parties'.[8] The European Court of

---

(c) any relevant rules of international law applicable in the relations between the parties.
4. A special meaning shall be given to a term if it is established that the parties so intended.
Article 32 *Supplementary means of interpretation* Recourse may be had to supplementary means of interpretation, including the preparatory work of the treaty and the circumstances of its conclusion, in order to confirm the meaning resulting from the application of Article 31 or to determine the meaning when the interpretation according to Article 31:
(a) leaves the meaning ambiguous or obscure; or
(b) leads to a result which is manifestly absurd or unreasonable.

[7] According to Ian Brownlie, the general rule on interpretation supported by the Convention is to give precedence to 'the intention of the parties as expressed by the text'. See BROWNLIE, *supra* n. 5.

[8] *Restrictions to the Death Penalty*, IACtHR 8 September 1983, Advisory Opinion, Series A No. 3, § 50.

Human Rights has said on numerous occasions that the European Convention on Human Rights is a 'living instrument which (...) must be interpreted in the light of present-day conditions',[9] and that the Convention should be interpreted in a manner which renders the rights not theoretical or illusory, but practical and effective.[10] Such an *effective and evolutionary* approach to interpretation is not necessarily contradictory to the Vienna Convention,[11] as it could be deemed part of an 'object and purpose' test, but it may certainly lead to results not originally contemplated by the parties to the Convention.

Is there a case to be made that given the special features of human rights treaties specific methods of interpretation are to be preferred?[12] The International Court of Justice gave credit to the idea that human rights treaties differ in character from traditional, contract-like international treaties. In its 1951 Advisory Opinion on the Genocide Convention, the Court identified the object of the Convention as:

> to safeguard the very existence of certain human groups (...) In such a convention the contracting States do not have any interests of their own (...) Consequently, in a convention of this type one cannot speak of individual advantages or disadvantages to States, or of the maintenance of a perfect contractual balance between rights and duties. The high ideals with inspired the Convention provide, by virtue of the common will of the parties, the foundation and measure of all its provisions.[13]

International human rights bodies have further developed this line of thinking. The UN Human Rights Committee has held that human rights treaties are not a web of inter-State exchanges of mutual obligations, but concern the endowment of individuals with rights, leaving little place for the principle of inter-State reciprocity.[14] The Inter-American Court stated that human rights treaties are not

---

[9] *Tyrer v. UK*, ECtHR 23 April 1978, Series A No. 26, § 31.

[10] *E.g.* see *Artico v. Italy*, ECtHR 13 May 1980, Series A No. 37, § 33.

[11] The section on interpretation in the Vienna Convention makes no explicit mention of either an effective or an evolutionary approach to interpretation. Antonio Cassese nevertheless argues that the authors of the Vienna Convention 'set great store by the principle of 'effectiveness' (...), a principle 'plainly intended to expand the normative scope of treaties, to the detriment of the old principle whereby in case of doubt limitations of sovereignty were to be strictly interpreted'. See A. CASSESE, *International Law* (Oxford, 2006) 179. See also, more cautiously, BROWNLIE, *supra* n. 5, 606. An evolutionary approach stresses the need to take into account realities and attitudes prevailing when the dispute arises, rather than opinions expressed during the preparatory work of the treaty.

[12] For a critical review of examples of the use of evolutionary interpretation by dispute settlement bodies in other areas of international law and particularly in WTO law, see FRENCH, *supra* n. 1, 295-300.

[13] *Reservations to the Convention on the Prevention and Punishment of the Crime of Genocide*, ICJ 28 May 1951, Advisory Opinion, General List No. 12, p. 12.

[14] UNITED NATIONS (UN), Human Rights Committee, General Comment 24 (Fifty-second session), *Issues relating to reservations made upon ratification or accession to the Covenant or the Optional*

multilateral treaties of the traditional type concluded to accomplish the reciprocal exchange of rights for the mutual benefit of the contracting States:

> Their object and purpose is the protection of the basic rights of individual human beings irrespective of their nationality (...). In concluding these human rights treaties, the States can be deemed to submit themselves to a legal order within which they, for the common good, assume various obligations, not in relation to other States, but towards all individuals within their jurisdiction.[15]

According to the Court, the Inter-American Convention is 'a multilateral legal instrument or framework enabling States to make binding unilateral commitments not to violate the human rights of individuals within their jurisdiction'.[16] The European Court of Human Rights speaks of 'objective obligations' that benefit from collective enforcement[17] and has explicitly dealt with the implications for the purposes of interpretation of the treaty:

> In interpreting the Convention regard must be had to its special character as a treaty for the collective enforcement of human rights and fundamental freedoms (...). Thus, the object and purpose of the Convention as an instrument for the protection of individual human beings require that its provisions be interpreted and applied so as to make its safeguards practical and effective (...). In addition, any interpretation of the rights and freedoms guaranteed must be consistent with the 'general spirit of the Convention, an instrument designed to maintain and promote the ideals and values of a democratic society' (...).[18]

Because human rights treaties confer rights on individuals, human rights bodies strive to interpret treaties in such a way that the protection offered to individuals is real. In order to assess whether the protection offered is real, their investigation goes beyond the intention of the parties, into *reality*.

At this point, social science methodology becomes relevant. Clearly, whether human rights safeguards are 'practical and effective', cannot be determined on a legal basis only. Effective protection will only be achieved if human rights norms have a real impact on behaviour in a relevant social setting, i.e. when safeguards result in

---

Protocols thereto, or in relation to declarations under article 41 of the Covenant, UN Doc. CCPR/C/21/Rev.1/Add. 6 (1994), § 17. On the effects for interpretation of the non-reciprocal character of human rights treaties, see also M. TOUFAYAN, *Human rights treaty interpretation: a postmodern account of its claim to 'specialty'*, New York: Center for Human Rights and Global Justice Working Paper No. 2, 2005, p. 4.

[15] *The Effect of Reservations on the Entry into Force of the American Convention on Human Rights*, IACtHR 24 September 1982, Advisory Opinion, Series A No. 2, §.29.

[16] *The Effect of Reservations on the Entry into Force of the American Convention on Human Rights*, *supra* n. 15, 33.

[17] *Ireland* v. *United Kingdom*, ECtHR 18 January 1978, Series A No. 25, § 239.

[18] *Soering* v. *United Kingdom*, ECtHR 7 July 1989, Series A No. 161, § 87.

actual protection against abuse by potential perpetrators. The social sciences offer quantitative and qualitative methods for establishing to what extent human rights safeguards result in real protection and for analyzing what variables would need to be impacted upon (e.g. through legal intervention) in order to improve protection. The methods involve data collection and hypothesis testing, through statistical analysis, interviews, focus groups, historical comparison and so on. If the aim is to ensure effective protection, the findings of this research should inform the interpretation of human rights norms by the courts and the further elaboration of human rights law from the global to the local level.

The same point can be made in a different way. Human rights judges are well advised not to use the community of lawyers as the only source of interpretive authority. Usually, the 'ordinary' meaning of a treaty provision in international law is the meaning as understood by the relative disciplinary community, i.e. the community of (international) lawyers.[19] In human rights law, however, other interpretive communities[20] — using other assumptions to determine understanding - are equally relevant for the purposes of constructing the meaning of a human rights provision in such a way that effective protection is achieved.

This need to make use of interpretive angles offered by other disciplines is certainly not unique to human rights law. In international environmental law, the establishment and maintenance of a regulatory regime that ensures 'effective protection' equally requires the input from a knowledge-based community of experts that are capable of determining an appropriate response to an environmental threat.[21]

A fascinating illustration of a multidisciplinary approach to interpretation is the judgment of the Inter-American Court of Human Rights in the Awas Tingni case.

---

[19]   D. VAGTS, 'Interpretation and the New American Ways of Law Reading', 4 *European Journal of International Law* (1993) 472-505 at 484.

[20]   Stanley Fish defines interpretive communities as 'not so much a group of individuals who shared a point of view, but a point of view or way of organizing experience that shared individuals in the sense that its assumed distinctions, categories of understanding, and stipulations of relevance and irrelevance were the content of the consciousness of community members who were therefore no longer individuals, but, insofar as they were embedded in the community's enterprise, community property'. Fish continues: 'Of course, if the same act were performed by members of another community (...), the resulting text would be different, and there would be disagreement; not, however, a disagreement that could be settled by the text because what would be in dispute would be the interpretive 'angle' from which the text was to be seen (...). See S. FISH, *Doing what comes naturally: Change, Rhetoric and the Practice of Theory in Literary and Legal Studies* (Oxford, 1989) 141.

[21]   Compare P. HAAS, 'Banning chlorofluorocarbons: epistemic community efforts to protect stratospheric ozone', 46 *International Organization* (1992) 187-224.

3. THE *AWAS TINGNI* JUDGMENT[22]

The small Awas Tingni community (consisting of about 140 families), situated in a densely forested area of Nicaragua's North Atlantic coastal region, claimed that Nicaragua had violated the Inter-American Convention on Human Rights by granting logging concessions on the community's traditional lands to a Korean timber company. After a long spell of domestic litigation, the case moved to the Inter-American Court of Human Rights.

The Court approached the issue primarily from the angle of the right to property.[23] The legal question before the Court was whether the ostensibly classic individual right to property included in the Convention could be interpreted in such a way as to include an essentially collective right to land and land use of an indigenous community.[24]

The Court first pays tribute to the drafters of the treaty by referring to the preparatory work of the Convention in order to establish that it was not the drafters' intention to only protect private property. Obviously, it does not follow that the Convention therefore protects indigenous concepts of property. The Court simply

---

[22]   *Mayagna (Sumo) Awas Tingni Community v. Nicaragua*, IACtHR 21 August 2001, Preliminary Objections, Series C No. 66.

[23]   Article 21 of the Inter-American Convention on Human Rights, entitled 'Right to Property', declares that: 1. Everyone has the right to the use and enjoyment of his property. The law may subordinate such use and enjoyment to the interest of society. 2. No one shall be deprived of his property except upon payment of just compensation, for reasons of public utility or social interest, and in the cases and according to the forms established by law. 3. Usury and any other form of exploitation of man by man shall be prohibited by law.

[24]   The Court explains its approach to interpretation in the following paragraphs of the judgment: '145. During the study and consideration of the preparatory work for the American Convention on Human Rights, the phrase '[e]veryone has the right to the use and enjoyment of private property, but the law may subordinate its use and enjoyment to public interest' was replaced by '[e]veryone has the right to the use and enjoyment of his property. The law may subordinate such use and enjoyment to the social interest.' In other words, it was decided to refer to the 'use and enjoyment of his property' instead of 'private property'.

[146].   The terms of an international human rights treaty have an autonomous meaning, for which reason they cannot be made equivalent to the meaning given to them in domestic law. Furthermore, such human rights treaties are live instruments whose interpretation must adapt to the evolution of the times and, specifically, to current living conditions. 147. Article 29(b) of the Convention, in turn, establishes that no provision may be interpreted as 'restricting the enjoyment or exercise of any right or freedom recognized by virtue of the laws of any State Party or by virtue of another convention to which one of the said states is a party'. 148. Through an evolutionary interpretation of international instruments for the protection of human rights, taking into account applicable norms of interpretation and pursuant to article 29(b) of the Convention -which precludes a restrictive interpretation of rights-, it is the opinion of this Court that article 21 of the Convention protects the right to property in a sense which includes, among others, the rights of members of the indigenous communities within the framework of communal property, which is also recognized by the Constitution of Nicaragua'.

uses the *travaux préparatoires* to create an opening for an argument that is entirely built on an objective reading of the text.[25]

The Court moves away quickly from the historical context in which the Convention was adopted by stressing that in interpreting the text it needs to take into account present times and 'current living conditions'. The Court resolutely adopts an evolutionary approach[26] and finds that at the present time Article 21 also protects rights of members of indigenous communities in the context of communal property. Although the Court can more easily arrive at this conclusion given that indigenous rights to land are — at least theoretically — recognized in the Constitution of Nicaragua, it devotes no particular effort to demonstrate that its interpretation of Article 21 coincides with the current intent of the parties to the Inter-American Convention. As such the judgment fits well within the approach of human rights bodies to treaty interpretation, as outlined above. The Court autonomously establishes whether in a specific situation the State has provided the protection required by the treaty to the plaintiffs. The Court does not really verify whether State Parties in their mutual relationships are in agreement with the Court's understanding of the provision. It is impossible to tell from the judgment whether the intent of the State Parties coincides with the Court's view that the conventional right to property should cover communal concepts of property based on indigenous custom.

The multidisciplinary element in the Court's interpretative methodology comes into play when the Court needs to determine the exact meaning of the concept of 'communal property'. Remarkably, the interpretive community that the Court turns to for clarification is the indigenous community itself. It is the shared understanding of property of the members of the community that will determine what 'property' means in Article 21, in the context of this specific dispute. Inevitably then, the Court accepts that very different forms of property can potentially be accommodated under the Convention, depending on how the concept is socially defined. The Court's interpretation thus allows for a degree of plurality within the treaty.

---

[25] Compare Jan Klabbers who argues that the travaux préparatoires are 'commonly used to demonstrate that the drafting history does not stand in the way of a particular (often more teleological) interpretation which would be difficult to accommodate on the basis of the mere text of a treaty provision'. See J. KLABBERS, 'International legal histories: the declining importance of travaux préparatoires in treaty interpretation?', 50 *Netherlands International Law Review* (2003) 267-288 at 283.

[26] More generally on the use of an evolutionary interpretation by the Inter-American Court of Human Rights, see M. FERIA TINTA, 'Justiciability of economic, social and cultural rights in the Inter-American system of protection of human rights: beyond traditional paradigms and notions', 29 *Human Rights Quarterly* (2007) 431-459 at 443-444.

Although the right is defined generally and is applicable to all the State Parties in the region, its specific meaning may vary depending on local understanding.[27]

In order to determine the content of the communal concept of property prevailing within the Awas Tingni community, the Court took evidence from twelve witnesses presented by the Inter-American Commission, including Awas Tingni and other indigenous leaders from the Atlantic Coast and a number of anthropologists.[28]

The anthropologists gave evidence on a wide range of issues.[29] One witness had visited the area in order to assist the community in mapping the lands they used and was questioned on how boundaries with neighbouring communities could be decided. Others were asked about the forms of exploitation of the soil in the area and whether the community recognized individual forms of appropriation. It became clear that the community used a communal system of property, but that inside the communal system, individual usufructory use was allowed. This meant that community members could not sell or rent the territory to people from outside the community. However, inside the community, certain individuals used a lot for an extended period of time.[30] The anthropologists agreed that the community considered the land communal (also because they engaged in rotational subsistence farming that was almost semi-nomadic), but that internally, the community had mechanisms to assign possible use and occupation to its own members that did not allow alienation to others from outside the community. When the agricultural cycle of a cultivation plot ended, the plot reverted to the community.[31] The system was embedded in indigenous customary law, which was not written, but consisted of real practices that were carried out in different communities.[32]

In its judgment, the Court relied heavily on the evidence given by the anthropologists. The Court found that:

---

[27] The Court's approach in the Awas Tingni case should not be confused with the European Court of Human Rights' margin of appreciation technique that, although it also allows for variety, does so in order to defer to a domestic State's interpretation of a treaty, rather than to the interpretation given by a local community which may well contradict the State's view.

[28] Anaya and Grossman characterize the role of the social science and legal professionals who testified as one of giving context for the story told by the indigenous leaders, providing insights into its broader implications and validating the perspective of territory advanced by the indigenous leaders. See S. ANAYA AND C. GROSSMAN, 'The case of Awas Tingni v. Nicaragua: a new Step in the International Law of Indigenous Peoples', 19 *Arizona Journal of International and Comparative Law* (2002) 1-15 at 11.

[29] For a transcript of the oral pleadings, see 'Transcript of the Public Hearing on the Merits', 19 (No. 1), *Arizona Journal of International and Comparative Law* (2002) 129-306. The journal published a full special issue on the Awas Tingni case.

[30] 'Transcript of the Public Hearing on the Merits', *supra* n. 29, 171.

[31] 'Transcript of the Public Hearing on the Merits', *supra* n. 29, 242.

[32] 'Transcript of the Public Hearing on the Merits', *supra* n. 29, 184.

Given the characteristics of the instant case, it is necessary to understand the concept of property in indigenous communities. Among indigenous communities, there is a communal tradition as demonstrated by their communal form of collective ownership of their lands, in the sense that ownership is not centred in the individual but rather in the group and in the community. By virtue of the fact of their very existence, indigenous communities have the right to live freely on their own territories; the close relationship that the communities have with the land must be recognized and understood as a foundation for their cultures, spiritual life, cultural integrity and economic survival. For indigenous communities, the relationship with the land is not merely one of possession and production, but also a material and spiritual element that they should fully enjoy, as well as a means through which to preserve their cultural heritage and pass it on to future generations (...)[33]

The customary law of indigenous peoples should especially be taken into account because of the effects that flow from it. As a product of custom, possession of land should suffice to entitle indigenous communities without title to their land to obtain official recognition and registration of their rights of ownership.[34]

The Court concluded that although the Nicaraguan Constitution recognized indigenous rights to property in principle, the State had failed to delimit and demarcate the territories over which such property rights existed. This created a climate of permanent uncertainty among the members of the Awas Tingni Community. The Court consequently held that the State was under an obligation to delimit, demarcate and title the territory of the Community's property, and that, until it had done so, the State was to cease granting concessions that could affect the existence, value, use or enjoyment of the resources located in the geographic area in which the Community members lived and carried out their activities.[35]

The anthropologists helped in decoding the local concept of communal property. They were thus instrumental in ensuring that the Court gave a specific interpretation to the relevant conventional provision that was in conformity with the community's concept of property and thus ensured that the abstract protection guaranteed by the Convention was effective. It is striking that the regional court was more sensitive to the local reality than the domestic judges involved in the dispute at an earlier stage. In any case, the judgment amply demonstrates that there is room within the judicial process and more generally within legal reasoning, to integrate knowledge from the social sciences.

---

[33] *Mayagna (Sumo) Awas Tingni Community* v. *Nicaragua, supra* n. 22, 149.
[34] *Mayagna (Sumo) Awas Tingni Community* v. *Nicaragua, supra* n. 22, 151.
[35] *Mayagna (Sumo) Awas Tingni Community* v. *Nicaragua, supra* n. 22, 151-153. On 4 September 2007, Hurricane Felix hit land on the Northeast Coast of Nicaragua as a level 5 hurricane. The eye of the hurricane passed directly over Awas Tingni, resulting in complete devastation of all the homes in the community, as well as destruction of all nearby crops and transport routes.

Even in countries where the customs of local communities have been codified and the legal system is officially dual, the need to involve social scientists for the purposes of interpretation remains. A nice illustration can be found in a recent review[36] of the 2004 *Bhe* case[37] before the South African Constitutional Court. The case concerned the rights of inheritance of women. The Constitutional Court ruled unanimously that the customary law principle that as a general rule only a male relative of a deceased person qualifies as an intestate heir, violated the right to equality protected in the Constitution.

Inevitably, the Court needed to determine the precise content of the customary rules in order to assess whether they were in violation of the Constitution. In South African law, it is reportedly common to distinguish between 'official' customary law and 'living' customary law. Codified customary law can be found in sources of State law, such as statutes, case law and government documents. It is widely accepted, however, that the codified version is a distortion of the law as existing in the community.[38] Commentator Evadné Grant explains that in existing customary law, rules on succession are based on a concept of family property: the oldest son does not only inherit the deceased's property, but also his responsibilities and in particular the duty to support surviving family dependants. At the time of incorporation into State law, however, the customary rule was reduced to a mere individual right of the oldest son to inherit property, thus locking women in a subordinate legal position.

Regrettably, in its judgment the Constitutional Court of South Africa does not make use of the existing law within the communities. If it had done so, the Court could perhaps have avoided fully setting aside customary law. According to Grant, practices in some of the communities are changing; in some instances, families now reach agreement to enable the widow of the deceased to administer family property.[39] But in order to discover the existence of such practices, the Court would have had to rely on evidence of social practice, based on observation, as the validity of existing customary law is not dependent on written sources.

The relevant South African legislation also enables the Court to use assessors to advise on customary law, but the use of assessors raises concerns about representation, particularly in gender sensitive cases. As Grant points out, assessors

---

[36]   E. GRANT, 'Human rights, cultural diversity and customary law in South Africa', 50 *Journal of African Law* (2006) 2-23.

[37]   *Bhé and Others* v. *Khayelitsha Magistrate and Others; Shibi* v. *Sithole and Others; South African Human Rights Commission and Another* v. *President of the Republic of South Africa and Another*, Constitutional Court of South Africa 15 October 2004, Judgment, 2005 (1) SA 580 (CC).

[38]   *Bhé and Others* v. *Khayelitsha Magistrate and Others; Shibi* v. *Sithole and Others; South African Human Rights Commission and Another* v. *President of the Republic of South Africa and Another*, *supra* n. 37, 13.

[39]   *Bhé and Others* v. *Khayelitsha Magistrate and Others; Shibi* v. *Sithole and Others; South African Human Rights Commission and Another* v. *President of the Republic of South Africa and Another*, *supra* n. 37, 15-16.

are usually chosen from traditional leaders 'which in many cases would exclude women'.[40] Clearly, a correct assessment of the content of the law, as it applies within the communities - which is essential in cases where an appropriate balance needs to be struck between individual and community rights - requires the use of social science methodology.

Anthropologists have had an ambivalent attitude vis-à-vis the idea of global human rights in the past, but this may well have changed, as evidenced by a special 2006 issue of the *American Anthropologist*. In his editorial, Guest Editor Mark Goodale reflects on anthropology's engagement with human rights since the American Anthropological Association in 1947 famously refused to endorse the idea of a universal declaration of human rights. He identifies two schools in the contemporary anthropology of human rights.[41]

According to the first school of thought, anthropologists should use their knowledge of specific cultural processes and meanings to reinforce specific projects for social change, to help prevent further encroachments against particular marginalized populations or to do both. This could serve as a description of the role played by the anthropologists in the Awas Tingni case: they argued for an expansion of the interpretation of human rights to increase their effectiveness for the community under threat. Clearly, anthropologists acting as an expert witness on the existing law within a community are of a crucial importance to judicial decision-making in cases involving a dispute between States and communities.

The second school of thought builds on the ethnographic tradition and perceives human rights as a problem that must be studied empirically. The aim is to develop a comparative database that explains how human rights actually function, what they mean for different social actors and how they relate empirically (as opposed to conceptually) to other 'transnational assemblages'. The descriptive data produced through these studies could be used to make the implementation of human rights more effective or not. Goodale concludes that modern anthropology can thus tolerate or even encourage approaches that are either fundamentally critical of human rights regimes or politically and ethically committed to them.[42]

I have argued elsewhere that if human rights are to provide effective protection to marginalized local communities,[43] they will need to be localized. Localization implies taking the human rights needs as formulated by local people as the starting

---

[40]   *Bhé and Others* v. *Khayelitsha Magistrate and Others; Shibi* v. *Sithole and Others; South African Human Rights Commission and Another* v. *President of the Republic of South Africa and Another*, supra n. 37, 20.

[41]   M. GOODALE, 'Introduction to 'Anthropology and human rights in a new key", 108 *American Anthropologist* (2006) 1-8 at 3-4.

[42]   GOODALE, *supra* n. 41, 5.

[43]   For the purpose of this study, a local community is an inclusive group or organization, that refers to a geographic reality, unified by common needs and interests, that articulates claims in human rights terms.

point both for the further interpretation and elaboration of human rights norms, and for the development of human rights action, at all levels ranging from the domestic to the global.[44]

In human rights litigation involving disputes between the State and a local community,[45] a practical device for ensuring that human rights treaties properly address the problems identified by the community, is to rely on social scientists to establish what a globally or regionally defined right needs to protect specifically in order to ensure human dignity to the members of the community. The findings arrived at through the use of social science methodology can subsequently inspire the interpretation of the norms included in the global or regional human rights convention.

Variations in the interpretation of rights in order to ensure that human rights protection is locally effective are not at odds with maintaining human rights as a global language. On the contrary, universality stands to be enriched if input from varied societies is taken into account. During the proceedings in the Awas Tingni case, Expert Rodolfo Stavenhagen made this specific point as follows:

> (I)n certain conditions, in certain circumstances, in certain historic contexts, the rights of the human person are guaranteed and can be fully exercised only if the rights are recognized of the collectivity and the community to which this person belongs from birth, and of which he is a part, and which gives him the necessary elements to be able to feel fully realized as a human being. That also means a social and a cultural being (...). I consider that (...) the international community (...) has the challenge to develop new concepts and new norms that, without in any way injuring or encroaching on the human rights of the person, of the individual, on the contrary, would enrich them by recognizing the social and cultural reality in which these violations occur.[46]

The communities that go through a human rights crisis build up knowledge — a usage of human rights linked to concrete living conditions. The recording and transmission of this knowledge is essential if human rights are ever to develop into an effective global protection tool. One path to achieving this aim is taking the findings of social observation seriously in the context of treaty interpretation.

---

[44]   K. DE FEYTER, 'Localising human rights', in W. BENEDEK, K. DE FEYTER and F. MARRELLA (eds.), *Economic Globalisation and Human Rights* (Cambridge, 2007) 67-92, at 68.

[45]   Disputes also arise between a community and an individual, who can either be a member of the community or not. Also, in such cases, use should be made of the social sciences to determine the community's understanding of the rights in question. A judge can only properly decide to give priority to the right claimed by the individual, if the judge's assessment of the community perception is based on valid social observation.

[46]   'Transcript of the Public Hearing on the Merits', *supra* n. 29, 184.

4. SUBSEQUENT CASE LAW

The Awas Tingni judgment proved to be the first in a line of cases under the Inter-American Convention, in which the Court based its interpretation of concepts in the Convention on definitions inspired by social observation of community life.

The Yatama case[47] concerned the exclusion by the Supreme Electoral Council of Nicaragua of candidates presented by Yatama, an indigenous regional organization, from the municipal elections held in November 2000. An anthropologist called by the organization as an expert witness testified on decision-making processes within the communities, on the selection of candidates, and on the difficulties of reconciling these community practices with the requirements of the Electoral Law. She argued that Yatama had been 'forced to adopt organizational forms, such as that of a political party, which do not correspond to the 'oral tradition of these people".[48] The Court found that there is no provision in the American Convention that allows it to be established that citizens can only exercise the right to stand as candidates to elected office through a political party. Other ways in which candidates can be proposed were pertinent and necessary to encourage or ensure the political participation of specific groups of society, taking into account their special traditions and administrative systems.[49] The restriction that they had to participate through a political party imposed on the Yatama candidates was a form of organization alien to their practices, customs and traditions as a requirement to exercise the right to political participation. The State had not justified that this restriction obeyed a useful and opportune purpose, which made it necessary to satisfy an urgent public interest. On the contrary, this restriction implied an impediment to the full exercise of the right to be elected of the members of the indigenous and ethnic communities that formed part of Yatama.[50]

The Court also decided two cases involving the protection of ancestral property rights of indigenous communities in Paraguay. In the Yakye Axa case,[51] the Court again showed its willingness to accomodate plurality in its interpretation of the Convention. In order to effectively ensure the rights in the Convention, the scope and content of its articles needed to be assessed taking into account the 'specific characteristics that differentiate the members of the indigenous peoples from the general population'.[52] In its analysis of the content and scope of Article 21 of the

---

[47] *Yatama* v. *Nicaragua*, IACtHR 23 June 2005, Preliminary Objections, Merits, Reparation and Costs, Series C No. 127.
[48] *Yatama* v. *Nicaragua, supra* n. 47, 111. For a description of the 'community democracy' practised with the indigenous organization, see § 124 (12-16).
[49] *Yatama* v. *Nicaragua, supra* n. 47, 215.
[50] *Yatama* v. *Nicaragua, supra* n. 47, 218.
[51] *Yakye Axa Indigenous community* v. *Paraguay*, IACtHR 17 June 2005, Merits, Reparation and Costs, Series C No. 125.
[52] *Yakye Axa Indigenous community* v. *Paraguay, supra* n. 51, 51.

Convention this meant that the Court took into account, as it has done previously, the special meaning of communal property of ancestral lands for the indigenous.[53] The Court also relied on Article 31, paragraph 3 of the Vienna Convention on the Law of Treaties, in order to interpret the right to property in the Inter-American Convention in the light of ILO Convention No. 169.[54] According to the Court, the American Convention is a part of a system of international human rights law and therefore should be interpreted in line with that system (of which ILO Convention No. 169 is an element).[55]

In the Sawhoyamaxa case,[56] the Court followed a similar reasoning,[57] but was confronted with an additional problem, namely that the relevant indigenous community had not been living on the land that it claimed, but in very difficult conditions on a roadside near the area. The contested lands had been transferred to private owners, who used them for raising cattle.

Article 64 of the National Constitution of Paraguay embodies the right of the indigenous communities to collective or communal ownership of the land that is their traditional habitat. The State pointed out that it did not deny its obligation to restore rights to the community, but that the members of the Sawhoyamaxa Community 'claim title to a piece of real estate based exclusively on an anthropologic report that, worthy as it is, collides with a property title which has been registered and has been conveyed from one owner to another for a long time'.[58]

The Court once again stressed the need to look at the right to property differently in the context of a dispute involving indigenous communities:

> This notion of ownership and possession of land does not necessarily conform to the classic concept of property, but deserves equal protection under Article 21 of the American Convention. Disregard for specific versions of use and enjoyment of property, springing from the culture, uses, customs, and beliefs of each people, would be tantamount to holding that there is only one way of using and disposing of property, which, in turn, would render protection under Article 21 of the Convention illusory for millions of persons.[59]

The Court found that members of the community, who had unwillingly lost possession of their lands, when those lands had been lawfully transferred to

---

[53]   *Yakye Axa Indigenous community* v. *Paraguay, supra* n. 51, 124.

[54]   ILO Convention No. 169 concerning Indigenous and Tribal Peoples in Independent Countries (27 June 1989), entry into force on 5 September 1991. Paraguay ratified ILO Convention No.169 in 1993.

[55]   *Yakye Axa Indigenous community* v. *Paraguay, supra* n. 51, 126-128.

[56]   *Sawhoyamaxa Indigenous Community* v. *Paraguay*, IACtHR 29 March 2006, Merits, Reparation and Costs, Series C No. 146.

[57]   *Sawhoyamaxa Indigenous Community* v. *Paraguay, supra* n. 56, 59-60, 83,117.

[58]   *Sawhoyamaxa Indigenous Community* v. *Paraguay, supra* n. 56, 125.

[59]   *Sawhoyamaxa Indigenous Community* v. *Paraguay, supra* n. 56, 120.

innocent third parties, were entitled to restitution thereof or to obtain other lands of equal extension and quality.[60] The Court could not decide that Sawhoyamaxa Community's property rights to traditional lands prevailed over the right to property of private owners or *vice versa*, since only the domestic courts had jurisdiction to decide disputes among private parties.[61] The State nevertheless had to consider the possibility of purchasing or condemning these lands. If restitution of ancestral lands to the members of the Sawhoyamaxa Community was not possible on objective and sufficient grounds, the State was ordered to make over alternative lands, selected upon agreement with the indigenous community, in accordance with the community's own decision-making and consultation procedures, values, practices and customs. In any case, the extension and quality of the lands was to be sufficient to guarantee the preservation and development of the Community's own way of life.[62]

Finally, the Moiwana[63] case is of particular interest here, because it does *not* involve an indigenous people. Moiwana Village was settled by N'djuka clans late in the 19th century. The N'Djuka are a community of Maroons, descendants of African slaves who managed to escape to the rainforest areas during the colonization period, and set up new and autonomous communities. Anthropologists again testified orally and in writing on the social structure of the community, its relationship to land, death rituals and reparation system. In 1986, members of the armed forces of Suriname attacked Moiwana. State agents allegedly massacred over 40 men, women and children, and razed the village to the ground. Those who escaped the attack supposedly fled into the surrounding forest and then into exile or internal displacement. According to the Inter-American Commission, there had not been an adequate investigation of the massacre; no one had been prosecuted or punished and the survivors remained displaced from their lands. The Court accepted the Commission's argument that it should assert jurisdiction because, while the attack itself predated Suriname's ratification of the American Convention and its recognition of the Court's jurisdiction, the alleged denial of justice and displacement of the Moiwana community continued.[64]

In *Moiwana*, the Court extended the interpretation it had given to Article 21 in indigenous cases to a non-indigenous ethnic community. Moiwana community members did not possess legal title to the village lands and Suriname had argued that by default the property belonged to the State. The Court recognized that the

---

[60] *Sawhoyamaxa Indigenous Community* v. *Paraguay, supra* n. 56, 128.

[61] *Sawhoyamaxa Indigenous Community* v. *Paraguay, supra* n. 56, 136.

[62] *Sawhoyamaxa Indigenous Community* v. *Paraguay, supra* n. 56, 212.

[63] *Moiwana Community* v. *Suriname*, IACtHR 15 June 2005, Preliminary Objections, Merits, Reparation and Costs, Series C No. 124.

[64] See also C. MARTIN, 'The Moiwana Village Case: A New Trend in Approaching the Rights of Ethnic Groups in the Inter-American System', 19 *Leiden Journal of International Law* (2006) 491-504.

Moiwana community members were not indigenous to the region,[65] but were a tribal people that had lived in the area in strict adherence to N'djuka customs. Relying explicitly[66] on the evidence given by an expert anthropologist, the Court found that the tribal people's 'all-encompassing relationship' to their traditional lands was expressed through a communal concept of ownership that the State was under a duty to recognize, taking into account the need to consult neighbouring communities.[67]

Although the way of life of the N'djuka and in particular their relationship to community land closely resembles that of an indigenous people, the judgment may be taken as an indication of the Court's willingness to bestow the benefits of its multidisciplinary approach to the interpretation of the Convention on other communities living in multi-ethnic societies.

In *Dogan and others v. Turkey*,[68] the European Court of Human Rights dealt with the forced evictions by Turkey of fifteen members of the same Kurdish family from their village in the context of the violent conflict in the area between the security forces and the PKK (the Workers' Party of Kurdistan). The inhabitants of the village had been displaced in 1994 and by the time of the judgment had not been allowed to return, nor had they received any assistance to achieve an adequate standard of living in the urban town where they had resettled. The applicants mainly alleged that the forced eviction and the refusal to allow them to return by the authorities amounted to a violation of Article 1 of Protocol No.1 to the European Convention.[69]

In the judgment, Boydas village, from which the family originated, is described as an area of dispersed hamlets and houses spread over mountainous terrain, used for livestock family farming. The family did not own title deeds attesting that they owned property in the village. The first issue then that the Court needed to decide was whether the family held any possessions in the village that could come under the protection of Article 1, Protocol. No.1. The applicants submitted that in the rural area where they had lived a patriarchal family system prevailed, wherein adults married, built houses on their father's lands and made use of their father's property

---

[65] *Moiwana Community* v. *Suriname, supra* n. 63, 132.
[66] *Moiwana Community* v. *Suriname, supra* n. 63, 132.
[67] *Moiwana Community* v. *Suriname, supra* n. 63, 134.
[68] *Dogan and others* v. *Turkey*, ECtHR 29 June 2004 (rectified on 18 November 2004), Reports of Judgments and Decisions 2004-VI (extracts).
[69] The text of Article1 of Protocol No.1 to the European Convention on Human Rights runs as follows: 'Every natural or legal person is entitled to the peaceful enjoyment of his possessions. No one shall be deprived of his possessions except in the public interest and subject to the conditions provided for by law and by the general principles of international law. The preceding provisions shall not, however, in any way impair the right of a State to enforce such laws as it deems necessary to control the use of property in accordance with the general interest or to secure the payment of taxes or other contributions or penalties'.

as a natural requirement of the social system. In those circumstances, protection should be afforded under the Convention to all the economic resources jointly enjoyed by all the villagers.[70] The mayor of the village testified that the applicants had all been using plots of land in the context of the economic system and local traditions described above.[71]

The Court noted that it was undisputed that the applicants all lived in Boydaş village until 1994. Although they did not have registered property, they either had their own houses constructed on the lands of their ancestors or lived in houses owned by their fathers and cultivated their fathers' land. They also had unchallenged rights over the common lands in the village and earned their living from stockbreeding and tree-felling. Those economic resources and the revenue the applicants derived from them qualified as 'possessions' for the purposes of Article 1 of Protocol No. 1.[72] The Court concluded that restrictions on the exercise of the right could be justified because of security concerns, but had been disproportionate in that they had imposed an excessive burden on the family.

In *Dogan*, the European Court of Human Rights accepted the applicants' statements on the communal system of land use in rural Kurdish villages at face value, without seeking to establish whether the applicants' statements were corroborated by social science research. Under Article 38 of the European Convention on Human rights and under the Rules of the Court, the Court may adopt investigative measures, including the organization of hearings of persons as witnesses and experts. Such investigations can also be carried out on the spot; in other cases involving the destruction of Kurdish villages, the Court has held fact-finding hearings in Turkey, particularly when it was not satisfied that domestic authorities and courts had properly investigated allegations.[73]

5. LESSONS FOR HUMAN RIGHTS RESEARCH

If it is accepted that judicial bodies and legislators should aim to achieve effective human rights protection through an interdisciplinary approach, clearly the same holds for human rights research. Human rights research that concerns itself with analyzing whether human rights deliver effective protection and that wishes to contribute to the improvement of human rights protection must be interdisciplinary

---

70 *Dogan and others* v. *Turkey, supra* n. 68, § 137.
71 *Dogan and others* v. *Turkey, supra* n. 68, § 23-24.
72 *Dogan and others* v. *Turkey, supra* n. 68, § 139.
73 See P. LEACH, *Taking a case to the European Court of Human Rights* (Oxford, 2005) 62-66. For an example of a case involving evidence-taking from witnesses in Turkey, see *Ipek v. Turkey*, ECtHR 17 February 2004, Reports of Judgments and Decisions 2004-II (extracts). The Inter-American Court also has the power to conduct investigations on the spot (see in particular Article 34 (4) Rules of Procedure of the Inter-American Court of Human Rights, 1991).

in nature. Obviously, not all human rights research may be concerned with effective protection: one can do a legal analysis of a judicial decision or of a domestic law on the basis of its compatibility with international law, without worrying about how the outcome of this purely legal exercise affects human rights protection on the ground. On the other hand, even a purely legal analysis stands to be enriched by a discussion of the impact of the legal result on the relevant society.

Interdisciplinary research is notoriously difficult. Most scholars only engage in interdisciplinary work after completing disciplinary training. In practice, interdisciplinarity then means opening up to insights from disciplines that one is almost inevitably less familiar with. Klabbers notes that interdisciplinarity 'often presumes a flat, one-dimensional vision of the discipline-to-relate-with'.[74] In addition, interdisciplinary research is probably not mainstream in academic human rights research — but perhaps more usual in policy-oriented human rights research and in research work by non-governmental organizations — where the concern for achieving effective protection comes naturally.[75]

That does not mean, however, that interdisciplinarity in human rights research cannot be done. In a recent publication,[76] Oré discusses the pitfalls of interdisciplinary human rights research. Interdisciplinarity inevitably affects the research process and team composition. Researching effective protection of human rights inevitably requires a combination of skills and thus either a research team or cooperation with outsiders that can offer technical disciplinary advice. The dialogue between disciplines requires building a common ground, which may be made somewhat easier by the fact that all work within the human rights paradigm. What is required is that at least some of the members of the research team act as knowledge brokers that can translate insights and experiences across professional and disciplinary boundaries. If the process works, it can:

> (R)esult in critical breakthroughs that approach (...) 'transdisciplinarity' — when disciplines begin to assimilate concepts rather than merely sitting side by side. Through this research process, the research team evolves into its own community of practice, with its own innovative, 'transsdisciplinary' orientation on the research.[77]

---

[74] J. KLABBERS, 'The Relative Autonomy of International Law or the Forgotten Politics of Interdisciplinarity', 1 *Journal of International Law & International Relations* (2005) 35-48 at 37.

[75] For an example, see INTERNATIONAL CENTRE FOR HUMAN RIGHTS AND DEMOCRATIC DEVELOPMENT, *Human Rights Impact Assessment for Foreign Investment Projects* (Montreal, 2007), <www.dd-rd.ca>.

[76] G. ORÉ, *The Local Relevance of Human Rights: A Methodological Approach* (Antwerp, 2008), <www.ua.ac.be/dev>.

[77] L. LINGARD, C. SCHRYER, M. SPAFFORD and S. CAMPBELL, 'Negotiating the Politics of Identity in an Interdisciplinary Research Team', 7 *Qualitative Research* (2007) 501-519 at 506.

METHODS OF PHILOSOPHICAL RESEARCH ON HUMAN RIGHTS

Andreas Follesdal

1. INTRODUCTION

Human rights raise several profound philosophical issues, of justification, content and institutional implications. One of these is how we are to best conceive of the relationship between *philosophical* and *legal* understandings of human rights. *Philosophical* conceptions of human rights are often argued on the basis of moral premises of human dignity and the sanctity of life, while *legal* conceptions of human rights appeal to a variety of domestic constitutions and international conventions.

Their interrelation has occasioned much scholarly attention, for many reasons. One concern is what David Forsythe notes in his contribution to this volume: is there a risk that we pay too much attention to *legal* and other institutional forms of human rights, given that they are at most *means* to respect, protect and promote human dignity and social justice, somehow conceived? This question is particularly pertinent given two major challenges to human rights research.

On the one hand, there is a marked absence of *internal* critical challenges to legal human rights among many human rights scholars. One reason is that these scholars are 'normative' in one important sense: they are activists at heart and these proclivities may dull an appropriately sceptical attitude toward the best case for human rights institutions. This sense of 'normative' is importantly different from that of *normative* political philosophy, within which discipline this article contributes. Many human rights scholars pursue research aimed at promoting certain desired norms or values, namely human rights. There is then a risk that the research agenda is that of a solution — more legal human rights - in search of problems. If this description holds true, we should expect certain weaknesses, such as the bias against problems that the preferred solution cannot address.

Much philosophy of human rights is also normative, but in a different sense. Normative philosophical research aims to help ascertain the *justifiability* of various norms and values. The research method of Reflective Equilibrium is a process by which we start with our empirical and normative 'considered judgments' at different levels of generality, and modify or reject some of them, add new ones, in order to secure consistency, coherence, credibility and simplicity aimed at obtaining a *theory* for that issue. I explore this philosophical research method in section 4.

The other challenge stems from the growing scepticism among *external* critics, exactly about the efficiency and efficacy of such legal human rights. David Kennedy is perhaps among the most pointed critics, when he recently claimed that:

> The legal regime of 'human rights,' taken as a whole, does more to produce and excuse violations than to prevent and remedy them.[1]

If indeed critics are correct that legal human rights are poor means to promote philosophical rights, at least two strategies are open. We may agree with David Kennedy, to reconsider whether we should endorse legal human rights — or instead defend other, better means. In addition, we may want to reconsider whether the relationship between philosophical and legal human rights is indeed one of ends and means — or whether they are related in more intricate ways so as to rebut or at least recast the criticism.

In light of these challenges, I submit that there are at least two important reasons to think critically and philosophically about the relationship between the philosophical human rights or human dignity, and the legal human rights. Firstly, in order to assess Kennedy's claim and the efficacy of legal human rights in general, we need a better, philosophically well grounded conception of human dignity or philosophical human rights. Without a sufficiently clear goal, it will be impossible to select and shape the requisite indicators and scales.

Secondly, I shall suggest that there are prominent philosophical theories of human rights that hold that the goal — philosophical human rights, social justice or human dignity — must be specified with an eye to the fact that the subject matter to be achieved and assessed are certain institutions, including the allocation of legal rights and obligations. Thus some rights are not only the means, but also the objective to be secured. The normative goal — 'human dignity' and claims of justice among us as human beings — may depend profoundly on, and require, certain kinds of practices and institutions, in particular legal institutions. And such institutions and ties among us may in turn ground further claims among us. Thus, the substantive normative claims based on 'human dignity' may depend on whether there are institutional arrangements in place or that can be put in place — due to such considerations as our complicity in the threats and promotion of the living conditions of others.

The following presentation contributes to both of these large topics. To illustrate good philosophical research, I sketch two valuable contributions: in section 2 that of

---

[1]   D. KENNEDY, *The Dark Side of Virtue: Reassessing International Humanitarianism* (Princeton, 2004) 24.

Amartya Sen and in section 3, Charles Beitz's. Sen's philosophical account of human rights may for our purposes be seen to argue that the claims of individuals are essentially the same across all domains: individuals' actions, domestic — and global — institutions, and actions by corporate bodies such as multi-national corporations or NGOs. Any differences among obligations of different actors derive mainly from their different opportunities and are not due to variations in the content of the fundamental moral obligations these agents owe to others.

An alternative strategy is to argue that different philosophical human rights — or moral requirements more generally — apply to institutions and to individuals' actions. Indeed, different standards may be appropriate for different institutionalized practices. We may describe this as an 'object-dependent moral theory'.[2] For instance, the triggers that may warrant disobedience by citizens, or breaches of 'external' immunity in the form of humanitarian intervention, or exclusion of corporations from investment, may well be drastically different, even though the triggers are all called 'human rights violations'. Charles Beitz's theory belongs to this category.

Section 4 provides a brief sketch of the philosophical research method of 'Reflective Equilibrium', which I believe should apply to issues of human rights just as much as to other topics of philosophical inquiry. Section 5 goes on to use this method to compare the two approaches of Sen and Beitz, by way of indicating some of the challenges each of them face.

2. AMARTYA SEN

In Sen's view, human rights are significant ethical claims on others generally.[3] Human rights are claims that certain freedoms are very important, and that all have a moral obligation to consider what they should do to respect and protect those freedoms of everybody.

The starting point for Sen is thus freedoms — 'descriptive characteristics of the conditions of persons' (328), which in turn generate claims on others. Each of us must refrain from violating these freedoms ourselves, and we must also consider ways and means to prevent violations by others of these freedoms (322). The freedoms of concern must satisfy two conditions: They are important for the individual and they can be influenced 'by social help': 'others could make a material

---

[2]   For various reasons, some of which are suggested by T.W. Pogge, 'Moral universalism and global economic justice', 1 Politics, philosophy and economics (2002) 29-58, I prefer this terminology to monism/dualism/nonmonism (L. MURPHY, 'Institutions and the demands of justice', 27 *Philosophy and public affairs* (1999) 251-291), and 'universalist'/'contextualist' (D. MILLER, 'Two ways to think about justice', 1 *Politics, Philosophy and Economics* (2002) 5-28).

[3]   A.K. SEN, 'Elements of a Theory of Human Rights', 32 *Philosophy and Public Affairs* (2004) 315-356.

difference through taking such an interest' (329). Many urgent claims do not amount to human rights because they fail either of these conditions (329-330).

One of the strengths of Sen's concern for freedoms is that they express the real opportunities for individuals to achieve valuable combinations of human functioning. This choice of 'index' avoids problems with some alternative measures, such as income, which fail to accommodate our different abilities to convert material means into opportunities or freedoms.

Note three features of this account. Firstly, it is not easy to determine from this article[4] whether Sen would agree that institutional distributive justice is a special issue, compared to the obligations individuals have toward one another to promote their freedoms. One might for instance hold that certain freedoms of some people create particularly urgent claims on some others, due not only to the ability of the latter to assist, but owing to the relationship they stand in.

Secondly, Sen plausibly insists that legislation is only one of several valuable routes to respect and protect such freedoms. Indeed, his focus on freedoms, without apparent concern for whether institutionalized relationships may affect the normative weight of duties to secure such freedoms, is also borne out in his insistence that human rights are not centrally to be understood as legal demands or grounds for laws (326). He seems to be correct when he writes that 'It would be a mistake, I would argue, to presume in general that if a human right is important, then it must be ideal to legislate it into a precisely specified legal right.... The necessary change would have to be brought about in other ways' (345).

Thus Sen credibly points out that there are good reasons to also consider other 'routes' in addition to legislation. He notes the 'recognition route' of the non-enforceable 1948 Universal Declaration of Human Rights and later declarations, such as the right to development. And he also stresses the 'agitation route' to promote effective social pressure (344).

Thirdly, note that Sen's account does not provide an absolute obligation to undertake any specific action, but rather requires that individuals give 'reasonable consideration to a possible action' (338-39). This move helps him avoid criticism that his account is unduly demanding.

I conclude that Sen's conception of philosophical human rights as claims to certain freedoms seems to regard institutions and legal rules only as instruments to implement these claims. The freedoms are defended with an independently grounded approach and the instruments of legalization are presumably sometimes

---

[4]   - or others, such as A.K. SEN, 'Equality of what?', in A. K. SEN, Choice, Welfare and Measurement (Cambridge, 1980) 353-369; cf. responses by N. Daniels, 'Equality of what: welfare, resources, or capabilities?', 50 *Philosophy and Phenomenological Research (supplement)* (1990) 273-296; G.A. COHEN, 'Equality of what? On Welfare, Goods, and Capabilities', in M. NUSSBAUM and A.K. SEN (eds.), *The Quality of Life* (Oxford, 1993) 9-29. In Sen's defense, such considerations may find room among the 'many parameters that may be relevant to a person's practical reasoning.' (339).

apt, but sometimes not. In contrast, Beitz's theory of human rights provides a markedly different view. He holds that philosophical human rights are best understood to address institutions and certain institutions in particular.

3. CHARLES BEITZ

Over several decades and perhaps most clearly in an influential contribution in 2001, Charles Beitz has offered a philosophy of human rights that for our purposes offers a distinctly different perspective.[5] Beitz regards human rights as fundamentally addressed to certain institutional and political issues:

> The doctrine of human rights is a political construction intended for certain political purposes and is to be understood against the background of a range of general assumptions about the character of the contemporary international environment. .... as principles for international affairs that could be accepted by reasonable persons who hold conflicting reasonable conceptions of the good life (276).

He explicitly seeks to understand and justify human rights on the basis of 'the role they play in international relations' (Beitz 2001, 267, 277). That particular social function is to state conditions for institutions,

> the systematic violation of which may justify efforts to bring about reform by agents external to the society in which the violation occurs (280).

Beitz goes on to specify that human rights play three different related roles: 1. they constrain the constitutions of states and the rules of international organizations and regimes; 2. they describe the goals for social development appropriate for all contemporary societies; and 3. human rights furnish grounds of political criticism appropriate in global politics by a variety of international and transnational actors (277).

As an illustration, he indicates how this understanding helps frame the requisite arguments that must be presented and defended in order to justify particular human rights. Democratic institutions, for instance, are justified as instrumental to secure subsistence rights and other urgent human interests (279).

4. THE METHOD OF REFLECTIVE EQUILIBRIUM

One prominent mode of philosophical research on normative issues is known as the method of 'Reflective Equilibrium' ('RE'). The name is due to John Rawls'

---

[5]   C.R. BEITZ, 'Human Rights as a common concern', 95 *American Political Science Review* (2001) 269-282.

Andreas Follesdal

presentation in *A Theory of Justice* (1971), but the method can be traced to Aristotle. Some also argue that this research method is appropriate for a much broader range of philosophical issues — and is indeed characteristic of most scientific methodology.[6]

4.1. THREE MAIN FEATURES

For our purposes, the theory of reflective equilibrium as laid out by John Rawls has three main features.

4.1.1. The Aim of Arriving at Reflective Equilibrium is Practical: To Attain Agreement on Specific Moral Issues

For our purposes, the practical puzzles would be those that are central to the philosophy of human rights, e.g. whether Philosophical Human Rights are properly regarded as supreme in some sense, and in what senses, if any, they are 'universal' and whether it is morally defensible to hold corporations to standards that are properly called 'human rights'.

If the method secures agreement among us on such issues, we have a practical justification of our actions and moral judgments. The theory presupposes that there is a shared desire among the parties to arrive at such an agreement on the issues it is applied to.

In our case, the issue is how we should understand the relationship between philosophical conceptions of human rights and international legal human rights, as discussed in section 1 above.

4.1.2 The Starting Points of the Procedure are Non-Foundational Empirical and Normative 'Considered Judgments'

The judgments that the method takes as its starting point are of many different kinds:

- empirical information about particular cases and generalizations, e.g. about the risk of corruption in centralized governments, likely effects of opposition parties;
- moral judgments concerning *particular* cases ('particular judgments'), e.g. that markedly different educational or health care opportunities for girls and boys are unjust;

---

[6]   For elaboration and references, cf N. DANIELS 'Reflective Equilibrium', <http://plato.stanford.edu/archives/sum2003/entries/reflective-equilibrium/>.

- moral *principles*— such as a principle of equal respect for all humans; and
- 'second—order judgments': judgments concerning standards of reasoning, formal requirements on alleged moral principles, etc.

One of the distinguishing features of the Method of Reflective Equilibrium is that none of these considered judgments ('CJ') are regarded as impervious to change as a result of the procedure. That is, any considered judgment is in principle open for modification or rejection when confronted with other considered judgments. This may for instance occur as a result of theoretical considerations: if a particular judgment belonging to the original set of judgments is incompatible with a proposed general principle, it may on reflection be modified or indeed discarded. A principle with some degree of initial credibility can similarly be discounted if it yields conclusions incompatible with several particular judgments and with other general principles or with empirical findings.

In our case, the starting considered judgments concerning human rights include several general principles. One prominent source — among several - is the Preamble and articles of the UN 'Universal Declaration of Human Rights'.[7]

Philosophical human rights are *'universal'* in several senses. In particular, all human beings have such claims on others, or on their institutions, regardless of their gender, ethnicity, religion or nationality: the equal and inalienable rights of all members of the human family.

Philosophical human rights are also *'overriding'*, e.g. in the sense that they protect urgently important human interests and that they should therefore override other legal regulations: 'Whereas it is essential, if man is not to be compelled to have recourse, as a last resort, to rebellion against tyranny and oppression, that human rights should be protected by the rule of law,...'.

4.1.3. The Theory Claims That There Is a Rational Procedure by Which This Aim Sometimes Can Be Reached

The Method of RE holds that arguments among those who disagree on these matters can be conducted according to standards of practical reason accepted by all parties. These standards are the same as those used in scientific arguments more generally. Thus, if an agreement is achieved, it is not a 'mere' agreement, in the sense of being generated by some irrational mechanism. Rather, the agreement is in same sense *objective*. The theory assumes that the parties wish to proceed according to such a procedure.

---

[7]   UNITED NATIONS GENERAL ASSEMBLY, 'Universal Declaration of Human Rights', General Assembly resolution 217 A (III) of 10 December 1948.

4.2. ELABORATION

As I shall use the terms, 'reflective equilibrium' ('RE') is a relation that holds among the CJ of one or more persons. The relation is one of consistency and coherence, in a sense to be explained discuss. CJ in RE are ordered in such a way as to constitute a *theory*: the set of judgments has a logical structure. Thus the set is temporarily stable - at least in the sense that we are not aware of any internal inconsistency which compels change on logical grounds.

4.2.1. Partial, Wide, Ideal REflective Equilibrium

Depending on the scope of the RE, the CJ may include a small or large part of the person's total body of empirical and moral judgments. A total RE will include all the moral and empirical judgments of a person. Our main concern will be with limited REs, i.e. subsets of these judgments for a specific area in moral philosophy. These judgments involved in a limited or total RE will primarily be principles and particular judgments concerning ethics. This may be called a *Partial* RE. A *Wide* RE may also include judgments of empirical theories, such as 'background theories' of the person, of social psychology, biology, etc.; and theories of (moral) epistemology, standards of relevance for moral arguments, theories about the nature and force of moral utterances, and standards of coherence and consistency.[8] We might sometimes want to talk about an *Ideal* RE. This is a wide and total RE where the set of judgments is coherent and consistent with the person's complete ideal theory of the world, accounting for all her experiences. All the judgments are stable: they will not be withdrawn because they conflict with other judgments or with our experience. They are based on true beliefs and true accounts of the world, however 'true' may be defined.

4.2.2. The Method of REflective Equilibrium

The 'Method of RE' refers to how this equilibrium among judgments is achieved, starting with the various CJs that are inconsistent. The method of RE has sometimes been criticized as being very vague and unspecified:[9] which standards are applied and how does the process of adjustment proceed? I shall maintain that the method applies the ordinary standards of rational acceptability. The method centrally requires that we modify or reject each component CJ, and add new ones, guided by the objective to secure consistency and coherence, until RE is achieved. This method

---

[8]   Cf. N. DANIELS, 'Wide reflective equilibrium and theory acceptance in ethics', 76 *Journal of Philosophy* (1979) 256-282; DANIELS, *supra* n. 6.

[9]   Cf. J. RAZ, 'The claims of reflective equilibrium', 25 *Inquiry* (1982) 307-330 at 314.

of RE exploits the fact that normative judgments tend to be theory-dependent. In ethics such changes in CJ are likely to occur when the person(s) explore the implications and best premises for each CJ.

4.2.3. Justification by REflective Equilibrium

What sort of 'justification' does RE provide? The set of CJs in RE — and each CJ — is justified, in a practical sense, for the person at that time. If several persons agree on the judgments, the RE will be justified for them. They will be able to justify their actions and judgments to each other, on grounds they all assent to. Particular judgments and principles can be justified 'from above': from principles and second—order principles, respectively. Principles and second—order principles can also be justified 'from below': by the sets of particular judgments and principles that follow from   them.
To clarify this terminology, let us apply it to Rawls' theory of justice. Rawls' theory constitutes a limited RE: the judgments involved mainly concern the social justice of the major domestic institutions of societies.

Rawls assumes that the RE will somehow come to be shared by citizens. The set of judgments in RE does not include a theory of moral truth, moral epistemology or a theory of theory—constraints. Still, the theory relies on judgments properly belonging to such theories. The RE is not claimed to be ideal: the judgments are only claimed to be accepted in our time, by many members of Western democratic societies. Thus the RE is liable to change, as are the rest of our judgments, in light of new knowledge, increased reflection and new proposed theories. Rawls claims that his theory is a better RE, in the sense of being closer to an ideal RE, than the other prevailing political theories — particularly utilitarianism.[10]

4.2.4. Four Norms that Guide the Method of REflective Equilibrium

Four norms guide efforts to bring coherence and consistency to a set of CJ.

1) Logical consistency
Considered judgments that are found to be logically inconsistent cannot all be included in the RE: one or more must be adjusted.

2) Coherence
A second standard applied in the method of RE is to secure logical — and causal — structures between considered judgments, to increase the logical structure of the set

---

[10]   Cf. J. RAWLS, *A Theory of Justice* (Cambridge, 1971) 381.

of CJ we start out with. This standard also requires that new *principles* or concepts
— such as 'dignity,' 'vital needs' or 'human rights' — be introduced into the set of CJ
to ensure that particular considered judgments become logically related to each
other, so as to allow further checks of consistency.

There are very few restrictions on the introduction of these principles: they are
theoretical constructions or explications.[11] Specifically, no claim is made that these
principles are analyses of the 'meanings' of the ethical terms — not what people
have intended to assert all along, or the actual psychological or sociological *causes* of
the particular considered judgments, held implicitly or unconsciously by anyone.[12]

The point of introducing such principles or concepts is to improve the theoretical
structure of the set of CJ, and a new principle or concept is appropriate if it enables a
better RE, and inappropriate if it does not.

These two standards seem to underdetermine the direction of modification.
Starting with some CJ, it might seem that many consistent and coherent systems can
be generated, in very many ways. After all, any number of judgments may be
modified or rejected, and replaced with any from a wide range of new ones — as
long as they yield a consistent and coherent fit. There may be at least two responses
to this concern. Firstly, it is easier said than done to obtain such consistency and
coherence — especially when the resulting set of CJ must also fit in RE with a wide
range of empirical findings. Secondly, there are two further standards:

3) Maximize credibility

The third standard reduces the scope of possible modifications: the method must
maximize credibility, starting with the original set of CJ that we have some trust in.

4) Simplicity

Finally, the resulting system of judgments — about particulars and about principles
— must be *simple*. This standard may be easier to apply than to define. It seems
mainly to play a role when we are forced to choose between REs that are equivalent
according to the other three standards.

5. THE METHOD OF REFLECTIVE EQUILIBRIUM
APPLIED: SEN AND BEITZ

To illustrate the method of RE, we now consider some weaknesses of the two
accounts sketched above, by Sen and Beitz.

---

[11]   J. RAWLS, 'Outline of a decision procedure for ethics', 60 *Philosophical Review* (1951) 177-197 at
       184-185.
[12]   I here appear to differ with R. DWORKIN, 'The Original Position', in N. DANIELS (ed.), *Reading Rawls*
       (New York, 1973) 16-53, at 22.

5.1. ON SEN: WHY ARE PHILOSOPHICAL HUMAN RIGHTS OVERRIDING?

Amartya Sen's clear account of a philosophy of human rights has several strengths. For instance, it makes clear how philosophical human rights are needed to serve as a critical standard to assess legal human rights and helps avoid undue focus on such legal rules to the detriment of other modes of social change. Moreover, his focus on freedoms helps explain why philosophical human rights are *universal*: all individuals have reason to value such freedoms.

One challenge to his account concerns whether it helps justify the CJ that human rights should *override* other moral concerns and why legal human rights should override other legal regulations. Indeed, Sen notes that claims of human rights must be 'consolidated with other evaluative concerns' (322), so he may want to remain agnostic as to whether these philosophical norms should indeed override other concerns.

If we seek a defence for the overriding nature of such freedom-based claims and look at other parts of Sen's impressive contributions, answers are not easily forthcoming. His elaboration of 'basic functioning' - being well nourished, being free from malaria — and 'basic capabilities' — the combinations of such functioning the person can achieve[13] seems to capture many of the central interests human rights should protect and promote. But it remains unclear what reasons he provides to hold that such capabilities — and basic capability equality[14] — should override other preferences, concerns — and other legal regulations. Our considered judgments about human rights seem to imply that they merit more than 'reasonable consideration'.

In order to avoid this weakness, I submit that Sen's approach can develop further some of the arguments presented by Martha Nussbaum. She seeks to defend the view that certain, specified basic capabilities should be regarded as of overriding importance for a legitimate political order and links this view to human rights.[15]

5.2. ON BEITZ: THE COMPLEXITY OF OBJECT-DEPENDENT THEORIES AND OF MULTIPLE ROLES FOR HUMAN RIGHTS

Space does not permit a more thorough presentation of Beitz's views, beyond noting that several other authors (including David Forsythe in this volume) share his

---

[13]   A.K. SEN, 'Capability and well-being', in M. NUSSBAUM and A.K. SEN (eds.), *The Quality of Life* (Oxford, 1993) 30-53 and elsewhere.

[14]   SEN, *supra* n. 4.

[15]   E.g. M.C. NUSSBAUM, *Women and Human Development: The Capabilities Approach* (Cambridge, 2000).

approach to regard human rights as fundamentally concerned with institutions. I here note some areas where the method of RE indicates that further elaboration is required.

Such an object-dependent theory seems at first glance inconsistent, incoherent, and too complex, and thus at odds with the norms central to the method of reflective equilibrium. Why should the content of norms depend fundamentally on their objects? And in particular, a normative philosophical theory cannot rest with claims that different fundamental principles of distributive justice as a matter of fact apply to different spheres of life - as Michael Walzer and others have explored.[16] It may turn out that such empirical claims about actual variation in legal or social norms cannot be justified, because they rest on normative or empirical principles or claims that cannot withstand criticism in RE.

At least two sorts of responses can be made on Beitz's behalf. One is that institutions affect the fundamental content of individuals' claims on each other. For instance, those who contribute to producing certain goods, have particularly strong claims to a share of these benefits. Thus, within a political order, citizens may have stronger claims to receive a share of the economic and other benefits of the social practices they jointly enable — the 'common projects' they are part of. Arguably, many such social practices and institutions are now of global reach, and thus have implications for cross-border claims on the benefits.

I submit that this is one reason why legal rules, such as those that regulate and even constitute domestic and global relations, warrant different normative standards than the rules for interpersonal interaction.[17]

A second sort of response is that philosophical — and legal - human rights can arguably serve several important but very different roles, to help shape and maintain a just state and a just system of states.[18] These different roles may well require quite different sets of specific human rights, since they serve as triggers for a wide range of actions by many different actors, ranging from compliance with law by individuals to humanitarian armed intervention. Indeed, I submit that historically, human rights have served even further roles. They have been regarded as moral constraints on governors, *and* as conditions for political obligation, *and* as a trigger for regicide. Human rights have also served as conditions for international immunity from military intervention — and as triggers for various *non-military* foreign policies of a political unit, such as rights-based international assistance policies or as conditions on loans. Moreover, human rights serve additional functions in federal political

---

[16]   M. WALZER, *Spheres of Justice: A Defense of Pluralism and Equality* (New York, 1983); MILLER, *supra* n. 2.

[17]   Cf. POGGE, *supra* n. 1; J. COHEN and C. SABEL, 'Extra Rempublicam Nulla Justitia?', 34 *Philosophy and Public Affairs* (2006) 113-147.

[18]   A. FOLLESDAL, 'Justice, stability and toleration in a Federation of Well-ordered Peoples', in R. MARTIN and D. REIDY (eds.), *Rawls's Law of Peoples: A Realistic Utopia?* (Oxford, 2006) 299-317.

orders, e.g. to specify part of the scope of immunity for sub-units to protect their culture from central authorities and to protect minorities within a sub-unit from local government abuse. This is not an exhaustive list of functions, but for each of these functions the substantive human rights requirements might be quite different. In each case, the triggers labelled 'human rights' should reflect the risks and benefits of various actions, including the likelihood of mistaken assessment of violations and the relative prospects for success compared to alternative policies and mechanisms. These assessments will vary depending on the kinds of actions regulated by these different roles.

In closing I note another challenge to Beitz's account which follows from the fact of multiple roles of human rights. When we apply the method of RE we should ask whether this account is sufficiently coherent. If indeed human rights norms play at least nine different roles, and quite possibly more, we should ask what unites these different roles or functions. Which features make it helpful to call all of these different norms 'human rights', in a philosophical or legal sense? For instance, does it suffice that any practice where basic capabilities or vital interests are at stake, for some of its rules to be labelled 'human rights'? Or should that term only be used for the exercise of 'public' power — which means that corporations cannot commit human rights violations? A satisfactory philosophical theory of human rights should have a clear criterion, that is justified — and that helps bring order and consistency to our considered judgments.

6. CONCLUSIONS

This contribution has sought to explain and illustrate the philosophical research method of 'Reflective Equilibrium'. We first considered two different philosophical accounts of how to best conceive of the relationship between philosophical human rights and legal rights. They offered two different sorts of reasons to value institutions that promote human rights. Amartya Sen — at least in the article considered here - regards institutions primarily as instruments to carry out the independently justified philosophical human rights obligations we have against each other. Charles Beitz, on the other hand, holds the view that philosophical human rights primarily should be seen as standards to be applied to particular international institutions or practices, namely as criteria for various forms of inter-state intervention.

This contribution then laid out some aspects of the philosophical research method of Reflective Equilibrium, and used this method to explore some of the strengths and weaknesses of the two accounts. Some issues must be resolved in order to achieve a more satisfactory reflective equilibrium. We need a theory that helps explain why human rights norms are taken to be universal and overriding — or that offers good reasons to modify these considered judgments about human rights. I have suggested where each of these theories must be further elaborated in order to provide such accounts. Amartya Sen's theory must include further arguments for believing that human rights norms are overriding — or explain why the best account of human rights requires us to modify this belief. Charles Beitz's theory must offer some account of whether human rights should continue to be used to regulate a wide variety of institutionalized relationships and if so which roles his theory would endorse. We would want a theory that explains why each of these social roles are special cases of a more general account of human rights as standards for assessing powerful social actors.

I conclude, then, that these two theories are of great help in bringing our considered judgments regarding human rights toward more coherence and more consistency. Neither of them seem to have arrived at an ideal state of full reflective equilibrium. It remains to be seen whether they are competing accounts or whether the changes will render them components of a more justified and credible account of human rights.

ABOUT THE AUTHORS

Eva Brems

Eva Brems studied law at the universities of Namur, Leuven, Bologna and Harvard. She is a Professor of Human Rights Law and non-Western law at the University of Ghent. Her research in the human rights field covers most areas of human rights law. She is the author of numerous publications in this field in Belgian and international journals and books, and a member of the editorial board of several law journals. She is the chair of the Flemish section of Amnesty International in Belgium and an activist in several human rights organisations. She publishes on numerous cases and provisions of the European Convention on Human Rights and is the editor of *Conflicts between Fundamental Rights* (Antwerp, Intersentia, 2008).

Fons Coomans

Fons Coomans studied international relations and international law at the University of Amsterdam. He currently holds the UNESCO Chair on Human Rights and Peace at the Department of International and European Law at Maastricht University. He is the coordinator of the Maastricht Centre for Human Rights, and Senior Researcher at the Netherlands School of Human Rights Research. His publications include edited volumes on the *Extraterritorial Application of Human Rights Treaties* (Antwerp, Intersentia, 2004, with M.T. Kamminga) and *Justiciability of Economic and Social Rights — Experiences from Domestic Systems* (Antwerp, Intersentia, 2006).

Koen De Feyter

Koen De Feyter studied law at the University of Antwerp (UIA) (1983 Lic.jur.). In 1984 he obtained a Master in International and Comparative Law (LL.M.), University of Brussels, Program on International Legal Co-operation. In 1992 he obtained a Ph.D. in Law at the University of Antwerp. He wrote his thesis on 'The Human Rights Approach to Development'. He is a former Chair of Amnesty International Belgium (1998-1999). He is the present Chair of International Law at the University of Antwerp. He also acts as the spokesperson of the Law and Development research group, and is the coordinator of the Centre for Flemish Foreign Policy at the same University. He is the author of *Human Rights. Social Justice in the Age of the Market* (London, Zed Books, 2005) and edited *The Tension between Group Rights and Human Rights* (Oxford, Hart, 2008 — with G. Pavlakos),

Economic Globalisation and Human Rights (Cambridge, Cambridge University Press, 2007 — with W. Benedek and F. Marrella).

DABNEY EVANS
Dabney Evans is Executive Director of the Emory University Institute of Human Rights. She received her Master of Public Health degree in 1998. Since that time she has served as a lecturer in the Hubert Department of Global Health at the Rollins School of Public Health at Emory University. Evans teaches courses in 'Interdisciplinary Perspectives in Human Rights' and 'Health and Human Rights.' In addition, Evans has served as a training instructor to more than 1,000 public health practitioners from over 20 countries. Evans is a doctoral candidate at the University of Aberdeen in law. Her dissertation research focuses on the nondiscriminatory provision of the right to health in several countries.

ANDREAS FOLLESDAL
Andreas Follesdal is Professor of Political Philosophy and Director of Research at the Norwegian Centre for Human Rights at the University of Oslo. He got a PhD in Philosophy from Harvard University in 1991. His research largely concerns political philosophy of human rights and of the European Union. He has edited books on democracy, the welfare state, consultancy, and on the European constitution. He is Founding Series Editor of Themes in European Governance, and Founding Consulting Editor of Contemporary European Politics, both with Cambridge University Press.

MARCO FORMISANO
Marco Formisano graduated in Law at the University of Rome 'La Sapienza', with a specialization in EU Law. He also graduated from the same University in Political Science, specializing in Sociology. He holds a MA in European Studies (College of Europe) and a Master in International Human Rights Law (University of Oxford). Currently he is Associate Protection Research and Information Officer at the United Nations High Commissioner for Refugees in Geneva, where he carries out research on the human rights situation in country of origin for refugees. Before joining UNHCR, he has worked as researcher on human rights, migration, asylum, and justice and home affairs issues for the Centre of European Policy Studies and for the European Commission in Brussels.

DAVID P. FORSYTHE
David P. Forsythe is Charles J. Mach Distinguished Professor of Political Science at the University of Nebraska-Lincoln, USA. During fall term 2008 he held the Fulbright Distinguished Chair in Human Rights and International Studies at the Danish Institute for International Studies (Copenhagen). In 2006 he won the

Distinguished Scholar Award from the Human Rights Section of the American Political Science Association. Previously he won the Quincy Wright Award from the Midwest Section of the International Studies Association for his professional achievements. Among his publications are *Human Rights in International Relations*, 2nd edition, 2006, and *The Humanitarians: the International Committee of the Red Cross*, 2005, both by Cambridge University Press.

PAUL GREADY

Paul Gready is the Director of the Centre for Applied Human Rights at the University of York, UK. He has worked for Amnesty International and a number of other international and national human rights organisations, and has wide-ranging experience as a human rights consultant. His recent publications have mainly been in the fields of transitional justice, and human rights and development. Research on the former topic has been written up in the monograph *Aftermaths: Truth, Justice and Reconciliation in Post-Apartheid South Africa, due to be published in 2009* - previous books include the *No-nonsense Guide to Human Rights* (2006, with O. Ball), and *Reinventing Development? Translating Rights-based Approaches from Theory into Practice* (2005, edited with Jonathan Ensor).

FRED GRÜNFELD

Fred Grünfeld studied political science at the Free University in Amsterdam. He is currently extraordinary professor in the causes of gross human rights violations at the Centre for Conflict Studies at the Faculty of Humanities of Utrecht University and associate professor of International Relations and of the Law of International Organizations at the Maastricht Centre for Human Rights at the Faculty of Law of Maastricht University and at the University College Maastricht. His inaugural lecture in 2003 was on 'Early action of bystanders to prevent wars and gross human rights violations'. In 2007 he published with A. Huijboom *The Failure to Prevent Genocide in Rwanda; The Role of Bystanders* (Brill/Nijhoff, Leiden-Boston).

MENNO T. KAMMINGA

Menno T. Kamminga is Professor of International Law at Maastricht University and Director of the Maastricht Centre for Human Rights. He studied International law and international relations at Groningen University and The Fletcher School of Law and Diplomacy and obtained his Ph.D. at Leiden University. He chairs the Netherlands Government's Advisory Committee on International Law and is a member of the Netherlands Government's Advisory Committee on Human Rights. His latest book is *The Impact of Human Rights Law on General International Law*, ed. with Martin Scheinin, (Oxford, Oxford University Press, 2009).

TODD LANDMAN

Todd Landman studied at the University of Pennsylvania (BA Political Science 1988), Georgetown University (MA Latin American Studies 1990), University of Colorado at Boulder (MA Political Science 1993), and the University of Essex (PhD Political Science 2000). He is a Reader in the Department of Government and Director of the Centre for Democratic Governance at the University of Essex. He is author of *Studying Human Rights* (Routledge 2006), *Protecting Human Rights* (Georgetown 2005), and *Issues and Methods in Comparative Politics* (Routledge 2000,2003, 2008); co-author of *Measuring Human Rights* (Routledge 2009), *Governing Latin America* (Polity 2003), and *Citizenship Rights and Social Movements* (Oxford 1997, 2000); and editor of *Human Rights, Volumes I-IV* (Sage 2009). He has published articles in *International Studies Quarterly*, *The British Journal of Political Science*, *Human Rights Quarterly*, *Democratization*, *The British Journal of Politics and International Relations*, and *Political Studies*.

MEGAN PRICE

Megan Price is a doctoral candidate in Biostatistics at the Rollins School of Public Health at Emory University where she is a Dean's Teaching Fellow. She earned her M.S. in Statistics at Case Western Reserve University in 2003. Price recently joined the Human Rights Data Analysis Group, a Benetech initiative helping local groups to make scientifically-defensible arguments based on rigorous evidence of human rights abuses.

HANS-OTTO SANO

Hans-Otto Sano holds a PhD in Economic history and a MA history with a specialization in development studies. He has worked as Acting Director of the Danish Institute for Human Rights since May 2008, before that he was Research Director between 2002 and 2007. He is an expert on human rights and development. His recent research focuses on three topics: rights-based development, global governance, and human rights indicators. Before being employed at the Danish Institute for Human Rights in 1997, he taught international development at the University of Roskilde in Denmark. In that context, he also coordinated the teaching program on methodological issues. He is a co-editor of Stéphanie Lagoutte, Hans-Otto Sano and Peter Scharff Smith (eds.) *Human Rights in Turmoil. Facing Threats, Consolidating Achievements*. Martinus Nijhoff Publishers, 2006.

JAN M. SMITS

After his study of law in Leiden and Poitiers (1986-1991), Jan Smits received his PhD from the University of Leiden (1995) on a theory of how contractual liability can best be explained. In 1995 and 1996, he taught private law at the universities of Stellenbosch and Tilburg. He then was appointed at Maastricht University, first as an associate professor (1996-1999) and then (1999) to the Chair of European Private Law. He is now professor of European Private Law and Comparative Law at the University of Tilburg and research professor of Comparative Legal Studies at the University of Helsinki. His research interests lie in the fields of European private law, comparative law and legal theory. He is the editor of Elgar Encyclopedia of Comparative Law, Cheltenham-Northampton 2006 (Edward Elgar Publishing) and the author of The Making of European Private Law; Toward a Ius Commune Europaeum as a Mixed Legal System (Antwerp-Oxford-New York, Intersentia-Hart Publishing-Transnational, 2002).

MARIA STUTTAFORD

Maria Stuttaford obtained a Bachelor and a Masters degree in Social Science, from the University of KwaZulu Natal, South Africa and a PhD from London South Bank University, England. She is now an Associate Research Fellow in the Institute of Health at the University of Warwick, England and holds honorary appointments at the University of St Andrews, Scotland and University of Cape Town, South Africa. Her research is mainly in the area of health as a human right, focusing on: human rights based approaches to promoting health equity; access to health and social care and the underlying determinants of health; and where, when and how civil society organisations work towards achieving the right to health. She is the co-author, together with G. Lewando Hundt and J. Harrington, of *Sites for health rights: the experience of homeless families in England* in the Journal of Human Rights Practice (forthcoming) and, with C. Coe *The 'learning' component of participatory learning and action (PLA) in health research: reflections from a local Sure Start evaluation* in Qualitative Health Research (2007).

HATLA THELLE

Hatla Thelle obtained a Bachelor Degree in History and a Master Degree in Sinology at the University of Copenhagen. She holds a PhD in Chinese studies and social and economic history. She has been working in the Danish Institute of Human Rights since 1997 as a researcher and a programme manager. Her main field of interest is social rights protection and she has done extensive field work in China over the last ten years. Her publications relate primarily to protection of human rights in China, but also touch on social security and social policies worldwide. Apart from research she is engaged in cooperation projects with Chinese institutions. Her publications include 'Cong wu dao you: Zhongguo falv yuanzhu zhidu de fazhan (From Nothing to Something: Development of a Legal Aid System in China), 2008). In Chinese, in He Hairen (ed.), *Gongyi susong de xin fazhan* (*New Developments of Public Interest Litigation*). Beijing: Zhongguo Shehui Kexue Chubanshe and (together with B. Lindsnaes and H.O. Sano) 'Human Rights in Action. Supporting Human Rights Work in Authoritarian Countries', in Bell and Coicaud, Ethics in Action. *The Ethical*

Challenges of International Human Rights Nongovernmental Organizations (Cambridge, Cambridge University Press, 2006).

SUBJECT INDEX

Accuracy, viii, 188, 199, 200, 202, 204, 205, 206
Across countries, 24, 31, 34, 130, 132
Across sub-populations, 123
Aggregation, 140
Amnesties, 66
Analysis, 11, 19, 20, 22, 23, 24, 25, 26, 27, 28, 29, 30, 31, 32, 33, 34, 36, 37, 38, 39, 40,
    41, 42, 43, 47, 54, 55, 62, 63, 68, 70, 71, 72, 79, 82, 85, 86, 87, 88, 89, 92, 93, 97, 99,
    104, 107, 115, 121, 124, 126, 127, 130, 131, 132, 133, 137, 139, 140, 144, 145, 146,
    147, 148, 150, 152, 155, 159, 163, 165, 168, 170, 171, 175, 176, 178, 180, 181, 187,
    188, 189, 191, 192, 198, 201, 204, 205, 208, 209, 218, 226, 231, 250
    levels of, 164
Anthropology, 135, 197, 224
    anthropologists, 60, 221, 222, 224, 228
Argumentative discipline, 51, 57
Benchmarks, 89, 140, 141
Bias, 34, 35, 140, 147, 204, 205, 206, 233
Civil and political rights, 23, 32, 112, 119
Civil society, 99, 137, 138, 141, 142, 145, 146, 251
Comparative, v, 20, 22, 24, 25, 26, 28, 29, 31, 32, 33, 34, 35, 37, 38, 40, 41, 51, 52, 54,
    55, 57, 58, 69, 72, 84, 85, 86, 88, 89, 92, 98, 100, 107, 140, 163, 171, 195, 206, 213,
    221, 224, 247, 250, 251
    analysis, v, 29, 31, 32, 33, 41, 92
    methods, v, 31
    perspective, 69
    studies, 34, 37, 107
Comparisons, v, 21, 26, 29, 31, 33, 34, 86, 123, 130
Construct validity, 156
Content analysis, 41, 145
Contextual, 31, 38, 67, 69, 101, 173, 178, 180
    analysis, 67, 69
    factors, 69
Conventional wisdom, 13, 14, 75
Core
    content of human rights, 21

conventions, 97, 108
obligations, 122, 124, 136
Correlation, 39, 124, 132
correlation to the normative human rights texts, 132
Country of origin, 16, 114, 189, 190, 191, 192, 193, 195, 196, 209, 210, 248
Country of Origin Information (COI), 187, 189
Credibility, 14, 156, 191, 192, 193, 194, 197, 202, 208, 209, 210, 234, 239, 242
Crimes against humanity, 64, 66, 69
Culture, 33, 41, 73, 74, 98, 137, 153, 163, 167, 227, 245
Customary law, 221, 222, 223
Data, vii, 21, 25, 28, 31, 32, 39, 40, 41, 43, 48, 72, 82, 91, 92, 93, 94, 96, 97, 99, 100, 101, 102, 103, 104, 106, 107, 108, 109, 111, 112, 123, 126, 127, 128, 129, 130, 132, 133, 138, 140, 144, 145, 146, 147, 148, 150, 152, 153, 154, 155, 156, 165, 170, 171, 176, 180, 195, 196, 199, 200, 218, 224, 250
availability, 32
Decision-making, 55, 59, 94, 104, 109, 194, 210, 224, 226, 228
Deductive, 15, 26, 30, 203
reasoning, 30
Descriptive studies, 28
Desk top research, 15
Development studies, 95, 250
Dialogue, 47, 67, 139, 144, 147, 150, 152, 153, 173, 231
Diaries, 146, 155
Disaggregation, 129
data, 130, 132
Discrimination, vii, 49, 51, 91, 92, 100, 114, 115, 116, 117, 119, 120, 121, 122, 123, 124, 129, 130, 131, 132, 133, 137, 198, 209
discriminatory practices, 103
Domestic policies, 92
Duty-bearers, 91, 92, 99, 101, 102, 123, 141, 145
Economic, social and cultural rights, 112, 115, 130, 220
Economic, Social and Cultural Rights, 104, 115, 117, 120, 121, 122, 126, 136
Economists, 47, 49, 60
Effectiveness, 11, 37, 71, 72, 74, 90, 94, 178, 224
of legal obligation, 72
Emancipatory research, 150
Empirical, vi, ix, 20, 21, 24, 26, 29, 30, 31, 33, 34, 36, 38, 43, 47, 48, 51, 53, 54, 61, 70, 71, 77, 78, 80, 83, 84, 86, 90, 91, 92, 101, 109, 131, 190, 198, 233, 238, 239, 240, 242, 244
data, 91, 92, 101
epidemiological research, 131

evidence, 30, 43, 53, 70, 71, 91, 109

generalizations, 21, 26, 29, 31

questions, 36, 78

Epidemiological analysis, 111

Event-based data, 100

Evidence, v, vi, vii, 13, 20, 21, 24, 25, 26, 27, 28, 29, 30, 39, 40, 41, 42, 43, 59, 64, 65, 71, 82, 91, 92, 93, 94, 96, 97, 101, 103, 104, 109, 138, 140, 142, 161, 180, 182, 183, 189, 190, 191, 192, 193, 194, 197, 200, 203, 204, 205, 207, 208, 209, 215, 221, 223, 229, 230, 250

Evolutionary approach, 216, 220

Experiential learning, 148, 152, 154

External validity, 156

Global, 19, 21, 26, 31, 32, 33, 41, 61, 111, 112, 127, 128, 132, 133, 187, 218, 224, 225, 235, 237, 244, 250

Health, vii, viii, 11, 17, 56, 111, 112, 113, 114, 115, 116, 117, 118, 119, 120, 121, 122, 123, 124, 125, 126, 127, 128, 129, 130, 131, 132, 133, 135, 136, 137, 138, 139, 140, 141, 142, 144, 145, 146, 147, 148, 149, 150, 152, 153, 154, 155, 156, 238, 248, 250, 251

indicators, 111, 120, 123, 124, 125, 126, 130, 131, 132, 139

inequalities, vii, 111, 112, 113, 114, 124, 127, 129, 132, 133, 146, 153, 155, 157

sciences, 11

Hierarchy, 72, 79, 84, 85, 210, 214, 215

of sources, 79, 85

History, viii, 11, 22, 28, 30, 33, 35, 47, 60, 63, 68, 167, 169, 173, 174, 176, 177, 178, 179, 180, 182, 183, 184, 205, 220, 250, 251

analysis, 60, 180, 181, 182

Holism, 161, 162

Human Development Index, 124

Human dignity, 13, 19, 55, 56, 61, 63, 64, 65, 66, 67, 68, 69, 70, 71, 75, 225, 233, 234

Human rights, iv, v, vi, vii, ix, 11, 12, 13, 14, 15, 16, 17, 19, 20, 21, 22, 23, 24, 26, 28, 29, 30, 31, 32, 33, 34, 35, 36, 37, 38, 39, 41, 43, 45, 55, 59, 60, 61, 62, 63, 64, 65, 66, 67, 68, 69, 70, 71, 73, 74, 75, 77, 79, 80, 81, 82, 83, 84, 85, 86, 87, 88, 89, 90, 91, 92, 93, 94, 95, 96, 97, 98, 99, 100, 101, 102, 103, 104, 105, 108, 109, 111, 114, 115, 116, 117, 118, 119, 120, 121, 123, 124, 125, 130, 131, 133, 135, 136, 137, 138, 139, 140, 141, 142, 144, 145, 146, 147, 148, 149, 152, 153, 154, 155, 156, 159, 160, 161, 162, 163, 164, 165, 166, 167, 168, 169, 170, 171, 173, 174, 175, 176, 177, 178, 179, 180, 182, 183, 184, 185, 188, 191, 195, 197, 198, 200, 201, 206, 207, 209, 210, 213, 214, 215, 216, 217, 218, 219, 220, 221, 223, 224, 225, 227, 229, 230, 231, 232, 233, 234, 235, 236, 237, 238, 239, 241, 242, 243, 244, 245, 246, 247, 248, 249, 250, 251

research, 11, 92, 94, 95, 97, 230

Human Rights Quarterly, 13, 19, 20, 34, 73, 82, 93, 95, 96, 98, 117, 140, 160, 162, 163, 170, 220, 250

Hybridity, 160, 166, 167, 170, 184

Impact, vi, 12, 14, 16, 20, 34, 63, 70, 71, 75, 95, 99, 100, 139, 140, 165, 171, 173, 198, 217, 231, 249
assessment, 20, 95, 139, 140

Impartiality, viii, 16, 168, 170, 196, 200

Impunity, 69

Indicators, 16, 19, 92, 98, 100, 106, 113, 121, 123, 124, 125, 126, 131, 132, 133, 139, 140, 141, 198, 206, 234, 250

Indigenous communities, 219, 220, 222, 226, 227

Indivisibility, 91, 117, 137

Interdependence, 91, 117

Interdisciplinary, 13, 17, 24, 51, 59, 75, 80, 82, 84, 85, 86, 87, 95, 109, 133, 230, 231, 248
approach, 230
research, 17, 80, 85, 231
subject, 59, 75, 95
training, 109

International relations, 11, 237, 247, 249

Interviews, 15, 78, 85, 88, 94, 100, 107, 108, 139, 141, 144, 145, 146, 150, 154, 171, 181, 192, 200, 218
focus group, 154
in-depth, 27, 40, 141, 146, 147, 154, 155
qualitative, 97, 107
semi-structured, 154

Judgements, 24, 154, 176

Justice, 11, 56, 63, 64, 68, 69, 73, 98, 101, 104, 105, 107, 108, 159, 160, 161, 162, 163, 168, 169, 170, 172, 176, 196, 214, 216, 217, 228, 233, 234, 236, 238, 241, 244, 248, 249

Justifiability, 233

Justification, ix, 182, 233, 238, 241

Legal, v, vi, vii, 11, 12, 13, 14, 15, 17, 21, 23, 45, 46, 47, 48, 49, 50, 51, 52, 53, 54, 55, 56, 57, 58, 59, 61, 62, 63, 64, 65, 66, 67, 68, 69, 70, 71, 72, 73, 74, 75, 77, 79, 81, 82, 83, 84, 86, 87, 88, 89, 90, 91, 93, 94, 96, 98, 101, 103, 104, 105, 106, 107, 108, 109, 111, 121, 124, 133, 137, 141, 144, 161, 167, 168, 170, 171, 175, 178, 181, 182, 183, 188, 191, 192, 194, 195, 198, 199, 203, 204, 208, 209, 210, 213, 217, 218, 219, 220, 221, 222, 223, 228, 229, 231, 233, 234, 236, 238, 239, 243, 244, 245, 247, 251
approaches, 54, 61, 62
conceptions of human rights, 233
documents, 91, 96, 108

interpretation, 68, 213
norms, 61, 91
obligations, 23, 101
research methods, 109, 133
Legalistic, vi, 13, 62, 65, 67, 69, 74, 175, 176
language, 175
Legality, 62, 94
Legislation, 49, 57, 58, 61, 92, 94, 102, 103, 104, 105, 107, 108, 109, 179, 191, 198, 209, 223, 236
Legitimacy, viii, 62, 91, 159, 168, 170, 173, 174, 178, 179, 182, 184, 189, 192, 193
Levels of analysis, 164
Methodology, v, vi, 11, 12, 14, 15, 20, 45, 46, 50, 54, 77, 78, 81, 83, 84, 86, 87, 93, 94, 98, 100, 109, 124, 131, 137, 140, 148, 149, 159, 160, 162, 165, 166, 171, 176, 178, 179, 184, 188, 198, 201, 202, 208, 210, 213, 217, 220, 224, 225, 238
quantitative, 100, 184
Methods, iv, v, vi, vii, viii, 12, 14, 15, 16, 17, 19, 20, 24, 25, 27, 30, 31, 32, 35, 39, 40, 41, 42, 44, 45, 47, 48, 54, 77, 78, 79, 81, 84, 85, 87, 88, 89, 90, 93, 98, 104, 107, 108, 109, 111, 116, 123, 126, 131, 135, 137, 138, 139, 140, 141, 142, 144, 145, 146, 147, 150, 153, 156, 159, 160, 163, 165, 167, 168, 170, 175, 179, 180, 181, 188, 198, 214, 216, 218, 233, 250
participatory, 141
qualitative, 16, 27, 31, 39, 40, 85, 94, 136, 141, 148, 153, 156, 157, 165, 218
Moral, ix, 20, 24, 53, 59, 60, 61, 62, 63, 68, 72, 154, 169, 170, 176, 181, 233, 235, 238, 239, 240, 241, 243, 244
argument, 59, 60, 240
assumption, 59, 61
consequentialism, 72
principles, 239
Mortality, 111, 113, 126, 127, 128, 129, 132
infant, 115, 126, 127, 128, 129, 130, 132
Multi-disciplinary, 135, 137, 142, 156, 157
Narrative, 41, 154, 161, 166, 170, 176, 177, 179, 181, 182, 183, 184
Netherlands Quarterly of Human Rights, 13, 21, 82, 93, 95, 96, 99, 165
Neutrality, 188, 209
Non-governmental, 19, 36, 126, 163, 187, 196, 200, 202, 231
Non-Governmental Organizations, 36, 126, 171, 187, 196, 231
Normative, v, vi, ix, 12, 16, 21, 45, 46, 48, 49, 50, 51, 52, 53, 54, 55, 56, 57, 58, 59, 60, 77, 78, 80, 81, 86, 87, 88, 89, 91, 98, 116, 119, 121, 131, 147, 216, 233, 234, 236, 237, 238, 241, 244
content, 121, 131
external normative approach, 50

foundation, 91
human rights research methods, 131
interpretation, 116
legal scholarship, 45, 46, 50
political philosophy, 233
questions, 49, 77
Objectivity, viii, 16, 54, 168, 170, 173, 178, 179, 184, 197, 200, 205, 209
Obligation, vi, 23, 62, 71, 72, 73, 74, 75, 108, 122, 131, 136, 194, 222, 227, 235, 236, 244
to fulfil, 23, 122
to protect, 23
to respect, 23, 122
Observation, 27, 40, 59, 65, 91, 97, 109, 155, 198, 209, 210, 223, 225, 226
Participatory action research, 148
Perception, 20, 93, 96, 100, 207, 225
analyses, 93
surveys, 96, 100
Philosophical conceptions of human rights, 233
Philosophy, 11, 21, 53, 60, 198, 203, 205, 233, 235, 236, 237, 238, 240, 243, 244, 248
philosophical conceptions of human rights, 238
philosophical foundations, v, 20, 21, 215
philosophical interpretation, 91
Political, 11, 21, 22, 23, 24, 25, 26, 27, 28, 29, 30, 32, 33, 34, 35, 37, 38, 39, 40, 42, 43, 46, 53, 59, 60, 61, 63, 64, 65, 66, 69, 70, 71, 72, 73, 74, 83, 89, 91, 104, 105, 109, 114, 115, 116, 117, 135, 137, 145, 150, 151, 152, 159, 161, 162, 165, 166, 168, 169, 170, 175, 176, 177, 178, 179, 181, 182, 184, 189, 191, 197, 198, 207, 209, 226, 237, 241, 243, 244, 248, 249, 250
science, 11, 24, 42, 43, 74, 249
scientists, 60
theory, 21, 53, 60
Propositions, 20, 25, 30, 37, 43
Qualitative data, 97
Qualitative research, 100
Quantitative data, 39, 96
Questionnaire, vi, 78, 79, 81, 82, 83, 85, 87, 88, 138
Racial categories, 128, 130, 132
Reconciliation, 17, 34, 36, 41, 64, 69, 141, 159, 160, 161, 163, 164, 165, 167, 168, 169, 171, 172, 173, 174, 175, 176, 177, 178, 179, 180, 181, 182, 183, 184, 249
Reflective Equilibrium, ix, 233, 235, 237, 239, 245
Reliability, viii, 16, 32, 140, 144, 156, 171, 188, 192, 193, 199, 200, 202, 206, 207

Research, iv, v, vi, vii, viii, ix, 11, 12, 13, 14, 15, 16, 17, 19, 20, 22, 24, 25, 26, 27, 28, 29, 30, 32, 33, 34, 35, 36, 38, 39, 40, 41, 42, 43, 45, 46, 47, 48, 49, 50, 51, 52, 55, 57, 58, 70, 75, 77, 78, 79, 80, 81, 82, 83, 84, 85, 86, 87, 88, 89, 90, 91, 92, 93, 94, 95, 97, 99, 100, 101, 102, 103, 104, 105, 108, 109, 124, 135, 137, 138, 139, 140, 141, 142, 143, 144, 145, 146, 147, 148, 149, 150, 151, 153, 154, 155, 156, 159, 160, 162, 163, 165, 166, 167, 168, 169, 171, 172, 178, 179, 180, 184, 185, 187, 188, 189, 190, 195, 196, 197, 198, 199, 200, 201, 202, 203, 205, 206, 208, 209, 210, 212, 215, 218, 230, 231, 232, 233, 234, 235, 236, 244, 247, 248, 249, 250, 251
    design, 25, 33, 34, 35, 40, 43, 135, 138, 139, 140, 142, 147, 148, 155, 156, 157
    emancipatory research, 136, 151, 153
    governance, 95
    method, 12, 13, 15, 29, 40, 48, 50, 52, 57, 58, 77, 79, 80, 81, 83, 84, 85, 87, 89, 90, 94, 135, 138, 159, 162, 165, 167, 178, 184, 187, 188, 190, 195, 208, 211, 233, 235, 238, 245
    operational, 135, 153, 157
    participatory action research, 146, 148, 149, 150, 153, 154, 155, 156
    qualitative, 135, 157
    questions, vi, 20, 30, 32, 77, 79, 93, 146, 156, 188, 195, 198, 199
    statistical, 99
Rights, iv, v, vii, viii, ix, 11, 12, 13, 14, 15, 16, 17, 19, 20, 21, 22, 23, 24, 26, 29, 30, 31, 32, 34, 35, 36, 37, 38, 39, 41, 43, 45, 55, 57, 59, 60, 61, 62, 63, 64, 65, 66, 68, 69, 70, 71, 73, 74, 75, 77, 81, 82, 83, 84, 86, 87, 89, 90, 91, 92, 93, 94, 95, 96, 97, 98, 99, 100, 101, 102, 103, 104, 105, 107, 108, 109, 111, 114, 115, 116, 117, 119, 120, 121, 122, 123, 124, 126, 130, 131, 133, 134, 135, 136, 137, 138, 139, 140, 141, 142, 144, 145, 146, 147, 149, 152, 154, 155, 156, 159, 160, 161, 162, 163, 164, 165, 167, 168, 170, 171, 173, 174, 175, 176, 177, 178, 179, 183, 184, 188, 191, 192, 198, 201, 207, 209, 214, 215, 216, 217, 218, 219, 220, 222, 223, 224, 225, 226, 227, 228, 229, 230, 231, 232, 233, 234, 235, 236, 237, 238, 239, 242, 243, 244, 245, 247, 248, 249, 250, 251
    -based approach to development, 100
    -based development, 99, 100, 250
    discourse, 63, 65, 69, 95, 100, 109, 177, 178
    holders, 145
Social sciences, v, 19, 20, 21, 23, 24, 25, 28, 30, 39, 40, 41, 42, 43, 48, 49, 61, 104, 131, 146, 218, 222, 225
    social science methods, 20, 26
    social science research, v, 19, 26, 43, 99, 109, 230
Sociology, 11, 22, 135, 154, 197, 198, 248
Socio-political, 109
    context, 101
    data, 109

Statistics, 39, 40, 100, 104, 105, 107, 108, 126, 129, 190, 250
  statistical significance, 31, 40
Synergistic approach, 111, 116, 117, 118, 130, 131, 133
Testimony, 166, 171, 173, 174, 175, 178, 180, 183, 191, 192, 193, 204, 208, 209
  oral, 183
Transitional justice, 161, 162, 172, 174, 249
Treaty interpretation, ix, 213, 217, 220, 225
Truth and Reconciliation Commission (TRC), 159
Truth as genre, viii, 160, 167
Truth Commissions, viii, 17, 34, 159, 160, 163, 164, 170, 178, 180
Typology, 124
Validity, 14, 15, 32, 89, 93, 94, 140, 151, 153, 156, 180, 193, 223
Vienna Convention on the Law of Treaties, 86, 213, 214, 227

MAASTRICHT SERIES IN HUMAN RIGHTS

The *Maastricht Centre for Human Rights* supervises research in the field of human rights conducted at Maastricht University's Faculty of Law. This research is interdisciplinary, with a particular focus on public international law, criminal law and social sciences. The titles in the Series contribute to a better understanding of different aspects of human rights *sensu lato*.

Published titles within the Series:

1. Ineke Boerefijn, Fons Coomans, Jenny Goldschmidt, Rikki Holtmaat and Ria Wolleswinkel (eds.), *Temporary Special Measures. Accelerating de facto Equality of Women under Article 4(1) UN Convention on the Elimination of All Forms of Discrimination against Women* (2003)
   ISBN 90–5095–359–X

2. Fons Coomans and Menno T. Kamminga (eds.), *Extraterritorial Application of Human Rights Treaties* (2004)
   ISBN 90–5095–394–8

3. Koen De Feyter and Felipe Gómez Isa (eds.), *Privatisation and Human Rights in the Age of Globalisation* (2005)
   ISBN 90–5095–422–7

4. Ingrid Westendorp and Ria Wolleswinkel (eds.), *Violence in the domestic sphere* (2005)
   ISBN 90–5095–526–6

5. Fons Coomans (ed.), *Justiciability of Economic and Social Rights* (2006)
   ISBN 978–90–5095–582–9

6. Jan C.M. Willems (ed.), *Developmental and Autonomy Rights of Children: Empowering Children, Caregivers and Communities. 2nd revised edition* (2007)
   ISBN 978–90–5095–726–7

7. Alette Smeulers and Roelof Haveman (eds.), *Supranational Criminology: Towards a Criminology of International Crimes* (2008)
   ISBN 978-90-5095-791-5

8. Hans van Crombrugge, Wouter Vandenhole and Jan C.M. Willems (eds.), *Shared Pedagogical Responsibility* (2008)
   ISBN 978-90-5095-813-4

9. Hildegard Schneider and Peter Van den Bossche (eds.), *Protection of Cultural Diversity from a European and International Perspective* (2008)
    ISBN 978-90-5095-864-6